RENEWALS 458-4574.
DATE DUE

Women and German Drama

For women, according to the contemporary Austrian dramatist Elfriede Jelinek, writing for the theater is an act of transgression. The idea that drama as a grand public genre resists women writers has become established in recent scholarship. But Jelinek herself has won the Büchner Prize, the most prestigious award in German letters, and there is a wealth of dramatic work by women from the twentieth century and before: both facts seem to contradict the notion of women's exclusion from drama. So why has drama by women appear to have been written against the odds, and why has it, until very recently, been missing from literary histories? This book looks in detail at women's playwriting in German between 1860 and 1945, and at its reception by critics. Many of the works considered have never before been analyzed by modern scholarship; others, notably the plays of Marieluise Fleisser and Else Lasker-Schüler, are well known, but are read here for the first time in the context of earlier dramatic work by women. Sarah Colvin seeks modes of reading that do justice both to the dramatic texts as *performance* texts, and to the sense of "otherness" experienced by the woman writer in a male-dominated literary and theatrical environment. She concludes that an understanding of the techniques developed by women playwrights of the nineteenth and early twentieth centuries can enrich our reading not only of Fleisser and Lasker, but of contemporary dramatists such as Jelinek. If all the world's a stage, playwrights can theoretically be seen as in control of the world they create; this book asks to what extent women dramatists manage to use the space of the drama to reflect the world that *they* experience.

Sarah Colvin is Reader in German at the University of Edinburgh.

Studies in German Literature, Linguistics, and Culture

Edited by James Hardin
(*South Carolina*)

Women and German Drama

Playwrights and Their Texts, 1860–1945

Sarah Colvin

CAMDEN HOUSE

First published 2003
by Camden House

Camden House is an imprint of Boydell & Brewer Inc.
PO Box 41026, Rochester, NY 14604–4126 USA
and of Boydell & Brewer Limited
PO Box 9, Woodbridge, Suffolk IP12 3DF, UK

ISBN: 1–57113–274–0

Library of Congress Cataloging-in-Publication Data

Colvin, Sarah.
 Women and German drama: playwrights and their texts, 1860-1945 /
Sarah Colvin.
  p. cm. — (Studies in German literature, linguistics, and culture)
Includes bibliographical references and index.
ISBN 1–57113–274–0 (alk. paper)
  1. German drama — Women authors — History and criticism.
2. German drama — 19th century — History and criticism. 3. German
drama — 20th century — History and criticism. I. Title. II. Studies
in German literature, linguistics, and culture. III. Series.

PT619 .C65 2002
832'.8099287—dc21

                                                        2002015195

A catalogue record for this title is available from the British Library.

This publication is printed on acid-free paper.
Printed in the United States of America

Unseren Schwestern des 20. Jahrhunderts rufen wir zu:
Vollendet, was wir begonnen!
— Minna Cauer, 1898

Contents

Acknowledgments

I AM INDEBTED to St John's College, Oxford, for the Junior Research Fellowship 1995–97 that enabled me to prepare much of the material for this project, as well as to the German Academic Exchange Service (DAAD) for a three-month postdoctoral scholarship which made it possible to carry out essential archive work. Publication of the finished volume was assisted by a generous grant from the Modern Humanities Research Association.

I received a great deal of intellectual encouragement and advice in the process of writing this book, particularly from Professor Susanne Kord (Georgetown), Professor Helen Watanabe-O'Kelly (Oxford), and Professor Ritchie Robertson (Oxford), to all of whom I owe a long-term debt of thanks.

Mark Taplin and Christl Reissenberger (Edinburgh) were an ever-present source of support, and for that, too, I am extremely grateful.

Introduction

Natürlich ist es kein Zufall, wenn die Ansicht besteht,
eine dramatische Begabung der Frau existiere nicht.[1]

IS THERE A TRADITION of women's playwriting in German? Or can we only read theater texts by women in the context of a male-centered literary and theatrical history?[2] Now that painstaking scholarship has shown that dramas by women do exist before the mid-twentieth century, these are the questions being asked by those interested in the "act of transgression" ("Überschreitung der Grenzen") that writing for the theater — according to Elfriede Jelinek — still equates to for women.[3]

This book addresses the second of those questions in particular, and suggests modes of reading for theater texts by women that do justice to both the dramatic genre and the cultural "otherness" of the female author, which — even if we regard the ghettoization of women's writing as undesirable, and even if we feel we have met the notion of "others" too often — it is not useful to ignore. I am looking for a mode of reading that is literary-historically aware, without taking men's theater as its critical yardstick. If we concentrate on drama by women as a thing in itself, as one fascinating part of the history of Western theater rather than a quirky supplement to drama by men, then patterns can begin to emerge, and the first question — whether there is a tradition of women's playwriting — can start to answer itself.

Any critical investigation is indebted to those critics who have gone before, whether for the inspiration provided by work its writer finds congenial, or for the stimulation culled from disagreement. This book is particularly indebted to the literary-historical recovery work of Susanne Kord (*Ein Blick hinter die Kulissen: Deutschsprachige Dramatikerinnen im 18. und 19. Jahrhundert*).[4] Anne Stürzer's *Dramatikerinnen und Zeitstücke: Ein vergessenes Kapitel der Theatergeschichte von der Weimarer Republik bis zur Nachkriegszeit,*[5] Katrin Sieg's *Exiles, Eccentrics, Activists: Women in Contemporary German Theater,*[6] Dagmar von Hoff's *Dramen des Weiblichen: Deutsche Dramatikerinnen um 1800,*[7] Anne Fleig's *Handlungs-Spiel-Räume: Dramen von Autorinnen im Theater des ausgehenden 18. Jahrhundert,*[8] and Heike Schmid's *Gefallene Engel: deutsch-*

sprachige Dramatikerinnen im ausgehenden 19. Jahrhundert[9] demonstrate various modes of reading dramatic texts by women in the context of the literary histories of different periods.

All these texts testify to the growing interest in German language drama by women, which makes it a surprise when Helga Kraft, in her recent historical overview *Ein Haus aus Sprache: Dramatikerinnen und das andere Theater*, still maintains that the achievements of women playwrights "schlummern weitgehend im Verborgenen."[10] This is true in the sense that German-language dramatists writing before the 1950s, with the exception of Marieluise Fleisser and Else Lasker-Schüler, are not yet convincingly present in the mainstream or "canon," and their plays are rarely available in modern critical editions (although this situation is improving all the time). However, women's achievements in drama are already far less hidden than was the case, say, ten or fifteen years ago, thanks to the investigative and analytical efforts of scholars in the field, and bibliographies of authors and works now exist which immeasurably facilitate library and archive work.

This study looks at a number of works which have never before been considered in detail in modern literary criticism: for example, Elsa Bernstein-Porges's *Johannes Herkner*, Gertrud Prellwitz's *Seine Welt*, Mathilde Paar's *Helene*, Laura Marholm's *Karla Bühring*, and Julie Kühne's remarkable play *Elfriede Laub oder Weib und Mensch*. My investigation of women's playwriting begins around the same time as the late-nineteenth-century women's movement in Germany, and ends with the rise of national socialism (Nazism) in the twentieth, which effectively curtailed that movement. My intention is to illustrate a wider phenomenon — the significance for women writers of the play as form — while remaining historically and culturally specific in the choice of material. Many dramatists whose work could not, for reasons of space, be included in this book (such as Nahida Lazarus 1849–1928, Emilie Mataja 1855–1938, Rosa Mayreder 1858–1938, Juliane Déry 1864–99, Lily Braun 1865–1916, and Marie Madeleine von Puttkamer 1881–1944, to name just a handful) were nonetheless present in my reading and thought processes, and are therefore at least implicitly a part of it.

Of the two most recent studies to have engaged with the subject of German-language drama by women, Heike Schmid's follows the now fairly established notion that the relation of drama to theater as a public institution renders the form problematic for women, who were assigned in gendered terms to the private sphere: "Nicht ohne Grund verschließt sich die 'öffentliche' Form des Dramatischen Frauen in weit stärkerem Maß als weiblichere, 'privatere' Formen der literarischen Produktion"

(16). Anne Fleig, by contrast, casts doubt on the real relevance of the theoretical division between public and private for writing women, at least in the late eighteenth century: "In Hinblick auf die gelebte Praxis der Autorinnen muß [. . .] das Konzept polarisierter Geschlechtscharaktere [. . .] als überholt gelten" (281). It could of course be argued that the nineteenth century, with its increasingly rigid polarization of the genders, was a more difficult time for women playwrights than the eighteenth, but the quantity of dramatic texts they produced shows that women did not allow themselves to be excluded from the genre. This book develops the notion that, despite the problems women have faced in theater (as an undeniably male-dominated institution even now), the space of the drama *per se* does not resist the woman writer.[11] I illustrate this argument with examples from a period in which notions of gender and sexuality, and women's ideas about themselves were developing — dramatically, in every sense of the word — and I consider the notion that drama (including unperformed drama!) in fact provides a particular, embodied or corporeal kind of space. It is a space which might, even within the terms of gendered discourse, be read as congenial to, rather than exclusive of, women dramatists.

Michaela Giesing describes the theater as an institution as "verweigerter Raum" for women writing in German around the turn of the nineteenth century.[12] She illustrates her point with reference to the lack of dramas by women in the repertoires, and the resistance to the idea (and reality) of female directors.[13] But women's absence in theater as authors finds its counterphenomenon in the repetitive presence of women as dramatic characters. When Gail Finney published her book *Women in Modern Drama*,[14] she was sufficiently accustomed to this pattern to elide the word "characters" after the word "women" in her title: for the book deals not with women as writers, but exclusively with women as protagonists, written by men. In the same year, Dagmar von Hoff introduced her book *Dramen des Weiblichen* with the words "Frauen schreiben keine Dramen. Sie neigen höchstens zu dramatischen Empfindungen. Dies ist ein allgemeiner Topos, der Drama und weibliches Geschlecht als unüberwindbare Gegensätze festlegt."[15] Von Hoff notes that women are welcome in theater as actors, as written-for rather than writing subjects. However, she shifts the emphasis from the problems encountered by women playwrights to the undeniable reality of their dramatic production, when she devotes her volume to Karoline von Günderrode and other dramatists around 1800. The real, productive existence of women dramatists at this time is further testified to in Karin Wurst's *Frauen und Drama im 18. Jahrhundert*,[16] and in Ruth Dawson's essay "Frauen und Theater."[17]

Even if the institution of theater is male-dominated, and even if women have tended to be the object rather than the subject of performed drama, women do write plays. So why, scholars ask, have those plays so often been overlooked?

The Gender of Drama

Von Hoff makes the theoretical link between gender and genre, when she maintains "daß Geschlecht und Gattung in einem besonderen Verhältnis stehen, wobei das Drama als männliches Feld deklariert wird."[18] This of course begs the question: declared as masculine by whom? To which the answer is: by literary historians, who until quite recently tended to be men.

Hegel hierarchized the drama as the most high-status of all the literary forms: "die höchste Stufe der Poesie und Kunst überhaupt";[19] it figures, therefore, as a masculine genre, while poetry and the novel have tended to be seen as lower-status and feminine. Susanne Kord problematizes this distinction with reference to shifting positions in the genre hierarchy — for example, the rise in the status of the novel (and hence its "de-feminization") after Goethe's *Wilhelm Meister*. But Kord, too, reads gender and genre as analogous, taking gender in Butler's sense "als variable Kategorie. Wie die Kategorie Geschlecht wird Genre als natürlich und unveränderbar beschrieben; realiter handelt es sich bei beiden Kategorien um ein soziales Konstrukt."[20]

Those like Hegel, who based their theories of drama's superiority as genre on Aristotle, simply assumed that "dramatist" meant "male dramatist." But during periods in literary history when gender issues are particularly prominent (which seem, interestingly, to occur around the turns of centuries) the gender of drama and the dramatist becomes an issue. Von Hoff traces connections between theories of gender and theories of the drama around 1800; she notes Hegel's demands on the "dramatic poet," namely, "daß er die volle Einsicht habe in dasjenige, was menschlichen Zwecken, Kämpfen und Schicksalen Inneres und Allgemeines zugrunde liegt."[21] This she compares with Novalis' observation, "Die Frauen wissen nichts von Verhältnissen der Gemeinschaft — Nur durch ihren Mann hängen sie mit Staat, Kirche, Publikum etc. zusammen."[22] Taken together, these two notions support the theory that drama is a space unsuited to women. While men have right of access to both the private and the public sphere ("Inneres und Allgemeines"), women are limited to domestic space, and their connection with public life is second hand, through their husbands, fathers, brothers or sons.

Although this has been called complementarity (in German, the "Ergän-zungstheorie"),[23] it is nothing of the sort. In fact, it is an appendage theory by which men own *both* public *and* private space; and they choose to keep their women, like their other appendages, tucked away in private.

Critical theories of drama in the later nineteenth century endlessly reiterate male ownership of the genre. At the turn of that century there is something like an epidemic of overtly gendered dramatic theory, which focuses above all on the dominant body of the playwright. Writing in 1903, Johannes Wiegand characterized the playwriting subject as what we might now call the alpha male:

> Zweifellos fordert das Drama vor allem einen Kampfmenschen, den es gelüstet, sich mit der Welt auseinanderzusetzen. Er personifiziert alle Gegensätze seines "Ichs" in Gestalten, die um die Herrschaft miteinander ringen. Andererseits aber erfordert das Drama auch eine Herren-natur, die unbarmherzig und konsequent mit ihrem lebendigen Material, den handelnden Menschen, umzuspringen weiß.

Wiegand goes on to construct (with rising excitement) images of a dra-matic masculinity that is "rücksichtslos [. . .] mit harter Hand," and cli-maxes: "Es muß in einem ununterbrochenen raschen Flusse zu [. . .] wilden Katarakten führen"[24] — he interprets the dramatist's interaction with his material, as well as the performance text's interaction with a no-tional audience, as an act of dominance that is sexually charged.

A woman dramatist, in this mode of thinking, would be akin to a woman on top in the act of intercourse: something to be read not only as unnatural, but as undesirable in the context of a system of gender hierarchy. Not merely intellectual, but *corporeal* masculinity is seen to be under threat from women playwrights. Interestingly, it is precisely corporeality that is regularly presumed missing from women's dramatic writing. Wiegand's contemporary, Dr. Ella Mensch, theorizes that play-writing emerges

> aus dem Blick für das, was hinter der zerstreuenden Mannigfaltigkeit der Dinge steht. [. . .] das gesteckte Ziel auf dem kürzesten Wege zu errei-chen, ist die Aufgabe des dramatischen Künstlers. Es will mir nun schei-nen, als wenn diese Methode des kürzesten Weges, bei dem allein die Gestalten auf der Bühne ihre Körperlichkeit behalten oder erhalten, dem ganzen psycho-physischen Organismus der Frau nicht läge.

She enlarges on this with reference to women's procreative role. True creative potency ("das Drama in seiner höchsten Potenz"), she argues pseudoscientifically, is precluded by the energy expenditure involved in the act of giving birth. One must assume that she does not envisage women

engaged in both activities — childbirth and playwriting — at one and the
same time, even though this is the only context in which her arguments
make sense. Apparently aspiring to masculine womb envy, Mensch con-
fides: "Ich glaube überhaupt nicht, daß eine Frau, die glückliche Gattin
und Mutter ist, der Welt noch viel als Dramenschriftstellerin zu sagen
hat."[25] At the same time as assigning women to the traditional feminine
sphere of the (subjugated) body, Mensch removes corporeality from
women's drama; comparing Elise Schmidt's successful play, *Judas Ischariot*
(Berlin 1848), with the work of male contemporaries, she notes: "die
geringere Körperlichkeit stellt es in Schatten gegen die genannten Män-
nerdramen."[26] Theodor Lessing argues for a missing corporeality in the
writing of another successful dramatist, Elsa Bernstein: "ihrem Drama fehlt
weder Hirn noch Nerv, wohl aber Blut, Galle, dramatische Impetu-
osität."[27] The female body, the familiar argument runs, is passively procreative rather than active and creative; women's playwriting is therefore
anaemic and unimpassioned.

There is a crucial contradiction here. Are we to understand that women
cannot write the body because they *are* the body? The neoclassical gender
discourses of the eighteenth and nineteenth centuries assign women to the
sphere of the domestic and corporeal, and promote men to the realm of
intellect and the spirit. But the notion that female drama has "Hirn" and
"Nerv," but lacks "Blut, Galle," paradoxically theorizes women's playwriting
as *logos*, the "high" intellectual, rather than the physical form. It seems that
the discourses of genre and gender have driven their perpetrators into *Herr-
und-Knecht*-style difficulties (Hegel's theory, whereby the dominance of the
"master" is always already under threat from the enforced — that is, fake —
abjection of the *Knecht*).[28] This is what Kord demonstrates via the writings
of an anxious A. W. Schlegel: "Wie das Geschlecht 'weiblich' erscheint das
Drama als potentiell höchste Gattung [. . .], die aber gleichzeitig die größte
Gefahr läuft, zur Hure abzusinken."[29] Drama, Schlegel is telling us, is similar
to the feminine; perhaps because of its connection to the corporeal (theater),
and certainly because, like femininity, it is owned and defined by men.
Following the *Herr-und-Knecht* pattern, drama constantly threatens to
subvert that defining ownership, which must, therefore, be endlessly reiterated. Drama, the critics insist, is a masculine genre *even* in its physicality. The
gentleman protests too much.

All this does, however, highlight something interesting in the notion of
the performance text. Drama combines the "masculine" element of ra-
tio/language with the "feminine" element of the body. If corporeality is
theater's essence, the masculine might even appear at a disadvantage.[30]

The theories of Mensch and Wiegand draw on a cultural belief system that positions men as central and women as supplemental. The currency of such an idea is illustrated, crassly, in comments such as from the unfortunate gynophobe Alexander Mar. Mar climbs on his hobbyhorse while reviewing a play by Gunnar Heiberg in 1895:

> das Weib [ist] [. . .] nicht reif für die aktive Thätigkeit [. . .]. Das Weib ist eben das Supplement des Mannes, genau so, wie der siebzehnte Band des Konversations-Lexikons das Supplement zu den sechzehn schon existierenden Bänden bildet. Bestehend ist hierbei die Thatsache, daß die sechzehn Bände für sich auch eine Daseinsberechtigung haben, [. . .] der siebzehnte Band ist [. . .] für sich allein ziemlich wertlos.[31]

The relevance of this attitude for women as playwrights is that if women are supplemental, then they are there to reflect the man's image back at him, not to seek to create an image of their own. They risk transgressing this rule when they create images of women and of men in drama. "Theories of the Other," Marney notes, "traditionally place the male in the active role of the performer and the female in the passive role of witness."[32] When women seek to become performers, problems will arise: actresses and dancers were long assumed to be sexually available because of their public performances. Not only acting and dancing, however, but also writing for public consumption can be construed as performance — the woman writer is, after all, demanding rather than providing an audience. A comment from Hans Pauli in 1896 suggests (unconsciously) that women's literary activity turns men into peeping Toms:

> In der That ist so ziemlich in der gesammten Frauenlitteratur das ästhetische und das objektive psychologische Interesse gering neben der reizvollen Art, wie sich eine Autorin mit Bewusstsein selber offenbart oder unbewusst selber verräth.[33]

Pauli undermines the importance of women's writing using the specifically feminine adjective "reizvoll," and then develops the corporeal connotations of that adjective with the verb "offenbaren" coupled with "selber": the woman who writes, we understand, exposes *herself* to the sexually proprietorial male gaze. He thereby simultaneously denies responsibility for his own sexualized gaze, and counters the threat of the illicitly performing woman by reiterating the pattern of gender dominance that objectifies her.

It is interesting that, at this time, women actors appear to disturb the notion of woman as passive, suffering and (willingly) subjugated far less than women writers do. In an essay for the newly-established journal *Die*

Frau of 1893, Paul Schlenther theorizes acting as peculiarly suited to women (or vice-versa):

> Die Schauspielkunst fordert das Geschmeidige der Frau, ihre große Fähigkeit, sich in ein fremdes Wesen zu versenken, sich einem fremden Wesen zu unterwerfen. Sie fordert die kleinen reizenden Verstellungskräfte der Frau und ihre große Kraft des Leidens.[34]

This documents a far less hostile attitude to women as actors than Pauli reveals towards women as writers,[35] but it does not change the fact that women who took up acting as a career in the late nineteenth century risked assumptions that they had "gone public" sexually as well as artistically. When women go on public display, their bodies are perceived as available, rather than owned; a fragment of dialogue from Mathilde Paar's "Künstler[in]drama" of 1882, *Helene* (discussed in detail in chapter 2), points this up nicely. Helene is a singer, and the speakers here are Warbek, her ex-husband, and Lothar, her husband-to-be:

> WARBEK. Würdest Du Dir ein Weib von den Brettern nehmen?
>
> LOTHAR. Vielleicht — wenn ich sie liebte!
>
> WARBEK. Und würdest Du Dein Weib, wenn es talentvoll wäre, die Bretter betreten lassen?
>
> LOTHAR. Nie![36]

Writing earlier in the century, the actor and playwright Johanna Franul von Weissenthurn articulated the difficulties of taking the step from actor to dramatic author:

> Oeffentlich als Verfasserinn aufzutreten, — der Schritt ist gewagt; er führt auf eine Bahn, die die sanfte Weiblichkeit scheuen sollte — er führt zum Krieg. [. . .] Ich habe allerdings wider die Kleiderordnung gefehlt und — statt Strümpfe zu stricken, ein paar Federn stumpf geschrieben. Die Männer sehen nun ein Mahl die Federn lieber auf unsern Köpfen und wollen nicht dulden, daß wir sie in die Dinte tauchen; [. . .] hab' ich mich mit meinem Schreiben ein wenig in die Sphäre der Männer verstiegen, so verspreche ich dagegen mit Geduld in den Schranken des Weibes zu bleiben, wenn sie mich deßhalb unsanft behandeln.[37]

Weissenthurn suggests that the "problem" when women cross the gendered boundary into public space as writers is felt essentially by men, and only at second hand — through the abuse they receive or fear receiving for their transgression — by women. While she is clearly nervous of the reception that awaits her as a playwright, Weissenthurn never doubts that the ability to write plays is inherent in women. She even suggests they may be more suited to it than men:

> Der Schauspiel-Dichter bedarf ein eigenes [= besonderes, S. C.] Talent; fehlt ihm dieses, so bringt er gewiß, trotz aller Gelehrsamkeit, kein brauchbares, auf die Zuschauer wirkendes Stück zur Welt. Dieses Talent ist, glaub' ich, ein Gefühl des Schicklichen und Wahren; eine lebhafte Einbildung, die alles, was sie auf das Papier wirft, in dem Augenblick von den Geschöpfen ihrer Phantasie schon ausführen sieht und dann im Stande ist, richtig zu beurtheilen, ob es die gehörige Wirkung hervorbringen wird. Da man nun dieses richtige Gefühl unserm Geschlecht im hohen Grade zugesteht, womit wir oft schneller eine verborgene Ursache entdecken, als der tief denkende Mann sie durch Schlüße bestätigt und es eine vorzügliche, nöthige Gabe zum Dichten, wie auch zur Schauspielkunst ist; warum soll nun dieß Talent sich bey uns in bloß alltäglichen Dingen äußern? (vi)

A century later, the prose writer and playwright Lily Braun, too, rejects the notions of women's passivity, literary or sexual, that are the starting point for masculinist theories of playwriting. Braun gives a reading of women's supposed absence in the realm of the drama that is exactly opposed to Wiegand's, when she suggests that

> die Individualität des Dichters muß hier [= in der Dramatik] hinter die Individualität der Geschöpfe seiner Phantasie zurücktreten, während von der dichterischen Leistung der Frau im allgemeinen gilt, daß sie umso wertvoller ist, je stärker die Persönlichkeit ihres Schöpfers sich in ihr ausprägt.[38]

Where Wiegand found women's subjectivity too weak to drive the drama, Braun finds it (potentially) too strong.

Braun's and Weissenthurn's arguments suggest that, while the difficulties women have encountered in the real world of theater must not be underestimated, researchers in theatrical history should be cautious of the notion so frequently cited by critics such as Johannes Wiegand and Ella Mensch, that the space of the drama resists women *per se*.

The Stage and the Self

The actor and philosopher Bruce Wilshire, in his successful book *Role-Playing and Identity*, summarizes his view of theater's significance like this: "My fellow human beings are a picture of *myself*. Theater, at its best, enables us to acknowledge this" (his italics).[39] Wilshire is working with Paul Schilder's notion of human perception of others as mirrors of the self.[40] But the metaphor of the mirror has since been problematized: Sigrid Weigel, for example, argued in 1988 that women see reflected images of themselves through lenses fashioned by a masculinist culture and society, and that such images can therefore only be distortions:

> Da die kulturelle Ordnung von Männern regiert wird, aber die Frauen ihr dennoch angehören, benutzen auch diese die Normen, deren Objekt sie selbst sind. [. . .] Für das Selbstverständnis der Frau bedeutet das, daß sie sich selbst betrachtet, indem sie sieht, daß und wie sie betrachtet wird; d.h. ihre Augen sehen durch die Brille des Mannes. [. . .] Ihr Selbstbildnis entsteht ihr so im Zerr-Spiegel des Patriarchats.[41]

Following Weigel, the simple recognition of oneself as human that Wilshire identifies as theater's primary gift to men would be an entirely different experience for women. In the "mirror" of patriarchy that in this case is theater, women are likely to see themselves as passive objects, and as supplemental. The question is, whether women dramatists can rewrite their image to give it human or subject status.

If we believe the turn-of-the-century theorists, drama requires a powerful writing subject to drive its action: a dominant self, possessing what Mensch describes as "die dichterische Fähigkeit, sich in fremde Gestalten zu verwandeln, in etwas, das man nicht mehr selbst ist und doch wiederum durch sein Selbst das Ganze zu beherrschen."[42] Self and subjectivity, however, are difficult notions. Postmodern theories have postulated the "dissolution of human subjectivity into textual play"; the notion of unique personal identity is "a philosophical and cultural mystification."[43] So is it still feasible, or useful, to consider the text from the point of view of a writing subject or self?

Patricia Waugh has engaged with the feminist counterargument that women have never been part of the "grand narratives" of Western culture that postmodernism shows to have broken down; that while the male self might once have been perceived as monolithic, the fragmentation of female subjectivity would be the fragmentation of a whole that never was:

> Those who have been systematically excluded from the constitution of that so-called universal subject — whether for reasons of gender, class, race, sexuality — are unlikely either to long nostalgically for what they have never experienced or possessed (even as an illusion) or to revel angrily or in celebratory fashion in the "jouissance" of its disintegration. [. . .] women have, in practice, always experienced themselves in a "postmodern" fashion — decentred, lacking agency, defined through others.[44]

It seems to me that it is both permissible and useful to engage with women writers' self-expression, so long as we recognize that "self" as a mutable rather than a fixed subject, in dialogue both with its own social and cultural context and (through our reading) with ours.

Judith Gardiner reminds us that "a central question of feminist literary criticism is, Who is there when a woman says 'I am'?"[45] In the field of drama the answer is — at least notionally — a theater audience.[46] Jane Plastow claims a part for drama (in this case specifically postcolonial drama) in "the creation of identities and a sense of self-worth." She argues that the latter is one of the many things taken from colonized peoples, "a people without some sense of communal identity become [sic] fundamentally disempowered and negated at a profound level of their personal sense of being."[47] As add-ons, excess, or "others" in societies that have defined humanness as essentially male, women, too, have found themselves without "communal identity." The notion of sisterhood still has far more specific and negative connotations for many people than the ideal of human solidarity, brotherhood. I disagree fundamentally with Judith Butler when she maintains that it is "crucial to resist the model of power that would set up racism and homophobia and misogyny as parallel or analogical relations."[48] While it is clearly unhelpful to suggest that racism, homophobia, and misogyny are identical processes, it seems equally unhelpful to ignore the structural similarities that can exist between different forms of oppression. That would risk encouraging the kind of insular thinking which can, for example, forgive homophobia where it would never forgive racism, or vice versa. Drama has been used by the politically and racially oppressed, by gay and lesbian writers, and by feminists — among others — to explore societies, ideologies, discourses, and their limits. This book limits itself to asking whether drama has a special significance for the constitution of self(-worth) specifically for women, and more specifically for women writing in German in the later years of the nineteenth and earlier years of the twentieth century; but it does so in the context of drama's widest potential as a genre.

Drama and Its Language

Performance — and this, I think, is crucial — is *already inherent in* the dramatic text. We might see an analogy between the theater/drama binary and the sex/gender dichotomy deconstructed, now famously, by Judith Butler.[49] Butler's argument is that "biological sex" does not preexist socially imposed gender — one is not, in de Beauvoir's words, "born a woman" before "becoming" one, because sex, just as much as gender, is an arbitrary category for organizing human existence. There is a similar chicken-and-egg difficulty with the distinction between drama and theater. Drama (the text) is generally taken to pre-exist theater (the performance), but one might just as well argue that an *idea* of theater, at least, must necessarily pre-exist the dramatic text. Keir Elam has put it like this:

> The written text constrains the performance in obvious ways [. . .] But it is equally legitimate to claim that it is the performance, or at least a possible or "model" performance, that constrains the dramatic text in its very articulation. [. . .] The written text [. . .] is determined by its very need for stage contextualisation, and indicates throughout its allegiance to the physical conditions of performance.[50]

I do not take this to mean, as Bennett does, that "the use of nonlinguistic sign systems in theater automatically strips language of its semiotic privilege."[51] But, since my investigation bases upon the hypothesis that performance texts are a significantly specific form, it will not do to read drama simply as if it were a novel in dialogue. Elam uses Benveniste's distinction between *histoire* (defined as "objective," past narration; epic) and *discours* (a "subjective" mode situated in present time) to characterize the drama: "the drama is invariably presented in the form of *discours*, a network of 'pragmatic' utterances."[52] This problematizes modes of reading performance texts as if they were epic narratives: "the adaptation of literary-critical and, above all, narratological models to the drama [. . .] will inevitably sacrifice the very level — that of pragmatic discourse — at which it characteristically unfolds" (*E*, 144). Dramatic action, then, is not *described* (in the manner of the novel), but arises out of *interactions*, most of which are linguistic. Speech produces the drama's action. In the analyses that follow, I accord the action that is language more attention than the external events that have tended to be read by literary criticism as the "action" of drama.

Elam cites J. L. Austin's now-famous theory of (non-dramatic) speech acts, which brings "philosophical attention to bear [. . .] on the pragmatic status of speech as an interpersonal force in the real world" (*E*, 157). Adapted for the drama, this theory can help us describe stage interactions. In Austin's terminology, an utterance may perform, for example, an illocutionary act (that is, a deed performed in saying something, such as "I swear"), and/or a perlocutionary act (that is, the result of the words spoken, such as when someone is persuaded to do something).[53] Of course, speech acts may or may not be effective; they depend on an interlocutor or audience to provide the reaction that will determine their efficacy. The "felicity conditions" provided by the context of an utterance decide whether it will be felicitious/effective or infelicitous/failed.[54] Speech may be ignored, misunderstood, manipulated, or overruled by physical violence. Elam points out that comedy in particular uses failed or infelicitous speech acts, especially involving misunderstandings (*E*, 163–4), although one might argue that tragedy often does the same.

Elam's groundbreaking work on the semiotics of the drama does not take account of the relevance of gender to the *discours* that characterizes performance texts. The basis of literary drama is linguistic interaction; and linguistic interaction is, as a large number of studies have shown, an exceptionally fruitful field for the investigation of gendered categories and gender performance.[55] The very words and metaphors with which language functions make linguistic interaction, in life and in the performance text, fraught with gendered meanings that we as audience are reading even when we are not aware we are doing it. Rhetorical tropes in dramatic language can function as signals of whole matrices of meaning. To take a famous example: when, in Schiller's *Maria Stuart*, Paulet calls the Queen of Scots "diese Helena" (I.i.84), he thereby categorizes Maria as a "Helen of Troy," that is, as a dangerous, inflammatory woman. We as audience or readers will tend to accept the authority of Paulet's words, and not to ask critically "who says women's sexuality is dangerous?" Tropes work, generally speaking, because they are not alienating; on the contrary, they present us with a "given" (such as the Helen of Troy story) and encourage us to substitute the meaning of that story in another context. It is crucial that we never ask how appropriate the substitution is.

The discourse conditions under which a play is written are worthy of consideration, even if that consideration is speculative. Discourse conditions encompass both conventional metaphor and tropes (which all too often serve to valorize the masculine and diminish or even demonize the feminine)[56] and socio-cultural beliefs about language itself. Not only the language that is used, but our beliefs about language use affect our readings of others' speech, as some later twentieth-century scholarship shows. Dale Spender, for example, gives this overview of beliefs about linguistic activity in her germinal study *Man Made Language*:

> English speakers believe — and linguists appear to be no exception — that men's speech is forceful, efficient, blunt, authoritative, serious, effective, sparing and masterful; they believe that women's speech is weak, trivial, ineffectual, tentative, hesitant, hyperpolite, euphemistic, and is often marked by gossip and gibberish.[57]

Spender goes on to investigate the widespread belief in women's talkativeness, and specifically that they talk *more* than men. Despite assumptions of this kind, she notes that there "has not been one study which provides evidence that women talk more than men, and there have been numerous studies which indicate that men talk more than women" (*S*, 41). So how do we account for the discrepancy between social belief and empirical evidence? Spender suggests the following explanation:

> The concept of women as the talkative sex involves a comparison: [. . .] we have erroneously assumed that the measurement of women as talkers is in comparison to men. But this appears not to be the case. The talkativeness of women has been gauged in comparison not with men but with *silence*. . . . When silence is the desired state for women [. . .] then any talk in which a woman engages can be too much. (*S*, 42)

In fact, Spender suggests — following Pamela Fishman — that the only time when women's talk is acceptable in a mixed group is when they are doing (to use Fishman's term) "shitwork"; that is, maintaining or establishing a level of conversational interaction for the benefit of male interlocutors: "Females [. . .] do the support work. They restrict their own opportunities for expression by concentrating on the development of male topics" (*S*, 48–9). No wonder their linguistic activity is perceived as trivial.

Spender is assessing the use of the English language in the 1970s, but the theories she develops also provide an intellectual stimulus for reading German-language dramas of the 1860s and after. The late nineteenth- and early twentieth-century theories of Mensch, Wiegand, Schlenther, or Mar suggest that a belief in women's passive, supportive, supplementary status vis-à-vis men is not new at the time Spender is writing. Popular prejudice — discourse conditions, sociocultural beliefs — affect the process of creation. Virginia Woolf, for one, had distinct views on this subject, summed up in the notorious image of the Angel in the House, who "never had a mind or a wish of her own, but preferred to sympathise always with the mind and wishes of others," and who whispers to the writing woman "be tender; flatter; [. . .]. Never let anyone guess that you have a mind of your own. Above all, be pure!"[58] In the case of late nineteenth- and early twentieth-century women dramatists it is difficult to say to what extent the notion of "proper" linguistic space for women as "trivial," "supportive," or "pure" affects their sense of what kind of play they *ought* to be writing; that is, how far they feel they should be performing gender while they write. The question is nonetheless interesting. And it is safe to say that beliefs about gender and language at this time mean that women's *discours*, including their dramatic writing, will necessarily run the risk of being perceived as trivial.

Reading Women's Drama

In this study, I propose to focus on a reading even of unperformed plays that takes into account their potential as performance texts. I prefer not to distinguish in terms of the critical reading process between performed and unperformed dramas (although details of recorded performances will be given); instead I explore the significance of the notional body on the stage as a latent possibility in the text, and the function of language, particularly the speech act, in the interaction between characters. Rather than following the "theater or drama?, serious or trivial?" line of enquiry, I prefer to ask Elin Diamond's questions regarding theatrical representation: "Who is speaking and who is listening? Whose body is in view and whose is not? What is being represented, how, and with what effects? Who or what is in control?"[59]

This study is roughly, but only roughly, chronological in its organization. More important than the precise chronology of the plays is how they illustrate the dramatists' impulse to articulate (or to obscure) female selfhood or subjectivity in the bodies they interpellate,[60] through dramatic language, into a stage world, that "area of experience that is both within and beyond the norms of structured social life, where possibilities of change and transformation [. . .] can be rehearsed and enacted."[61] As dramatists, they are the creators of that world and, theoretically at least, in control of it; it will be interesting to observe how far they are able to use stage space as an emancipatory alternative to real life.

Some of the writers I consider are well known, and their works are widely available; others are almost completely unknown. Wherever possible I provide brief life details for the lesser-known dramatists; where biographical information is not available, the plays must be left to speak for themselves, and for their creators.

Notes

[1] Else Hoppe, "Die Frau als Dramatikerin," in *Die Literatur* 10 (1929), 563–64 (563).

[2] "Gibt es eine weibliche Theatertradition, die es uns ermöglichen wurde, diese Dramen in einem anderen Kontext zu lesen als in dem der männlichen Literatur- und Theatergeschichte?" Susanne Kord, "Frühe dramatische Entwürfe — Drei Dramati-

kerinnen im 18. Jahrhundert," in *Frauen Literatur Geschichte*, ed. by Hiltrud Gnüg und Renate Möhrmann, 2nd completely revised ed. (Stuttgart: Metzler, 1999), 231–47 (233).

[3] "Als Frau für das Theater zu schreiben, ist eine maßlose Herausforderung, eine Überschreitung der Grenzen." Interview with Jelinek, Web Page, cited in Helga Kraft, "Mimesis unterminiert: Drama und Theater von Frauen," in Gnüg/Möhrmann, eds., 1999, 279–98 (279).

[4] Susanne Kord, *Ein Blick hinter die Kulissen: Deutschsprachige Dramatikerinnen im 18. und 19. Jahrhundert* (Stuttgart: Metzler, 1992). Kord offers analyses of an enormous range of texts, and lists dramatists and dramas in an extensive bibliography.

[5] Anne Stürzer, *Dramatikerinnen und Zeitstücke: Ein vergessenes Kapitel der Theatergeschichte von der Weimarer Republik bis zur Nachkriegszeit* (Stuttgart: Metzler, 1993). Stürzer looks at the plays of Anna Gmeyner, Ilse Langner, Hilde Rubinstein, Eleonore Kalkowska, Christa Winsloe, and Maria Lazar, and pays particular attention to the problems of exile and "inner emigration."

[6] Katrin Sieg, *Exiles, Eccentrics, Activists: Women in Contemporary German Theater* (Ann Arbor: U of Michigan P, 1994). Sieg gives analyses of dramas and performances by Marieluise Fleisser and Kerstin Specht; Erika Mann; Else Lasker-Schüler; Gerlind Reinshagen; Elfriede Jelinek; and Ginka Steinwachs.

[7] Dagmar von Hoff, *Dramen des Weiblichen: Deutsche Dramatikerinnen um 1800* (Opladen: Westdeutscher Verlag, 1989).

[8] Anne Fleig, *Handlungs-Spiel-Räume: Dramen von Autorinnen im Theater des ausgehenden 18. Jahrhunderts* (Würzburg: Königshausen und Neumann, 1999).

[9] Heike Schmid, *Gefallene Engel: deutschsprachige Dramatikerinnen im ausgehenden 19. Jahrhundert* (St. Ingbert: Röhrig, 2000). Schmid provides fairly brief readings of plays by five dramatists of the period: Elsa Bernstein-Porges, Juliane Déry, Margarete Langkammer, Anna Croissant-Rust, and Clara Viebig. Her focus is on the "verschiedene Subjektpositionen weiblicher Charaktere" (21), although to this reader it did not become clear what precisely Schmid means by this.

[10] Helga Kraft, *Ein Haus aus Sprache: Dramatikerinnen und das andere Theater* (Stuttgart: Metzler, 1996), 3. Kraft's book is historically wide-ranging, but must be used with care as there are some minor errors: for example, Charlotte von Stein's drama *Die zwei Emilien*, recorded by Kord (*Ein Blick hinter die Kulissen,* 430), is misrecorded by Kraft as *Die zwei Familien* (Kraft, 31).

[11] "The woman writer" is an approximate, unsatisfying term, and refers in this study specifically to white women writers from German-speaking areas (which is still a generalization!).

[12] Giesing, "Theater als verweigerter Raum: Dramatikerinnen der Jahrhundertwende in deutschsprachigen Ländern," in *Frauen Literatur Geschichte: Schreibende Frauen vom Mittelalter bis zur Gegenwart*, original ed. ed. by Hiltrud Gnüg und Renate Möhrmann (Stuttgart: Metzler, 1985), 240–59.

[13] On the subject of repertoires and women directors, see also Michaela Giesing's new essay for the revised edition of *Frauen Literatur Geschichte*, "Verhältnisse und Ver-

hinderungen — deutschsprachige Dramatikerinnen um die Jahrhundertwende," in Gnüg/Möhrmann, eds., 1999, 261–78 (265).

[14] Gail Finney, *Women in Modern Drama: Freud, Feminism, and European Theater at the Turn of the Century* (Ithaca: Cornell UP, 1989).

[15] Von Hoff, 9.

[16] Karin Wurst, *Frauen und Drama im 18. Jahrhundert, 1770–1800* (Cologne: Böhlau, 1991).

[17] Ruth P. Dawson, "Frauen und Theater: Vom Stegreifspiel zum bürgerlichen Rührstück," in *Deutsche Literatur von Frauen*, ed. by Gisela Brinker-Gabler, vol. 1 (Munich: Beck, 1988), 421–34.

[18] Von Hoff, 10.

[19] Hegel, "Die dramatische Poesie," in Hegel, *Ästhetik*, ed. by Friedrich Bassenge, vol. 2 (Berlin: Aufbau, 1965), 512. Cited in von Hoff, 21.

[20] Kord, *Sich einen Namen machen: Anonymität und weibliche Autorschaft, 1700–1900* (Stuttgart: Metzler, 1996), 68–69.

[21] Hegel, 7. Cited in von Hoff, 22.

[22] Novalis, *Werke, Tagebücher und Briefe* ed. by Hans-Joachim Mähl und Richard Samuel, vol. 2 (Munich: Hanser, 1978), 765. Cited in von Hoff, 23.

[23] See Sylvia Bovenschen, *Die imaginierte Weiblichkeit: Exemplarische Untersuchungen zu kulturgeschichtlichen und literarischen Präsentationsformen des Weiblichen* (Frankfurt a. M.: Suhrkamp, 1979), 60.

[24] Wiegand, *Die Frau in der modernen Literatur: Plaudereien* (Bremen: Schünemann, 1903), 60–61.

[25] Dr. Ella Mensch, "Der Misserfolg der Frau als Dramenschriftstellerin," in *Bühne und Welt* 13 (1910–11), 155–59 (157–59).

[26] Mensch, "Der Misserfolg der Frau," 157.

[27] Lessing, "Zwei Münchener Dichterinnen: Ernst Rosmer und Helene Böhlau," in *Die Gesellschaft* 13/III (1898), 16–28 (24).

[28] G. W. F. Hegel, *Phänomenologie des Geistes*, in *Gesammelte Werke*, ed. Wolfgang Bonsiepen and Reinhard Heede, vol. 9 (Hamburg: Meiner 1980), 114.

[29] A. W. Schlegel, *Vorlesungen über dramatische Kunst und Literatur*, 2 vols. (Stuttgart: Kohlhammer, 1966–67), I, 39. Cited in Kord, *Sich einen Namen machen*, 71.

[30] "die Theorie/ der Geist, traditionell Domäne des Mannes, ist [. . .] zur Schaffung eines Schauspiels denkbar ungeeignet: dazu gehören eher weiblich besetzte Eigenschaften wie Spiel, Körperlichkeit." Kord, *Sich einen Namen machen*, 71.

[31] Mar, "Ein merkwürdiges Buch. 'Der Balkon.' Drei Akte von Gunnar Heiberg," in *Die Gesellschaft* 11 (1895), 1511–21 (1515–16).

[32] Julie Marney, "Performing Subjectivities: Feminism, Postmodernism and the Practice of Identity," unpublished doctoral dissertation, University of Edinburgh, 2000, 32.

[33] Pauli, "Frauen-Litteratur," in *Neue Deutsche Rundschau* 7 (1896), 276–81 (276).

[34] Paul Schlenther, "Frauenarbeit im Theater," in *Die Frau* 1 (1893/4), 150–55 (155).

[35] The reasoning provided for women's success as actors is not always this benevolent, as Renate Möhrmann points out: Bernhard Bauer, for example, in his book *Komödiantin — Dirne?* of 1927 argues that women are natural liars and therefore natural actors. See Möhrmann, *Die Schauspielerin: Zur Kulturgeschichte der weiblichen Bühnenkunst* (Frankfurt a. M.: Insel, 1989), 18.

[36] Paar, *Helene: Schauspiel in vier Akten* (Berlin: Luckhardt, 1882), 14.

[37] Weissenthurn, "Vorrede," in *Schauspiele*, vol. 1 (Vienna: Degen, 1804), v–viii.

[38] Braun, *Das geistige Leben des Weibes. Sonderdruck aus "Mann und Weib." Herausgegeben von Professor Dr. R. Koßmann und Privatdocent Dr. Jul. Weiß* (n.p. 1908), 274.

[39] Wilshire, *Role-Playing and Identity: The Limits of Theater as Metaphor* (Bloomington, IN: Indiana UP, 1991 [1982]), 26.

[40] Wilshire refers specifically to Paul Schilder's *The Image and Appearance of the Human Body* (New York 1950). See Wilshire, 26, note 4.

[41] Sigrid Weigel, "Der schielende Blick: Thesen zur Geschichte weiblicher Schreibpraxis," in *Die verborgene Frau*, ed. Inge Stefan and Sigrid Weigel (Berlin: Argument, 1988), 83–137 (85).

[42] Dr. Ella Mensch, *Die Frau in der modernen Literatur: Ein Beitrag zur Geschichte der Gefühle* (Berlin: Duncker, 1898), 77.

[43] Fredric Jameson, "Postmodernism and Consumer Society," in *Postmodern Culture*, ed. Hal Foster (London: Pluto, 1985), 111–26 (115).

[44] Patricia Waugh, *Practising Postmodernism, Reading Modernism* (London: Edward Arnold, 1992), 124–29.

[45] Judith Kegan Gardiner, "On Female Identity and Writing by Women," in *Writing and Sexual Difference*, ed. by Elizabeth Abel (Brighton: Harvester, 1982), 177–92 (178).

[46] In the practice of theater, the author's subjective stance is of course filtered through the subjectivity of others, particularly of the director. Here I am concerned with the *idea* of performance before an audience which is part of the creative process for the dramatist.

[47] Plastow, "Introduction," in Jane Plastow and Richard Boon, eds., *Theatre Matters: Performance and Culture on the World Stage* (Cambridge: Cambridge UP, 1998), 1–10 (1).

[48] Butler, *Bodies That Matter: On the Discursive Limits of "Sex"* (New York: Routledge, 1993), 18.

[49] In Butler, *Gender Trouble: Feminism and the Subversion of Identity* (New York: Routledge, 1990).

[50] Keir Elam, *The Semiotics of Theatre and Drama* (London: Routledge, 1994 [1980]), 209. Hereafter referred to in the text as *E*.

[51] Benjamin Bennett, *Theater as Problem: Modern Drama and its Place in Literature* (Ithaca: Cornell UP, 1990), 15.

[52] Emile Benveniste, *Problems of General Linguistics*, transl. Mary Elizabeth Meek (Miami: U of Miami P, 1970 [1966]), 237–40. Cited in Elam, 144. Even "epic" theater follows this pattern to a great extent, despite its deliberate use of elements of "histoire."

[53] Elam, 158. Austin's terminology has since been adapted and expanded, but these two types of speech act remain the most useful descriptors of linguistic action for our purposes.

[54] "Happy" and "unhappy" are Austin's terms. Other speech act theorists, especially John R. Searle, helped develop the notion of felicity conditions; for example, see Searle, *Speech Acts: An Essay in the Philosophy of Language* (Cambridge: Cambridge UP, 1969), 60–65. See also Elam, 162.

[55] Dale Spender's *Man Made Language* (2nd ed., London: Pandora, 1985), and Deborah Tannen's work, including *Gender & Discourse* (New York: Oxford UP, 1994) are well known examples.

[56] For a thorough discussion of the development of such metaphors and tropes in German language drama see Sarah Colvin, *The Rhetorical Feminine: Gender and Orient on the German Stage* (Oxford: Clarendon, 1999).

[57] Spender, 33. The inclusion of passages from this study in Deborah Cameron's standard textbook *The Feminist Critique of Language* (London: Routledge, 1998) testifies to the continued influence of Spender's work. *Man Made Language* is hereafter referred to in the text as *S*.

[58] Woolf, "Professions for Women," in Woolf, *Collected Essays* (London: Chatto & Windus, 1966), vol. 2, 284–89.

[59] Diamond, *Unmaking Mimesis: Essays on Feminism and Theatre* (London: Routledge, 1997), ii.

[60] Interpellation is the process by which, according to sociolinguistic theory, the body comes into being through being named. See Judith Butler, *Bodies That Matter*, 225.

[61] Susanne Greenhalgh, "Occupying the Empty Space: Feminism and Drama," in *Teaching Women: Feminism and English Studies*, ed. by Anne Thompson and Helen Wilcox (Manchester: Manchester UP, 1989), 170–79 (171).

1: Marie von Ebner-Eschenbach and Helene Druskowitz: Experiments in Dramatic Form

THE NOTION THAT DRAMA is a masculine genre dogs the critical reception of women playwrights. The young Alexander von Weilen, son of Marie von Ebner-Eschenbach's literary acquaintance, Joseph von Weilen, demonstrates the ubiquity of the idea at the turn of the nineteenth century. Commenting in 1890, when Ebner was sixty years old and well established as a prose writer, Alexander glibly assesses her achievements: "Den wenigen Dramen, welche die Ebner verfaßt, fehlt nichts als — die Hand des Mannes, welche allein die Gewalt fordernde Form zu beherrschen vermag."[1] Even though he writes with the flourish of one presenting a revelation, von Weilen is making no pathbreaking contribution to turn-of-the-century criticism. He is merely parroting the established notion that the role of the dramatist is the role of the dominant male. Nonetheless, an idea repeated often enough can become reality, and Weilen's predictable assertion that Ebner, as a woman, simply could not also be a dramatist, finds its unfortunate echo in the fact that, by 1890, she *was* no longer writing dramas. At most she still wrote comic one-act plays, but she had abandoned her more serious aspirations in the genre,[2] and was received for almost a hundred years much as Otto Krack described her in 1898: "Die Bühnendichterin kann sich mit der Erzählerin nicht messen."[3]

Ebner certainly once had dramatic aspirations. At the age of fourteen, Marie Dubsky, later von Ebner-Eschenbach (1830–1916), told her family she intended to be the German Shakespeare of the nineteenth century.[4] The significance of her ambition should not be underestimated. Ebner wanted to write historical tragedy, a particularly high-status literary form, associated in Germany with Schiller and Goethe; at age fourteen she felt able to align herself with the most influential dramatist in Western literary history, Shakespeare. Her dearest wish, then and later, was to see her work performed at Vienna's Burgtheater. With a fine disregard for nineteenth-century cultural beliefs regarding the role and capacity of women, the young Ebner intended her work to be neither trivial nor supportive.

Her early literary projects reflect her ambitious attitude of mind: they are historical dramas in the classical style, composed in iambic verse. Five are on record, and she completed and published two, namely *Maria Stuart in Schottland* (published at her own expense in 1860), and *Marie Roland* (1867). *Strafford* is now lost; *Cinq-Mars* (also titled *Richelieus Ende*) and *Jacobäa von Jülich-Cleve* are fragments. Neither of the completed tragedies is yet available in a more recent edition.

Ebner never managed to have a full-length play performed at the Burgtheater. Eduard Devrient, the artistic director in Karlsruhe to whom she sent her *Maria Stuart* under the pseudonym "M. v. Eschenbach" was initially enthused by the piece; he performed it in Karlsruhe in 1861 and entered it for the prestigious Schiller Prize in 1863.[5] Devrient was surprised to discover that the author of *Maria Stuart* was a woman ("Also eine Dichterin. Das ist überraschend bei diesem männlichen Geiste"),[6] and he declined to perform her next tragedy, *Marie Roland*.

Maria Stuart was not considered for production at the Burgtheater, although Heinrich Laube, as artistic director, did accept Ebner's short comedy *Die Veilchen* for performance in May 1863.[7] In June of that year we find her doing her sums in her diary, with some amazement at the financial consequences of the two projects: "Vom Burgtheater für die *Veilchen* 80fl. Von Michaelson 100fl = 180fl. Ab: Druckkosten 20fl. Rest: 160fl. *Maria Stuart* hat beinah so viel *gekostet*" (*T I*, 13 May 1863; Ebner's emphasis). Another one-act piece, *Dr. Ritter*, written for the Kärntnertortheater on the occasion of Schiller's 110th birthday, moved to the Burgtheater on 23 February 1869 and had six performances.[8] After this, there was a gap of almost 30 years before — chiefly in response to her success as a prose writer — the Burgtheater performed two of Ebner's romantic one-act plays, *Ohne Liebe* (1898) and *Am Ende* (1900). *Am Ende* can be described as her most successful play, produced 27 times to 1953. It deserves more critical attention than it has been given, or can be given here. Under the veneer of a conventional sentimental plot (wronged wife forgives aging playboy husband and takes him back into her home), *Am Ende* is a complex portrayal of gender relations, of abjection and dominance; a play as ambiguous as its title.

After *Maria Stuart*, *Marie Roland* was Ebner's next hope for the Burgtheater. Laube read the play soon after it was finished in January 1867, and responded so positively that Ebner was incoherent with joy: "Von Laube kommend. Alleluja! Danke Dir mein Gott! Du bist mir doch gnädig u. huldreich über alles Verdienst, über alle Erwartung" (*T I*, 26 January 1863).[9] But the timing was unlucky. 1867, the year in which Ebner finished the play, was also the year in which the position of artistic influence at the Burgtheater changed hands, less than amicably, from Heinrich Laube to Eligius Freiherr von Münch-Bellinghausen, also known as Münch and by his literary pseudonym Friedrich Halm. When Münch was appointed as *Intendant* of the Burgtheater in 1867, he also took responsibility for its artistic directorship. Laube resigned in protest.

Like Laube, Münch was himself a dramatist, and both men were friends of and literary advisers to Ebner-Eschenbach. Before the split with Laube, Münch, too, had expressed admiration for *Marie Roland* (*T* I, 31 January 1867; 2 February 1867). From early 1867, Ebner had been working with Laube on revising the drama for performance. When, in July of that year, it became clear that Münch would be the Burgtheater's next *Intendant*, she foresaw disaster for her play — "Leb wohl Marie Roland! — es ist einmal wieder eines meiner Kinder gestorben bevor es auf der Welt war" (*T* I, 11 July 1867). Sure enough, Münch did not continue Laube's work on the piece: as Ebner had predicted, *Marie Roland* fell victim to the men's private fracas.[10] By November 1867, she was playing the role of intermediary between them, but she was unable to prevent Laube's resignation. Her reaction to the death of Münch in 1871 indicates how profoundly this quarrel influenced her relations with him — "Daß in den letzten Jahren unsere früher so freundschaftlichen Beziehungen getrübt werden mußten, durch den unseligen Kampf mit Laube, werde ich Zeit meines Lebens nicht verwinden" (*T* II, 26 May 1871).

In December 1868, Münch had also rejected Ebner's new full-length comedy *Das Waldfräulein*. Laube, however, expressed interest in the piece, for his new project: the Viennese Stadttheater, which opened in 1872. Laube conceived of this theater as a rival institution to the Burgtheater, its intended audience Vienna's growing class of wealthy bourgeoisie, rather than the "old" Viennese nobility who enjoyed exclusive use of the Burgtheater's boxes till 1867.[11]

Das Waldfräulein opened at the Stadttheater on 13 January 1873. Laube had predicted a success for the piece. In one sense, he was right, at least as far as publicity for his own new theater was concerned: word had got around that a comedy satirizing Viennese high society, written by a member of that society, was to be performed. The interest aroused by the première was such that mounted police officers were brought in to supervise the arriving carriages.[12] Laube may also have hoped that a Stadttheater audience would warm to the play's satirical portrayal of Vienna's upper classes. If so, he miscalculated. Ebner's diary entry for the opening night suggests that they did not: "Nach dem letzten Aufzuge hörte ich mehr Zischen als Applaus" (*T* II, 13 January 1873). Even if the hissers in the

audience were not as numerous as she perceived,[13] the play was subsequently attacked by Vienna's theater critics, and Ebner herself lampooned
as a scribbling bluestocking.

The Tragedy of a Queen: *Maria Stuart*

For a writer like Ebner-Eschenbach, fired by her enthusiasm for Schiller's
historical dramas, Mary Stuart seems an obvious choice of character
around which to build a classical, iambic, five-act play.[14] Schiller's *Maria
Stuart* of 1800, like his predecessor Haugwitz's *Maria Stuarda* of 1684
(which in turn is based on Vondel's play of 1646),[15] deals with events
leading up to the death of the Queen of Scots, as prisoner of Elizabeth
I of England. However, Ebner stages events from a far earlier period in
Mary's life: the period she spent as ruler of her own kingdom, Scotland,
which was also the time of her marriage to Henry Darnley and later to
James Hepburn, Earl of Bothwell.

> In meine Hände legtest Du ein Scepter
> Das wie ein Schwert geformt: als wie ein Schwert
> Zu schwingen und zu brauchen.[16]

When Ebner's Mary Stuart evokes her royal power with reference to the
sceptre and the sword, images of the power of the author's pen (often
equated with phallic power)[17] spring to mind. Marie and her character
Maria, as writer and queen respectively, share a directive calling. We
might identify this as hubris on the part of the young playwright: there
is self-reference that recalls Goethe's far more famous "gab mir ein Gott,
zu sagen, was ich leide."[18] But the text puts a twist in the notion of
female power that Maria Stuart's speech evokes. Immediately after Maria
has spoken, we hear an offstage explosion that signals the murder of
Darnley, her husband; an event masterminded by men (Murray and
Bothwell), and utterly beyond the Queen's control. A woman's calling
to a position of authority is shown to be incomplete.

Mary Stuart's authority is a highly problematic issue in the play.
Where for Schiller it was the Queen of Scots' sexuality that provoked
men to action, for Ebner it is her royal status: Ebner's Maria is defined,
paradoxically, not only as a woman — and therefore subordinate — but
as a ruler, and therefore dominant. This drives the men around her to
both action and distraction. Darnley is tortured by a sense of inferiority,
as is her second husband Bothwell later; and her brother Murray will not
rest till Mary is cast from the throne and he himself has charge of the
male heir (later James VI and I).

Much of the play is given over to the battle for dominance, which is also a battle about the gendered definition of individuals, by themselves and those around them. Early on, Darnley is encouraged by the Scottish lords to establish mastery over Maria:

> Tritt vor sie als Gebieter — ford're von
> Der Überwundenen Gehorsam! Dies
> Begehren wir. (7)

Words like "Gebieter" and "Gehorsam" immediately call to mind the traditional rights of the man in marriage. But for Maria's supporters at court, the definition "queen" supplants the definition "woman" — Lennox spells this out:

> Ich werd' ihr raten als ein Weib zu *dulden,*
> *(für sich).* Bis sie als eine Kön'gin *handeln* kann.
>
> (8; Ebner's emphasis)

The two verbs, "dulden" and "handeln," reflect perfectly the contradictory notions of feminine passivity and royal activity that complicate the position of the Queen of Scots. Maria herself insists on the conjunction, when she complains to the men who are holding her captive after the murder of Rizzio:

> Die Rücksicht, Lord, gewähret dem Geschlecht —
> Und ehrt in der gefang'nen *Königin* — das *Weib*
>
> (14; Ebner's emphasis)

and again in her reproaches to Darnley:

> Nicht blos [*sic*] die Königin — das Weib in mir
> Hast Du beschimpft. (24)

But where Maria conjoins her sex and her status, the men around her are keen to separate the two elements. Darnley curses her:

> Sei groß als Königin,
> Als Weib sei Du verachtet! (24)

and Bothwell, in his Machiavellian courtship of the Queen, disguises his hunger for power by privileging her sexual definition, as woman:

> Ich liebe Dich — nicht wie
> Ein Unterthan die Fürstin liebt — o nein!
> So wie ein Mann das Weib, das er begehrt. (25)

Later, however, when the insecurity of his dominance over a woman who is also a queen is driving Bothwell mad, he tries to use the category "woman" (in its meaning "subordinate, passive") to control her movements:

BOTHWELL.   Du bleibst. Der Krieg ist nicht für Weiber.

MARIA.   Für Königinnen ist auch Krieg und Ruhm. (54)

When the battle against the English forces is lost, the two of them take up the rhetorical cudgels again, this time implementing exactly switched categories: Maria pleads for mercy on the grounds that she is a (weak) woman, while Bothwell chooses to present her as a powerful queen:

MARIA.   Erbarmen, Bothwell! Gib Dein Weib nicht Preis
            Dem Uebermuthe siegender Empörer —

BOTHWELL.   Bist Du nicht Königin? Beschütz' Dich selbst. (59)

At issue throughout the play is Maria's capacity to define herself, as opposed to the power of others to define her. Alongside her own self-definitions "Königin" and "Weib" (terms which are hijacked by both Darnley and Bothwell), the men of the play use "Buhlerin" (Darnley, 11), "Verbrecherin" (Darnley, 11; Murray, 62), and "Mörderin" (Lennox, 46; Erster Soldat, 61). Drawing on biblical and mythological traditions, Ruthven calls her "Jesabel" (5), and Bothwell "Syrene" (59). It is worth noting that the only other woman in the play, Lady Argyll, defines Maria differently: for her, she is "die Vielgeschmähte" (39) — the woman who is much maligned in the linguistic battle that is central to this drama. Interestingly, Lady Argyll also turns around the normal usage of the classical metaphor "siren" to categorize a man, rather than a woman. In the sexual relationship between Bothwell and Maria, she casts *him* as the seductive/destructive force:

Er hat
Dein Herz bethört und Deinen Sinn verblendet —
Dein Ohr umstrickt mit seinen Liebesschwüren. (40)

Lady Argyll's metaphor is remarkable and unusual — she turns around the mythological story of Ulysses and the sirens. The available stock of images in language and cultural tradition tends to work against women, not for them, and must be turned around if they are to function rhetorically against men. The rabidly gynophobic speech in which Bothwell finally vents his insecurity perfectly illustrates how a stock of misogynist images feeds neurosis and paranoia. When Mary kneels in her despair to ask for death at his hand, Bothwell explodes:

Ha! Neue Künste nun? Vergeblich. Weib!
Ich bin gefeit gen [= gegen] alle. Ich durchschaue
Dich ganz, Syrene mit dem Kinderauge,
Und mit der Brust voll Arglist und voll Tücke!
— Was Du verheißest, ist Glückseligkeit,
Was Du gewährest, Höllenqual und Pein,
Dein Wort ist Balsam — Gift sind Deine Thaten —
Deine Geschenke, Goldesechtheit lügend —
Bei der Berührung Moder — ekler Staub! (59)

Given that Ebner has made it perfectly clear that Bothwell was never interested so much in Maria's person as in the power that went with it, we ought not to feel much sympathy for him here. So it is odd that this long speech is so poetic and impassioned. In fact, the speech is practically pre-written for Ebner in the German literary idiom: consciously or not, it is pastiche. The misogynist images Bothwell conjures are (disturbingly) so readily available in the literary vocabulary that they seem to flow effortlessly from Ebner's pen, and their effect is (again, disturbingly) effective even in the mouth of a character who ought not to command our sympathy. Bothwell characterizes Maria not only as a siren, but as Frau Welt, the popular medieval figure whose enticing exterior conceals foulness and decay. The associations with this figure are serious and dreadful: she incorporates the worldly sinfulness that can rob men of their eternal souls.[19] Where Mary Stuart in Schiller (and in Haugwitz) finishes the play as a kind of saint, Ebner's Queen of Scots finishes the play — at least in the eyes of the men on stage[20] — as a kind of devil. Ebner's reading of male psychology and social reality is, it seems, considerably less optimistic than Schiller's.

The linguistic battles in the play interact interestingly with actual or threatened physical violence. One of the problems raised by Ebner's Maria is that, as Queen, she commands a level of authority not generally accorded to women. Early on in the play, when Douglas seeks to engage linguistically with the Queen, Murray suggests that this Gordian knot must be cut with violence:

Nicht ich, bei Gott! nicht ich, erwarte Heil
Von der Comödie, in welcher Douglas
Die Rolle des Vermittlers spielen will!
Nur der Gewalt erliegt Maria Stuart. (9)

Bothwell's philosophy is similar: he arrives at Maria's court, where he is to be tried for the murder of Darnley, with a troop of henchmen who are armed to the teeth, thus physically threatening the linguistic authority of the court. Lady Argyll protests: "Er bringt *Gewalt*, die es gefährlich macht / Ihn zu verurtheilen" (40; Ebner's emphasis). Judgments pronounced in court are, generally speaking, particularly effective linguistic acts (they have concrete results) — but Bothwell specializes in resisting the power of the speech act. His characterization in the play as a peculiarly masculine man depends as much on his relationship to speech as it does on his willingness to use physical violence. We can see this if we focus on speech acts in the text.

Commands or imperatives are an easily identifiable type of illocutionary speech act. Darnley, who is an "unmasculine" man (Maria defines him as "unmännlich," 23), is unable to issue effective imperatives. When he commands Maria to give him a key — "Gieb!" (11) — she simply refuses, and thus renders his attempted command infelicitous. Bothwell, by contrast, makes his first impression on the Queen by resisting an imperative issued by her. Maria commands that he be reconciled with Murray, but Bothwell, rather than simply refusing to obey the command, goes so far as to deny her ability to issue it to him:

> Du kannst mit Trug
> Und Lüge Dich versöhnen, doch von mir
> Die Lüge fordern — kannst Du nicht. *(er geht ab)* (16)

His removal of his bodily presence, as a sign of her powerlessness over him, is a particularly effective form of resistance. Maria's immediate response to this is to recognize the significance, in gender terms, of what has happened: Bothwell has denied her linguistic and corporeal authority, and thereby asserted his masculinity: "Er ist ein *Mann* / In dieser Schaar von Feiglingen und Schlangen!" (16; Ebner's emphasis).

Unsurprisingly, given his masculine status in the play, Bothwell's own speech is peppered with imperatives, which are generally felicitous; Bothwell is the confident owner of the language he uses, so much so that he is not afraid to take risks. In asserting his love for the Queen, he both identifies and dismisses the danger inherent in that linguistic act:

> Ich [. . .] setze nun mein Dasein auf ein Wort —
> Und sprech' es aus wär's auch mein Untergang:
> Ich liebe Dich! dies Wort ist Hochverrath. (25)

Maria's powerlessness to exercise authority in the face of such assertive masculinity is reflected not only in her disjointed speech: "Nicht so — verlasse mich — ich will's!" (25), but also in the fact that Bothwell yet again ignores her command. The "no means yes" that he assumes here denies Maria's capacity to speak effectively: what she says is not impor-tant, but how he chooses to interpret it. Significantly, only one character in the play is Bothwell's linguistic master, and that is Murray, the play's Iago. By a perlocutionary (persuasive, manipulative) speech act, Murray is able to effect Bothwell's murder of Darnley — he thereby brings about Bothwell's downfall and his own, Murray's, triumph.

The Tragedy of a Revolutionary: *Marie Roland*

Ebner's later play, *Marie Roland,*[21] reveals a similar concern with linguis-tic authority, but displays less traditional gender divisions. From the first scene of the first act of *Marie Roland*, it is clear that the central protago-nist is linguistically and corporeally in control. A fellow Girondin (disap-provingly) observes her relationship with her husband, Roland:

> Sie schreibt *für* ihn,
> Und spricht für ihn, und handelt wohl für ihn.
> > (3; Ebner's emphasis)

Marie Roland confounds gendered expectations because hers is, em-phatically, a "body that matters."[22] The entrance of another Girondin, Louvet, confirms this: Louvet's greeting recognizes primarily Marie Roland, and only secondarily the others who are gathered:

> LOUVET. Gegrüßt, Marie Roland,
> > *(zu den Uebrigen)*
> > und Ihr.

Marie Roland's speech acts are, as we might expect, largely illocutionary and perlocutionary: she commands, demands, and persuades. Emphasis is given to the notion that her speech provokes action, "Handeln" or "That," as opposed to the endless, "Reden" or "Gedanken" that the male Girondins have been engaged in. Importantly, they accord to her the authority to speak effectively: Vergniaud turns to Marie Roland for a decision with the words,

> Entscheide Du, [. . .]
> Du bist die Seele der Gironde, und stets
> Erschien Dein Wunsch ihr ein Gesetz. (5)

Unlike Maria Stuart, then, Marie Roland is in a position to produce felicitous results when she speaks. She is not in thrall to powerful male speech in the way that her dramatic predecessor, Maria Stuart, was: when Buzot confesses his love to the married Marie Roland in a scene not dissimilar to that where Bothwell confessed his to the married Queen of Scots, Marie Roland is well able to hold her own. In the earlier play the linguistic and corporeal power was Bothwell's — Maria Stuart is unable to prevent his assertion of the rights of a (male) lover over her — but here the authority is with Marie Roland: "Mein erstes Wort ist stets mein letztes Wort. [. . .] geh'!" (10).

Despite her control of language, Marie Roland cannot avoid being defined by it. Like Maria Stuart, she is caught in the web of misogynist metaphor. For Robespierre, she is not a siren (as Maria was for Bothwell), but the related mythological figure Circe (18); she is also called "Buhlerin" (10) and often simply "Weib" (which, here as in Ebner's earlier play, has derogatory, reductive connotations not associated with "Mann").

Marie Roland is crucially unlike Maria Stuart, however, when she moves into negative *self*-definition. Ebner's later heroine damns *herself* in language: she describes herself as "hochmüthig" (12), as "Mörderin" (26), and as a "schuldbelad'nes Weib" (36).[23] This, it seems, is the price of the gender-bending authority she has enjoyed. Gender norms dictate that women must assume an abject, not a dominant linguistic position. Ebner's Queen of Scots has abjection forced on her by the men who plot against and overthrow her; Marie Roland, the Queen of the Girondins ("Königin der Girondes," 13), practices self-abjection.

Where Maria Stuart, in her final words to Murray as the guardian of her son, pleads simply for kindness, Marie Roland's instructions to her daughter's caretaker, Lodoïska, are different; she insists that her child be subjugated in such a way as to compensate, it seems, for her own lack of humility:

> Sie ist mein Kind, hat einen starken Willen,
> Schon regt sich ihre junge Eitelkeit.
> Bekämpf' den Fehler! beuge ihren Stolz!
> [. . .] Milde werde sie! (36)

In the context of the drama and of nineteenth-century gender norms, Ebner is here preserving her heroine's ideal status. Marie Roland, we infer, has recognized the necessity of enforcing passive gentleness in women, even though she herself lived life as an active revolutionary. In another context — that of the writer's subjectivity — we might identify a chain of compensatory actions here. The dramatist (who, as a woman playwright, is offending against gender norms) forces abjection on her character (who, as a historical leader of men, has offended against gender norms), who in turn forces abjection on her daughter (who is to be prevented from the start from offending against gender norms).

Is this, and the miserable defeat of Maria Stuart, to be understood as the "return to order" that characterizes tragic closure? In both plays, Ebner returns us to an all-too-familiar order in which linguistically dominant women are disempowered and silenced. So how can we read Ebner-Eschenbach's choice and use of the historical tragedy as form?

Because this form conventionally deals with persons and events of historical significance, Ebner's decision to use it does encourage us to view her heroines (if we did not already) as bodies that matter. As a form, historical tragedy traditionally brings the dramatist, too, a certain weight — the events portrayed lend the writer the authority of historical necessity. Brecht later turned this around, turning necessity into necessity-for-change; and Ferrel Rose has, from a modern reading perspective, identified a need-to-change in *Maria Stuart*: "an imperative that society must change before anyone, male or female, can govern with any humanity."[24] But Ebner's drama does not really anticipate epic theater, and her tragic endings do not deliberately alienate; instead, as I have argued, they strive to conciliate, returning unruly women to the gendered fold. This is not in itself a dramatic weakness — it might even be read as a strength, since a return to order is understood to provide satisfying closure.

Of non-historical tragedies by women, Susanne Kord has made this important observation, which is worth citing at length:

> Allen nicht geschichtlichen Trauerspielen von Frauen sind zwei Aspekte gemeinsam: das Bewußtsein der Abhängigkeit der Frau und die Abwesenheit von Lösungsvorschlägen. Denn alle Lösungsvorschläge, ob philosophischer [. . .] oder politischer [. . .] Natur, basieren auf der Vorstellung einer Welt, die im Prinzip funktioniert und an der nur einiges verbessert werden muß. In Trauerspielen von Frauen [. . .] existiert diese Welt nicht oder nur für Männer.[25]

We can apply this to the historical tragedies *Maria Stuart* and *Marie Roland*. Ebner does provide closure, but it is not of a type that can be read as satisfying for a female self or subject. The earlier play ends with the absolute triumph of men: Bothwell escapes heroically from his pursuers, while Mary is dispatched by Murray to England, into the clutches of Elizabeth, who will eventually execute her and thus damage her own reputation, not Murray's, by doing the dirty work. In Scotland, Murray remains as regent to the infant James, who will eventually join both queens' kingdoms [!] under male rule. *Marie Roland* concludes, it is true, with the apotheosis of the heroine; but it is an apotheosis that can only be bought at the cost of remorseful self-accusation, and with the promise that proper, gentle, abject feminine behavior will be imposed on the next generation: her daughter.

An Experiment in Comedy: Ebner's *Waldfräulein*

Tragedy is not the only dramatic mode in which a resolution is demanded. Comedy, at least as much as tragedy, relies on a set of social codes. It will inevitably overstep the established mark — that is an important part of what makes comedy funny — but every transgression makes sense only in the context of knowledge of the code or boundary that is being overstepped. The overstepping of boundaries necessitates a particularly clear return to order at the end of the play if satisfying closure is to be achieved. Especially in romantic comedy, this return to order or "happy ending" has tended to be marriage.

It is less easy than it might appear to shake off such traditional shackles: if comedy oversteps the wrong kind of boundaries it risks being perceived as alarming or offensive, rather than as humorous. Kord has already noted the difficulty posed by marriage as closure for writers who knew very well, often from their own experience, that married happiness for women "hing realiter bestenfalls am dünnen Faden männlicher Toleranz."[26] But, as Regina Barreca confirms, "in order to be read and for their comedy to be acknowledged as such, women writers have accepted the basic conventions associated with the genre."[27] While engagement and marriage are maintained in many comedies by women as the "proper" form of closure, the ideality of the situation is seldom left undisturbed: Kord has written of the "Relativierung des traditionellen Happy Ends, mit allen damit verbundenen Zweifeln an der Ordnung, die in der Komödie dargestellt wird."[28] There tends to be an implicit end beyond the happy ending, a deictic hint at a less-than-blissful future in conventional marriage.

One clear attraction posed by comedy for women writers is its status. There is no doubt that comedy is regarded as a less grand mode than historical drama or tragedy. In this sense, as trivial, it slots more easily into the category "feminine"; it appears, on the surface at least, to offer space more readily for the woman writer. This may have been a consideration in Ebner-Eschenbach's decision, while she was completing her last historical tragedy, *Marie Roland*, to start work on a full-length comedy called *Das Waldfräulein*.[29] In October 1871, it was intimated to her that Laube (now at the Stadttheater) intended to stage both dramas,[30] but only the comedy was performed. Laube's choice was almost certainly populist — even in his days at the Burgtheater, Laube did not believe that his public wanted to be subjected to historical drama — and it was a choice that did not appear to surprise Ebner.

The two plays, as emerges from the diaries, were written in overlap (*T* I, 28 June 1867). Even though one is a historical tragedy and the other a contemporary comedy, they show thought-provoking similarities in their content and structure. In both plays we have a central female protagonist who is fiercely and self-consciously righteous: in the tragedy, Marie Roland herself, and in the comedy, Sarah Hochburg, the country girl or "Waldfräulein" turned Viennese débutante. This righteousness — which is a quality of humane virtuousness rather than self-righteousness — is expressed in both cases on two levels, one of which could be described as stereotypically masculine, the other as stereotypically feminine. On the masculine side, Marie Roland, leading the Girondins in revolutionary France, practices determined political integrity; while Sarah Hochburg, "das Waldfräulein," identifies with and supports the late nineteenth-century democratic endeavor in Austria. Both women show by their actions that they are braver than most of the men around them, and put the unmasculine male to shame.[31] Both are straightforward, straight-talking, impatient of personal adornment, resolute and fearless, with a strong sense of personal honor. They stand out against, in Marie Roland's case, the intellectual "wetness" of her fellow Girondins, and, in Sarah Hochburg's case, the men of the Viennese *monde*, who routinely lie and cheat and are cowardly and vain. As well as ideal masculine traits, however, both heroines also display a sexual continence that is traditionally idealized in women. Marie Roland chooses her duty to and friendship for her much older husband over her passionate love for Buzet. Sarah is less severely tested, but proves her virtue when she expresses disbelief and horror at the loose sexual mores that prevail in Vienna's high society.

Both characters are shown to be crucially *different* from those around them. Historically, views are divided on Marie Roland: she has been seen as an inspired leader, and as a ruthless terrorist.[32] Ebner depicts her as a passionate political revolutionary, whose power to lead stems from a remarkable belief in herself, which is also a belief (initially at least) that she is *unlike* those she condemns. In the comedy, the nickname "Waldfräulein" signals the heroine's status in and simultaneously outside of Viennese society: she is a Simplicissimus figure, a naïve outsider whose alienated gaze allows her to see far more than those who are fully socialized, or sophisticated.

Ebner gives her *Marie Roland* an interesting twist by re-directing the focus in the course of the play to the similarities, rather than differences, between Marie and her most hated adversaries on the Republican and Royalist sides: Danton, and the deposed (and executed) queen Marie-Antoinette. It is important that those similarities are not only apparent to the audience, but are recognized by the protagonist: in her confrontation with Danton in the crucial last scene of the third act (Ebner called this scene "die wichtigste im ganzen Stück," *T* I, 7 April 1866), and later during her final hours in the conciergerie, in a cell that is right next to the one the French queen inhabited before *her* death on the guillotine. In the less somber world of *Das Waldfräulein*, Sarah Hochburg, too, changes her tune: she finally marries not her democratic uncle (though this is briefly in the cards) but a young aristocrat she has fallen in love with. Neither heroine, then, preserves her status as other than those she has condemned. Both give up their (masculine) roles as central performer: Sarah — after one last projected performance at the altar — to be a wife to her Count; and Marie Roland — after one last projected performance on the guillotine — to permit the more feminine, self-sacrificing Lodoïska to raise her, Marie Roland's, daughter.

There is evidence that Ebner-Eschenbach was more than usually dismayed at the failure of her *Waldfräulein* at the Stadttheater. Vienna's critics focused on its central character and her failings, but also on the author. Sarah Hochburg is characterized as "kühn" and "frech," with an "Anlage zum Blaustrumpf," while another critic finds that "der Gedanke an irgendeine persönliche Rache der Authoress in allernächster Nähe liegt."[33] In her diary Ebner noted, with a mixture of resentment and self-flagellation:

> Das Waldfräulein ist gewiß ein sehr schwaches Stück. [. . .] Aber den Hohn mit dem es überschüttet wird hat es nicht verdient u. die Autorin weiß nicht wie sie zu der persönlichen Gehässigkeit kommt, die ihr wie auf Signal von allen Journalen, allen, ohne Ausnahme bewiesen wird. (*T* II, Anhang Jänner 1873)

Ebner was not unused to criticism, and Vienna's theater critics at the time were certainly not known for wearing kid gloves. Her sensitive reaction here is therefore surprising, unless we view *Das Waldfräulein* as in some sense an "other" *Marie Roland*. We can see the comedy as an attempt to create something more accessible and popular, from which Ebner may have promised herself the appreciation from a theater audience she so badly wanted.

But the aggressively gender-specific responses to *Das Waldfräulein* in the Viennese press suggest that she overlooked the real problem, common to both plays: how gender is performed. In both dramas, the protagonist is loved by two men: Marie Roland by Buzot and by her husband, Roland; Sarah Hochburg by her democratic uncle Robert and by Count Paul, whom she eventually marries. In each case the triangle includes a worthy older man and a younger, more passionate beloved, and in each case the older men are prepared to sacrifice themselves for the women they love. Roland offers to dissolve his marriage to Marie so she can marry Buzot — he even insists he will do so gladly, for the sake of her happiness, although he would be giving up his own. Later in the play he commits suicide when he hears of her death, something he has always sworn he will do. Roland, in short, offers the kind of unilateral fidelity conventionally reserved for ideal *women* in literature (such as Kleist's Käthchen, or Dickens's Agnes in *David Copperfield*). In *Das Waldfräulein*, Uncle Robert behaves analogously when he gives up Sarah, who has promised to marry him, so that she can be engaged to her younger beloved, Paul. Ebner is turning dramatic conventions on their heads: in these plays, the masculine resoluteness of the women is matched by the feminine selflessness of the men.[34]

And that is not the end of it. Remarkably, in these relationships it is the women who take on a role that in the Rousseau-influenced nineteenth century is peculiarly masculine: that of the educator. Buzot explains that his love for Marie Roland derives in great measure from the political education he received at her hands (29). When the "Waldfräulein" Sarah Hochburg arrives in Vienna, we hear Count Paul expressing an intention to educate her: "erziehen" is the word he chooses. But Ebner turns the tables on him — by the end of the play, we find Count Paul expressing gratitude to Sarah for all that *she* has been able to teach *him*: conventional expectations are ironized.

Dale Spender has shown that, despite beliefs in women's talkativeness, it is men who talk more in mixed gender situations.[35] Both of Ebner's heroines occupy a masculine position in linguistic terms, in that their speeches dominate — not only in terms of the number of lines they fill. These women protagonists speak their minds, are forceful and uncompromising in their opinions, and, most importantly (this distinguishes them from the earlier heroine, Maria Stuart), their speech is effective: it has results. Where exclamatory forms, usually with shocking effect, are characteristic of Sarah's linguistic style, Marie Roland's speech — like Bothwell's in *Maria Stuart* — is remarkable for its frequent use of the imperative: it is active speech, and it produces action in the men who hear it. Both take risks when they speak — Sarah in Vienna's hidebound high society, Marie Roland in post-revolutionary Paris — but both put personal honor and their social responsibilities before personal welfare and the demands of convention. Structurally speaking, it is only the difference of mode in these plays — comic or tragic — that achieves the difference in ending — marriage or execution. Marie Roland risks (and suffers, in tragic mode) real death, where Sarah Hochburg risks (but avoids, in comic mode) social death.

Sarah and Marie Roland are not the only women who are taking risks. In allowing her heroines to dominate in this way, Marie von Ebner-Eschenbach was putting her own and her dramas' acceptability on the line. Yet there is no suggestion anywhere in Ebner's copious notes and diary entries that a radicalization of gender relations was a conscious part of her dramatic project. The closest she comes to stating her position around the time of writing these plays is in a note written to herself in December 1874:

> Das Wort Frauenemancipation ist so oft von dummen Leuten in den Mund genommen worden daß selbst die gescheidten nicht mehr wissen was sie davon denken sollen u. nichts mehr darunter verstehn als eine Carricatur [sic] u. Ausgeburt der Uebercivilisation. In der That bedeutet sie die Möglichste [sic] Ausbildung aller weibl Fähigkeiten inerhalb [sic] ihm von der Natur gezogenen Grenzen. (T II, Anhang 1874)

To the modern eye, the naïveté of Ebner's assumption that only Nature sets the boundaries of female emancipation leaps off the page. But this, it seems, is also the assumption that informs her portrayal of the heroines of *Das Waldfräulein* and *Marie Roland*. These two women set out to achieve what Nature, in giving them the qualities of intelligence and dynamism, appears to have made possible. For Ebner this constitutes good sense rather than radicalism, and in her plays the men who matter agree.

This is not to make the claim that Ebner was ignorant of the force of gendered convention; on the contrary, she shows herself keenly aware of it. In *Das Waldfräulein* "feminine" and "unfeminine" behavior are constantly at issue. As a playwright she is clearly also aware that only a return to gendered norms, in some form, can provide satisfying closure, in comedy or tragedy: both heroines undergo a process of "feminization" in the build-up to their structurally parallel fates. Marie Roland goes to her death retaining her belief in the social and political cause, but also embracing, for the first time, the values of femininity. In the manner of the stoic virgin martyr of early modern *Trauerspiel* she accepts the passive role that her execution forces on her,[36] she learns selflessness from the example of another, far more obviously fallible/feminine woman (Lodoïska), and grows gentler, less self-assured, and more forgiving (the point here is not whether these are to be classed as positive or negative traits; it is that they are to be classed as *feminine*). In *Das Waldfräulein*, audience satisfaction is achieved at the end of the play — and critical reviews testify to this — by the reduction of active, independent Sarah to a more traditional, passive object: she is formally handed over (literally led by the hand and given) by Uncle Robert, her fiancé and therefore her current owner, to her future husband and proprietor Count Paul. Sarah acquiesces because she is in love, and therefore — as convention has it — tamed.

Ebner has, then, gone to some lengths to make her heroines acceptable and sympathetic, and this might help explain her aggrieved response to the gender-specific criticisms heaped on *Das Waldfräulein*. The hopes of real theatrical success which had been raised by an initially very positive response, especially from Laube, to *Marie Roland*, were dashed by the political battle between Vienna's theater heavyweights, Laube and Münch. Those hopes rose again when Laube took on *Marie Roland*'s comic pendant piece, *Das Waldfräulein*, for the Stadttheater, and even suggested to Ebner that (as befits a woman playwright?) her real strengths lay in more lightweight theater: "Ich soll mich, sagt er, ganz auf das Lustspiel verlegen" (*T* II, 22 July 1872). At this time it may have seemed to Ebner that the "Gifthauchatmosphäre der Revolutionszeit" that her Karlsruhe contact, Devrient, complained of in *Marie Roland* (*T* I, 162), could be comically transmogrified and rendered acceptable in a play like *Das Waldfräulein*.

If this is true, Ebner overlooked a basic problem shared by both plays, which could not be solved with the pro forma "taming" of the heroine in marriage. In both *Marie Roland* and *Das Waldfräulein* — and this again distinguishes them from *Maria Stuart in Schottland* — the woman protagonist is not only central, but dominant both linguistically and in the terms of the action. Marie Roland runs the Girondins' revolution, and Sarah Hochburg runs the satirization of Viennese society that is *Das Waldfräulein* — Sarah is the character who directs the comedy, who tells us who to laugh at.

In her theoretical reflections on the comic, Susan Purdie has distinguished between two types of fool: the abject fool, and the masterful fool.[37] The abject fool we laugh *at* — he or she is the butt of our jokes — but the masterful fool we laugh *with*, because she (or far more likely he) is running the show. Conventionally, women are expected to be the butt of comedy, not its master — even with the recent ascent of women in stand-up, there are more jokes about women than by them. But there is no doubt that Ebner's Sarah is a masterful fool, who directs audience mirth. All this might explain the rather confused response that Ebner's play elicited from one Viennese critic:

Bei gar manchem Lustspiel, das wie toll belacht wird, fragt man sich
hinterdrein: "Warum habe ich eigentlich gelacht?" Wenn ich nachträg-
lich die einzelnen Gestalten und Szenen des "Waldfräulein" überdenke,
frage ich mich umgekehrt: "Warum habe ich über das und jenes nicht
gelacht?"[38]

For some reason, Ebner's comedy did not appear to this member of the
audience to be "properly" funny; and, applying Purdie's theory of jok-
ing, we find that for reasons of comedy's gendered nature, *Das Waldfräulein* is indeed "improperly" funny. Female behavior which for Ebner
was simply "die Möglichste [*sic*] Ausbildung [. . .] weibl Fähigkeiten
inerhalb [*sic*] ihm von der Natur gezogenen Grenzen" was, for Sarah
Hochburg's Viennese critics, an unacceptably masculine subject status as
didactic and masterful fool.

Woman as Abject Fool: Druskowitz's *Emancipationsschwärmerin*

Marie von Ebner-Eschenbach's dictum on the subject of women's emancipation, which, she argues, has been so abused as an idea that "selbst die
gescheidten [. . .] nichts mehr darunter verstehn als eine Carricatur u
Ausgeburt der Uebercivilisation" — would have found sympathy with a
fellow playwright with whom she even had some contact: Dr. Helene
Druskowitz.[39]

The name of Helene (von) Druskowitz,[40] despite a recent growth of
interest in this writer,[41] is still considerably less well-known than that of
Ebner-Eschenbach. Druskowitz disappeared almost completely from
literary critical discussion at the end of the nineteenth century;[42] therefore, some basic biographical details are not out of place. She was born
in Vienna in 1856, and died in 1918 in Mauer-Oehling near Salzburg,
having spent the last 27 years of her life in psychiatric care. In her youth,
Druskowitz was one of the first generation of "Zürcher Studentinnen"
(study at German and Austrian universities was at that time still impossible, but Zurich began admitting women students in 1867). In 1878,
Druskowitz was only the second woman to gain a doctorate in the humanities there, for her dissertation on Byron's *Don Juan*. In addition to
literary critical and philosophical works — including some attacks on
Nietzsche, for which she became notorious — she wrote a number of
dramas, some of which were published but none performed.[43]

Druskowitz's best-known play is her satirical comedy, *Die Emancipations-Schwärmerin* (1889).[44] It is, as the title suggests, the tale of a woman

whose enthusiasm for the new women's movement takes her beyond the bounds of what is reasonable — in the terms of not only society at large, but also in the eyes of her literary creator. Unlike Ebner, Druskowitz shows us a woman not as a masterful fool, but as an abject one.

At a first reading of the play, it seems odd that the dramatist, a supporter of the women's movement and (as a university graduate) its beneficiary, should launch an attack on the excesses of that movement via a character who shows some external similarities with herself. Alwine Dissen, the play's antiheroine, is — as Druskowitz was — a student of the arts with a preference for philosophy. Like Druskowitz she expresses her emancipation by, among other things, smoking, but she has nothing of the dominant subject status of Ebner's Sarah Hochburg. Alwine Dissen is not a masterful fool but an abject fool, the butt of the comedy, and as such the object of the (projected) audience's laughter and disdain. Even before we see her, Alwine is defined in the words of another woman character as "die lächerliche Emancipirte" (5). This is her interpellation into the world of the play, and her first stage appearance confirms or reiterates it: she immediately calls her hostess by the wrong name, revealing her abject inability to name and define correctly. She is risible in her choice of oversentimental, over-elaborate modes of address — again displaying the linguistic ineptitude that is the performance of the fool's abject status in language.[45] The intellectual pseudonym she bears, Aspasia, invites ridicule because it reflects her semi-educated status: Aspasia, the second wife of Pericles, was indeed an intellectual, but Alwine presumably does not know that her namesake was also mocked in Athenian comedy for being his concubine. Aspasia did not have citizenship in Athens and her marriage was not fully recognized. Alwine/Aspasia, like her ancient counterpart, believes she is an insider in the man's world of classical learning; but in fact she is not.

One odd feature of this character is that she is beautiful: women fools are, as a rule, ugly, because physical unattractiveness underlines their low status in a discourse that locates female value in physical beauty. The other "Emancipirten" in the play fit this, more usual, pattern: Amalie von Hörner and Miß Emily Turner both appear "in defekter Toilette" (25). What Druskowitz seems to be signaling in her portrayal of a beautiful fool is that Alwine Dissen is redeemable. Unlike Emily and Amalie, who in their appearance and behavior perform the impossibility of their ever being anything but the laughable "other" of normal, masterful discourse, Alwine has a certain value within that discourse despite her behavior because she is physically beautiful. Her son Percy reminds her: "Eine jugendliche, schöne Frau bist Du, der Stolz deines Sohnes" (25)— the genitive suggests that Percy has already understood the principle of masculine ownership of female bodies. Where Amalie and Emily are largely ignored or avoided, high-status men such as university professors are prepared to engage with Alwine. An exchange between Alwine Dissen and Professor Werent illustrates the dynamics well:

> FRAU DISSEN.   Keine Schmeicheleien! Man muß bei mir vom
>   Aeußeren gänzlich abstrahieren!
> WERENT *(bei Seite).* Was sollte da übrig bleiben? — Wenn das nur
>   möglich wäre! (38)

Werent — although he is himself a ridiculous character — here clearly plays the role of the masterful fool. Speaking "bei Seite," quasi *ad auditores,* is a sure sign of this: he directs audience mirth at Alwine, excluding her from the knowledge of the "obvious truth" that he shares with the audience, namely that her only interest lies in her beauty.

Alwine, however, is not only ludicrous, but also dangerous. Comedy is often linked to a sense of threat or danger; in laughter, that tension is released and the threat dispelled, because the superiority of the audience over the comic object is established. Usually the danger resides in the foolish character's will to upset the established social order (Charlotte von Stein's Daval in *Die Verschwörung gegen die Liebe* is a good example of this,[46] as are Molière's *Précieuses Ridicules*).

We learn from the play that there are two classes or types of woman emerging in the wake of the women's movement. One is the type embodied by Alwine, the type that is simultaneously risible and dangerous. Alwine poses a dual threat: on the one hand, she threatens to undermine the achievements of the women's movement through her ridiculous behavior; she is (as we are told by the ideal Dora Hellmuth, of whom more later) "eine gefährliche Persönlichkeit! Sie schadet der guten Sache, der sie zu dienen glaubt" (17). On the other, her singlemindedness in the pursuit of her academic studies translates into danger for her children: Alwine risks the future happiness of her daughter, Zelia, not only by trying to force her into academia — Zelia is a gifted artist, but a miserable scholar — but also by arranging her marriage to a worthless, posturing academic, whom Alwine is too foolish to see through. Only the good offices of Zelia's wise and authoritative lover, Moro, save the day. The consequences for Percy are even more extreme: he finds himself involved in a duel, trying to protect his mother from critics of her laughable behavior at the university. Alwine's response to the news of Percy's duel is, finally, an admission of guilt: "Dahin mußten meine Studien führen?" (71). That her intellectual ambition adversely affects her children, we infer, is proof that it is unnatural.

The other type or class of emancipated woman is exemplified in the figure of Dora Hellmuth. The name is not subtle, and a connection between this ideal character and Druskowitz herself might be deduced, as Hinrike Gronewold has observed, from the reversed initial letters of their names.[47] Unlike Alwine, Dora is focused: "Ich studire [*sic*] Medizin und wünsche eine gute Aerztin zu werden" (16), and femininely modest: "Ich muß mich nach meinen kleinen Mitteln richten und werde mich glücklich schätzen, einst in engerem Kreise Ersprießliches zu wirken" (17). Dora, too, has distinct and well articulated views on the *Frauenfrage*, which tempt us to read her as a mouthpiece for her creator:

> DORA. Mir jedoch scheint, wir Frauen müßten nun *handeln* und die Freiheit, die uns gewährt ist, nach Kräften benutzen, jede, die Talent für ein bestimmtes Gebiet besitzt, suche es zu bethätigen, denn nur dadurch, daß die Einzelne Talent zeigt, kann die Meinung von der Befähigung der Frauen im Allgemeinen eine höhere werden. Das Talent allein kann Beweise schaffen. Lassen Sie einer Aerztin eine schwierige Operation, die Diagnose und Beseitigung einer komplicirten Krankheit gelingen, und sie wird die Frauenfrage weit mehr fördern, als es hundert öffentliche Reden zu Gunsten unseres Geschlechts thun werden. (17; Druskowitz's emphasis)

Dora is the acceptable face of nineteenth-century feminism, and she is rewarded with approval and acceptance from the men in her social circle. She is popular at the university, beloved of the Zurich *monde*, and finally successful in her chosen career, when she becomes the preferred protegée of a distinguished physician.

The improbability of this rosy scenario is of less interest than the implicit message it sends. Women like Alwine, we understand, are putting men's backs up unnecessarily (and how much more women like Amalie Hörner and Miß Emily Turner, who do not even offer men visual pleasure in their beauty), and thereby damaging the cause of their sex. If they only would behave like Dora, everything would go swimmingly. It is, then, women's *fault* that the movement for their emancipation is not progressing as quickly or effectively as it should.

Even if we feel a certain sympathy for Druskowitz's position, and accept that any movement can be damaged by those who espouse it thoughtlessly and vehemently, we must not be distracted from the important shift in emphasis here. The focus of responsibility for the social re-positioning of women as full human beings is shifted off men and on to women themselves. If men reject the notion of emancipation, it is, we are led to infer, women's fault — they have failed to assert themselves with sufficient humility and dedication, à la Dora Hellmuth.

One might argue that this amounts to making women into active subjects: they are the engineers of their own fates. But those fates also depend entirely on the approval of men, which means that women, even women like Dora, have at best eternally deferred subject status.

The notion that male approval is not capricious and partisan, but wise, authoritative, and good, permeates this play. Mock is made, it is true, of the two professors, Werent and Teichert, but they are primarily associated with Alwine, and their function is to expose her foolishness and the shallowness of her academic learning, which manifests itself in her inability to recognize intellectual fraud. At those moments in the play when Alwine comes closest to wreaking real havoc, men step in to save the day. Moro saves Zelia from being forced down the academic path that terrifies her, and Moro exposes Werent as the intellectual charlatan he is, thereby rescuing Zelia from a disastrous arranged marriage. Moro speaks "mit Autorität" (46) in the face of Alwine's powerless expostulations; reveals himself, despite his quiet modesty, as far more knowledgeable in academic matters than she; and gently corrects her pseudo-learned gaffes:

> FRAU DISSEN. Nochmals Verzeihung, Moro, daß ich Ihre Bedeutung nicht sogleich erkannte. "Es irrt der Mensch, so lang' er lebt."
>
> MORO *(leise verbessernd).* "strebt." (49)

Zelia, then, is safe under the protection of this authoritative, gently instructive father-figure. Another father-figure, this time in a more literal sense, is necessary for the rescue of Alwine's unfortunate son, Percy, as well as for the final salvation of Alwine herself. By the middle of act 5, she has engineered a situation which can only be described as desperate: Percy is fighting a duel for her honor that endangers his own life, and the reception rooms are filled with her creditors, demanding repayment of monies owed for a failed publishing project.

At this moment her husband, Emil, who has significantly been absent in the USA all this time, arrives at the house in Zurich. The moment smacks of a vision or revelation: Alwine cries "Du? Emil, Du? oder ist es nur Täuschung?" (75). It provokes her into immediate self-accusation and confession: "Du wirst mir Vieles zu verzeihen haben! [. . .] ich bin unvorsichtig und gewissenlos gewesen! Ich muß Dir nun Alles gestehen" (76). Emil functions here not only as the *deus ex machina* who will resolve the dramatic situation, but as a divine patriarch who will judge, forgive, and remedy. Alwine begs him, "Richte nicht zu strenge, Emil!" (77), and responds to his judgement with adoration that shifts him from the position of husband to that of (heavenly) father: "Ach, wie gut Papa ist, wie himmlisch gut! Ein Engel an Hochherzigkeit und Großmuth!" (77). The function of the dramatic family as a microcosmic analogy, identified by Kord, is very clear here:

> In dieser Analogie symbolisiert der Vater den Staat bzw. das Staats-
> oberhaupt, Stellvertreter Gottes auf Erden; die Mutter fungiert als
> Untertanin des Vaters mit beschränkter Autorität über die Kinder; der
> Sohn als zeitweiliger Untertan und künftiger Herrscher bzw. Nachfol-
> ger des Vaters; die Tochter als permanente Untertanin erst des Vaters,
> dann des Ehemannes; die Familie als Staatsgefüge und Sinnbild der
> göttlichen Weltordnung.[48]

Indeed, Emil's sagacity is near-divine. When he reproaches his wife — "Du verkennst Deinen Beruf!" (76) — he is reminding Alwine, and the reader/audience, of nineteenth-century notions of women's "Berufung" or calling to domestic duties, self-abnegation, and motherhood.[49] Emil and Alwine agree that the current disastrous situation is the natural and inevitable result of her intellectual ambitions. Emil laments, "Dahin also mußte es kommen! [. . .] Da siehst Du die Früchte Deines Thuns. Das Schicksal hat es selbst übernommen, Dich zu bekehren" (76), and Alwine promises to change: "Die Leiden und Schrecken dieser letzten Stunden haben mich in mancher Beziehung verändert. Es soll in Zukunft anders werden" (77). Between them, Fate and Emil have restored order, and Alwine Dissen has been pulled back into line. She has undergone comic punishment, and will now be received back into the domestic fold under the watchful eye of her father-husband, to resume her duties as wife and mother, as she promises:

> Ich habe an fremdes Wohl gedacht und darüber das meiner Liebsten,
> meiner Nächsten vernachlässigt, ja das Leben meines Sohnes auf's Spiel
> gesetzt. Doch ich bin Euch zurückgegeben, meine Lieben! [. . .] Du
> sollst wieder zufrieden sein mit Deiner Frau, theurer Emil, Eure Mutter
> wird Euch nun erst wieder eine Mutter sein, meine Kinder. (79)

Why, we might ask, is Dora Hellmuth able to live a non-domestic lifestyle without interference from men or "das Schicksal," while Alwine Dissen is not? Dora is, certainly, a more modest character who has the feminine grace to play down her achievements rather than boasting foolishly (like a man, we might say, observing Druskowitz's characteriza-tion of the two professors). But this in itself does not yet explain how she can escape the "Berufung" to the private sphere that finally catches up with Alwine. The answer is simple enough: Dora is not married. Drusko-witz, like many women of her time, believed that academic and creative women must not marry: "Die Ehe ist keine Institution für begabte Frauen. Der begabte Mann mag in ihr einen Friedensport sehen, in dem er seine Kräfte erst recht sammelt und entfaltet; die begabte Frau zersplittert sich."[50] There is, as we shall see again in chapter 2, little or no scope for women to combine the public with the private sphere in this way.

Comedy, Tragedy, and the Woman Writer

According to Ferrel Rose, Ebner-Eschenbach once "stated without qualification that it was the male bias against women dramatists that forced her to abandon the genre."[51] In fact, it is impossible to assess whether Ebner or Druskowitz would have had more success as playwrights had they been men; not least because, as men, they would be unlikely to have written the same plays. There is a subtler problem in the reception of much writing by women than simple gender prejudice: namely, that a perspective on events that is based on female experience can perplex readers or audiences, male *and* female, who have been educated to expect and approve the masculinist viewpoint. Michaela Giesing has suggested that the content of German theater in the eighteenth and nineteenth centuries complicated things not only for the audience/reader, but for the writer. Male dramatists, she argues, established a convention of using suffering and passive women in their sign-systems, and therefore:

> Wollten Frauen die Gattung sich aneignen, dann verlangte dies, mit dem Muster des leidenden Weibs und der opfernden Heldin eine im bürgerlichen Drama überhöhte Erwartung doppelt zu unterlaufen. Dies konnte nicht im simplen Verkehren der Rollenmuster, dem Ersetzen der passiven durch aktive Heldinnen, gelingen.[52]

Giesing never spells out why the "Verkehren der Rollenmuster" — the replacement of passive with active heroines — might be a necessary (if impossible) precondition for women dramatists. She assumes that the female subject, in the active process of writing, cannot accept the "othering" of passivity onto women that is practiced by male writers. This, Giesing seems to be suggesting, would threaten the subject status of the woman writer, and interfere with the process of active creation. Not only the structure of theater as institution is a problem for women, but the discourse of the dramas which are played in it.

Certainly, Ebner's youthful ambition to be the female Shakespeare of the nineteenth century was unrealizable. Even if she had been able to appropriate the masculinist viewpoint perfectly, and to write flawlessly, the idea that a woman might take center stage in the most prestigious and authoritative of the literary genres was unthinkable. German drama is in its origins a didactic genre; and the notion of woman as pedagogue (to grown men) turns the world of nineteenth-century, Rousseau-influenced German gender theory on its head.

Ebner's last full-length dramas, *Untröstlich* (now lost),[53] and *Männertreue*, were both comedies. Laube produced *Untröstlich* under an authorial pseudonym, "Meier," at the Stadttheater in March of 1874; Ebner described critical responses to the piece depressedly, as "über die Maßen grob" (*T* II, 17 March 1874). *Männertreue* was staged in Coburg in November of the same year.[54] But Marie von Ebner-Eschenbach's burning desire to succeed as a playwright was pretty well extinguished. Her profound disappointment is documented in the story of a failed dramatist, called *Ein Spätgeborner*,[55] which she began writing in 1873, about a month after the painful failure of *Das Waldfräulein*.

The central character in *Ein Spätgeborner* finishes the story dead, and his near-dead body is found, significantly, outside the city: outside social bounds. Ebner herself did not die as a result of her failure as a dramatist — instead, she killed her own ambition (possibly in the figure of Andreas, the "Spätgeborner"). It is no coincidence that the plays she finally took refuge in (and the ones with which she was successful in gaining entry as a playwright to the Burgtheater) are short comic pieces, designed to be played as complement to the main dramatic event. They therefore come closest to obeying the gender imperative. Comedy is generally thought of as "trivial," and the role of one-act plays is supportive, usually of another, longer play. This kind of drama performs, so to speak, the theatrical "shitwork." The brevity of the comedies further fits the pattern that — in mixed company at least — women are not given access to significant amounts of linguistic space. Ebner's decision to change her work to suit the society she lived in was, as Rose has argued, "a better alternative to [= than, S. C.] her own artistic death."[56]

Like Ebner, Druskowitz wrote comedy in the hope of achieving dramatic success. Unlike Ebner, her reasons were financial as well as artistic, since Druskowitz's private means were very slight; but this presumably only made her wish to succeed more pressing. Significant here is that both women were writing to please; neither could afford, for whatever reason, to use her comedy to voice radical ideas that might offend.

Yet Ebner did offend, at least the critics, and Druskowitz, for all her efforts, never managed to get her play accepted for production. Neither the tragic nor the comic form seem to have provided a solution for these writers. Internally to the plays, all the central women characters — Mary

Stuart, Marie Roland, Sarah Hochburg, Alwine Dissen — rebel in some way against the order of gender, and all of them finish the play back in the grasp of that order. Maria Stuart's Scotland is re-appropriated for a male ruler, Marie Roland ensures the "taming" of the next female generation (her daughter) before she dies, Sarah Hochburg and Alwine Dissen are contained within marriage. Externally to the dramas, the situation regarding performance and reception is just as difficult. Ebner's comic *Waldfräulein* was no better received than her tragedies had been, and her masterful female fool is perceived as transgressive. Nor does Druskowitz's abject female fool do any better: *Die Emancipations-Schwärmerin* was not even accepted by a theatre.

One problem may have been that, for all its discrediting of certain directions in late nineteenth-century feminism, Druskowitz's play — like the three of Ebner's that I have discussed — is woman-centered. The men characters play important roles, but they are important primarily in their relation to the two central protagonists, Alwine Dissen and Dora Hellmuth. This reverses the pattern familiar from traditional masculinist drama, in which women characters (even central characters!) are important primarily in the context of their relationships with men — whether they are there to betray men, to seduce them, to expose them as insufficiently masculine, or to make them better. To the male-dominated institution of theater, plays about women are not plays that matter. That will become a leitmotif of this study.

Notes

[1] A. von Weilen, "Eine österreichische Novellistin," in *Über Land und Meer: Allgemeine Illustrirte Zeitung* (1890), 1003. Cited in Ulrike Tanzer, *Frauenbilder im Werk Marie von Ebner-Eschenbachs* (Stuttgart: Heinz, 1997), 58.

[2] For an account of Ebner's development, see also Sarah Colvin, "'Ein Bildungsmittel ohnegleichen': Marie von Ebner-Eschenbach and the Theatre," in *Harmony in Discord: German Women Writers in the 18th and 19th Centuries*, ed. by Laura Martin (Oxford: Lang, 2001), 161–82.

[3] Krack, "Schreibende Frauen," in *Die Zukunft* 24 (1898), 324–30 (325).

[4] Edith Toegel, "The 'Leidensjahre' of Marie von Ebner-Eschenbach: Her Dramatic Works," in *German Life and Letters* 46 (1993), 107–19 (108).

[5] Toegel gives the year as 1861, but Ebner's diary contradicts this. See Marie von Ebner-Eschenbach, *Tagebücher*, ed. by Karl Konrad Polheim (Tübingen: Niemeyer, 1989), I, 7 February 1863. Further references to the first (*T* I) and second (*T* II) volumes of the *Tagebücher* are given in the text.

[6] Eduard Devrient, *Aus seinen Tagebüchern, Karlsruhe 1852–1870*, ed. by Rolf Kabel (Weimar: Böhlau, 1964), 393.

[7] *Die Veilchen* had eight performances.

[8] Georg Reichard, "Die Dramen Marie von Ebner-Eschenbachs auf den Bühnen des Wiener Burg- und Stadttheaters," in *Marie von Ebner-Eschenbach: Ein Bonner Symposion zu ihrem 75. Todesjahr*, ed. by Karl Konrad Polheim (Berne: Lang, 1994), 97–122 (112).

[9] It is worth noting, in respect of all quotations from the diaries, that Ebner bowdlerized her own diaries thoroughly.

[10] *Marie Roland* was eventually performed at the Weimar Hoftheater under Freiherr von Löen. See Toegel, 117.

[11] After 1867 some boxes, with the exception of those on the first floor, were opened to those members of the bourgeoisie and intelligensia who could pay for them. See Karlheinz Rossbacher, *Literatur und Liberalismus: Zur Kultur der Ringstrassenzeit in Wien* (Vienna: J & V, 1992), 162.

[12] See the "Vorwort" by Karl Gladt in Marie von Ebner-Eschenbach, *Das Waldfräulein*, ed. by Karl Gladt (Vienna: Belvedere, 1969), 45.

[13] Gladt suggests they were not. See Gladt, 45. *Das Waldfräulein* went on to have eleven performances, which is at least a respectable performance record. Laube clearly did not feel under pressure to remove the play from the program immediately.

[14] On Ebner's and other Mary Stuart plays see also Sarah Colvin, "Disturbing Bodies: Mary Stuart and Marilyn Monroe in Plays by Liz Lochhead, Marie von Ebner-Eschenbach and Gerlind Reinshagen," in *Forum for Modern Language Studies* 35 (1999), 251–60.

[15] Friedrich Schiller, *Maria Stuart* (1800; repr. Stuttgart: Reclam, 1985); August Adolph von Haugwitz, *Schuldige Unschuld oder Maria Stuarda*, in *Prodromus Poeticus, Oder: Poetischer Vortrab* (1684), ed. by Pierre Béhar (Tübingen: Niemeyer, 1984); Joost van den Vondel, *Maria Stuart of Gemartelde Majesteit* (Keulen 1646).

[16] Marie von Ebner-Eschenbach, *Maria Stuart in Schottland* (Vienna: Mayer, 1860), 38. All further references are to this edition of the text.

[17] See Sandra M. Gilbert and Susan Gubar, *The Madwoman in the Attic: The Woman Writer and the Nineteenth-Century Imagination* (New Haven: Yale UP, 1979), 1–7.

[18] Goethe prefaced his late poem "Elegie" with the couplet: "Und wenn der Mensch in seiner Qual verstummt, / Gab mir ein Gott zu sagen, was ich leide."

[19] See, for example, the portrayal of Courasche as Frau Welt in Hans Jakob Christoph von Grimmelshausen, *Lebensbeschreibung der Erzbetrügerin und Landstörtzerin Courasche*, ed. by Klaus Haberkamm and Günther Weydt (Stuttgart: Reclam, 1971).

[20] In performance one could, of course, play this another way; but Ebner's text does not in itself invite it.

[21] Ebner-Eschenbach, *Marie Roland: Trauerspiel in fünf Aufzügen* (Vienna: Wallishausser, 1867). All further references are to this edition of the text.

[22] The phrase was coined by Judith Butler, *Bodies that Matter: On the Discursive Limits of "Sex"* (New York: Routledge, 1993), and describes a body/person (in masculinist society more usually male) that is generally perceived to be of import.

[23] Kord has suggested that what damns Marie in this play is not her public politics, but her private ruthlessness and lack of feeling. I would argue that both, political activity in the public sphere and personal rigidity, are immediately recognizable in late nineteenth-century eyes as unfeminine, and that Marie is therefore damned for both. See Kord, *Ein Blick hinter die Kulissen: Deutschsprachige Dramatikerinnen im 18. und 19. Jahrhundert* (Stuttgart: Metzler, 1992), 130–31.

[24] Ferrel Rose, "The Disenchantment of Power: Marie von Ebner-Eschenbach's Maria Stuart in Schottland," in *Thalia's Daughters: German Women Dramatists from the Eighteenth Century to the Present*, ed. by Susan L. Cocalis and Ferrel Rose (Tübingen: Francke, 1996), 147–60 (153).

[25] Kord, 121.

[26] Kord, 42.

[27] Regina Barreca (ed.), *Last Laughs: Perspectives on Women and Comedy* (New York: Gordon & Reach, 1988), 10.

[28] Kord, 44.

[29] Ebner-Eschenbach, *Das Waldfräulein*, in *Aphorismen — Erzählungen — Theater*, ed. by Roman Roçek (Vienna: Böhlau, 1988). All further references are to this edition of the text.

[30] *Tagebücher* II, 26 October 1871: "Ida sagt mir, daß Laube das *Waldfräulein* und die *Roland* geben will."

[31] This is a fairly standard dramatic function of the *femme forte*: compare Schiller's *Jungfrau von Orleans*, for example.

[32] See Toegel, 114.

[33] *Neue Freie Presse*, 15 January 1873. Cited in Gladt, 46.

[34] A comparably "inverted" gender situation is portrayed in Anna Croissant-Rust's later drama, *Der standhafte Zinnsoldat* (Berlin: Schuster & Loeffler, 1896). See chapter 2.

[35] Spender, *Man Made Language*, 2nd ed. (London: Pandora, 1985), 41.

[36] The classic example is Gryphius's *Catharina von Georgien* (1647), repr. ed. by Alois M. Haas (Stuttgart: Reclam, 1975). Schiller, too, uses this pattern, in his *Maria Stuart*.

[37] Purdie, *Comedy: The Mastery of Discourse* (New York: Harvester Wheatsheaf, 1993), 59–63.

[38] *Das Neue Wiener Tagblatt*, 15 January 1873. Cited in Gladt, 48.

[39] Ebner and Druskowitz met in 1881. The older writer invited the younger to stay at a spa in Bad Reichenhall, where Druskowitz also met Louise von François. Ebner later helped finance Druskowitz's treatment in a psychiatric clinic. See Hinrike Gronewold, "Helene von Druskowitz (1856–1918): 'Die geistige Amazone,'" in

Wahnsinns Frauen, ed. by Sybille Duda and Luise F. Pusch (Frankfurt a. M.: Suhrkamp, 1992), 96–122.

[40] The name appears both as Druskowitz and von Druskowitz. Helene's father was Fraune (Lorenz?) Druskowitz, her mother Madeline von Biba. She occasionally claimed to be the illegitimate daughter of a Bulgarian prince called Tedesco Ventravin. See Gronewold, "Helene von Druskowitz," 97. As a writer, Druskowitz also used the pseudonyms Adalbert Brunn, H. Foreign, E. René, Sakkorausch, Sacrosanct, von Calagis, and Erna.

[41] See for example, the fictional *Sakkorausch: ein Monolog*, by Elisabeth Reichart (Salzburg: Müller, 1994); Helene v. Druskowitz, *Der Mann als logische und sittliche Unmöglichkeit und als Fluch der Welt*, ed. by Hinrike Gronewold and Traute Hensch (Freiburg: Kore, 1988); and Gronewold, "Helene von Druskowitz."

[42] She is, for example, not to be found in the standard *Lexikon deutschsprachiger Schriftstellerinnen 1800–1945*, ed. by Gisela Brinker-Gabler et al. (Munich: dtv, 1986).

[43] For a list of the published dramas see Kord, 353. Gronewold and Hensch also list five unpublished and now lost dramas written after Druskowitz was admitted into psychiatric care. See Druskowitz, *Der Mann als logische und sittliche Unmöglichkeit*, 79–92.

[44] *Die Emancipations-Schwärmerin: Lustspiel in fünf Aufzügen*, in Druskowitz, *Die Emancipationsschwärmerin und Dramatische Scherze* (Dresden: Petzold, n.d [1889]). All further references are to this edition of the text.
The play is briefly discussed by Gronewold, "Helene von Druskowitz," 98–99, and by Petra Neubaur, "Vogue la galère: Die 'Frauenfrage' als Modeströmung: Skepsis und Ambivalenz in Helene Druskowitz's 'Die Emanzipations-Schwärmerin,'" in *Frau — Literatur — Wissenschaft im alpen-adriatischen Raum*, 11: *Zuschnitte/Moden* (May 1997), ed. by Bettina Wellacher, Jolanda Woschitz, Ulrike Oberheber, Elisabeth Frei (University of Klagenfurt, 1997).

[45] There is a long-established tradition by which abject fools in low comedy fail to hit a suitable linguistic register: usually they overcompensate, and their ineptitude is received as amusing. This is a feature, for example, of the farces of Christian Reuter; see Sarah Colvin, *The Rhetorical Feminine: Gender and Orient on the German Stage 1647–1742* (Oxford: Clarendon, 1999), 267–68.

[46] See Sarah Colvin, "'Lachend über den Abgrund springen': Comic Complexity and a Difficult Friendship in Charlotte von Stein's *Neues Freiheitssystem oder die Verschwörung gegen die Liebe*," in *Goethe at 250 / Goethe mit 250*, ed. by T. J. Reed, Martin Swales, and Jeremy Adler (Munich: iudicium, 2000), 199–208.

[47] Gronewold, "Helene von Druskowitz," 99.

[48] Kord, 42.

[49] These are in essence the same notions as were being propagated at the end of the eighteenth century by the likes of Johann Heinrich Campe, an enthusiastic follower of Rousseau, whose *Väterlicher Rath für meine Tochter* appeared in eight editions between 1782 and 1808. Campe proclaims: "Gott selbst hat gewollt [. . .] daß nicht das Weib, sondern der Mann das Haupt sein solle. Dazu gab der Schöpfer, in der Regel dem Manne, die stärkere Muskelkraft [. . .] und — in der Regel, meine ich —

auch die unverkennbaren Anlagen zu einem größern, weiterblickenden und mehr umfassenden Verstande [. . .] Es ist also der übereinstimmende Wille der Natur und der menschlichen Gesellschaft, daß der Mann des Weibes Beschützer und Oberhaupt, das Weib hingegen die [. . .] dankbare und sorgsame Gefährtinn und Gehülfinn seines Lebens sein soll." Campe, *Väterlicher Rath*, in *Sämmtliche Kinder- und Jugendschriften [. . .] Neue Gesammtausgabe der letzten Hand*, vol. 36 (Braunschweig: Schulbuchhandlung, 1832), 100.

[50] Druskowitz, *Die Emancipationsschwärmerin und Dramatische Scherze*, 106.

[51] This remark appeared in Ebner's notes for her autobiography, but was later cut. See Ferrel Rose, *The Guises of Modesty: Marie von Ebner-Eschenbach's Female Artists* (Columbia, SC: Camden House, 1994), 66.

[52] Giesing, "Theater als verweigerter Raum: Dramatikerinnen der Jahrhundertwende in deutschsprachigen Ländern," in *Frauen Literatur Geschichte: Schreibende Frauen vom Mittelalter bis zur Gegenwart*, ed. by Hiltrud Gnüg and Renate Möhrmann (Stuttgart: Metzler, 1985), 240–59 (258).

[53] She herself refers to it as *Die Untröstlichen*, "das kleine Lustspiel." *Tagebücher* II, 18 October 1873.

[54] Ebner was unwilling to have *Männertreue* performed at the Stadttheater, and deliberately prevented its performance by making difficulties about the casting. *Tagebücher* II, 4 October 1874 and 9 October 1874.

[55] Marie von Ebner-Eschenbach, *Ein Spätgeborner*, in *Erzählungen / Neue Erzählungen (Sämtliche Werke*, vol. 1) (Berlin: Paetel, 1920; facs. repr. Freiburg: Freiburger Echo, 1999), 11–73.

[56] Rose, "The disenchantment of power," 158.

2: Elsa Bernstein-Porges, Mathilde Paar, Gertrud Prellwitz, Anna Croissant-Rust: The Gender of Creativity

THE PESSIMISTIC CONCLUSION to the previous chapter was that neither the serious nor comic mode seemed to offer an emancipatory solution for the dramatic work of Marie von Ebner-Eschenbach or Helene Druskowitz. In all the plays considered, rebellious women protagonists are tamed — whether by fate or by society — and neither dramatist was able to find a mode (comic or serious) of presenting such characters that might guarantee their popular appeal.

But by the mid 1880s, the conventions associated with Naturalism — domestic settings, the working- or middle-class milieu, prose dialogue, often in dialect — had begun to make themselves felt. In the terms of gendered discourse, this brings drama closer to the women writer — both are now defined as natural and located tendentially in the domestic sphere, as Else Hoppe notes, with hindsight, in 1929: "seit dem Naturalismus [haben sich] Typus der Frau und Struktur des Dramas [. . .] nunmehr genähert."[1]

While it is true that, in the 1880s and 1890s, a number of German-language women playwrights began to acquire prominence, the continuing perception of drama as a space properly owned by men is nonetheless testified to in critical reactions to women's visible dramatic activity: reactions that range from interested astonishment to outright disapproval. In all cases the woman playwright is seen as the exception to a rule, and specifically as a phenomenon that crosses the bounds of gender. She is therefore in need of explanation or rationalization by critics.

The quickest and easiest way to explain away dramatic creativity in women is to cross-assign the writer to the proper, male, gender category: to redefine her as a "masculine" woman. The method is much used: Devrient remarks on Ebner-Eschenbach's "männlichen Geist";[2] in 1898, Otto Krack congratulates Emilie Mataja (1855–1938; alias Emil Marriot) for displaying "etwas Männliches, Entschiedenes, Selbstständiges" in her writing;[3] and Theodor Lessing finds Elsa Bernstein-Porges (1866–1949; alias Ernst Rosmer) "beinah männlich."[4] In all cases, the description is intended as a compliment, and in the two latter cases at least, the male pseudonyms, Emil and Ernst, used by the authors for their dramatic work can be read as a form of acknowledgment that they ought properly to be men.

In the mainstream literary criticism and theory of the late nineteenth and early twentieth centuries there is a clear, explicit insistence that drama is the realm of the male writer; it is gendered masculine. An influential proponent of this notion is a woman: Dr. Ella Mensch, herself a prose writer as well as a literary critic,[5] who paid special attention to the problem of women playwrights in her monograph *Die Frau in der modernen Literatur* (1898).[6] Mensch contests: "Die Kunstform des Dramas verlangt eine ausgesprochene Herrschernatur. Der Dramatiker ist aus demselben Material gebildet, welches die Natur für die grossen Helden und Staatsmänner verwendet" (73). "Herr," "Herrschaft" and "beherrschen" are words used strikingly often in drama criticism at this time. Mensch goes so far as to suggest that "Herrschen, kraft einer ausgeprägten Persönlichkeit herrschen, Einfluss auf das Weltbild gewinnen wollen, das ist der letzte, tiefste Grund für die Existenz des Dramendichters" (73).

This is not just masculinity; it is hypermasculinity, the apex of the hierarchical patriarchal ideal. Mensch is developing a definition of drama and the dramatist that depends on utter separation from all that is associated with the feminine. Drama is architecture; it erects a monolith; and it is therefore an unnatural act for a woman to write a play. This will (in Mensch's view) adversely affect the quality of the work:

> Bei der Arbeit des Architekten, die für das Drama verlangt wird, muß sie [= die Autorin, S. C.] aber dermaßen aus ihrer Natur heraus, daß ein solcher Emanzipationsprozeß, wenn er überhaupt vollzogen werden kann, nur zu leicht der Harmonie des Werks Gefahr bringt.[7]

It is interesting that Mensch describes the undesirable process of female playwriting as "Emanzipation." Such emancipation, she argues, endangers "Harmonie" — and harmony, in music, differs from melody in that it is complementary rather than dominant. Female playwriting, we understand, endangers feminine subordination under the masculine "Herr / Herrscher." In the field of literary endeavor, women are allowed to command what is scattered or trivial — a woman may, according to the literary critic Johannes Wiegand (who appears to have been heavily influenced by Mensch), be "Beherrscherin des Details." But the quality of leadership that characterizes the dramatist will (naturally) elude women: "im Drama, mit seiner logischen, konsequenten Führung der Handlung erreichten sie bisher so gut wie nichts."[8]

The impetus of this literary critical discourse of gender and drama is clear enough: women's creativity may not be monolithic, only trivial or scattered (that is, short prose or comedies, rather than full-length drama); it may not be dominant or demanding, only subordinate and supportive (for example, acting rather than playwriting). Yet women dramatists at this time — themselves defined in critical discourse as creatures without creative or dramatic genius — show a distinct inclination to explore the potential of female and male creativity in their work. Artists, especially women artists, are a favorite topic in plays such as Ada Christen's (alias for Christiane von Breden) *Faustina* (1871), Marie Itzerott's *Hilde Brandt* (1905), Laura Marholm's (alias for Laura Mohr-Hansson) *Karla Bühring* (1905), Mathilde Paar's *Helene* (1882), Anna Croissant-Rust's *Der standhafte Zinnsoldat* (1896), Gertrud Prellwitz's *Seine Welt* (1911), Elsa Bernstein-Porges's *Wir drei* (1893) and *Johannes Herkner* (1904).[9] The plays by Paar, Croissant-Rust, Prellwitz, and Bernstein-Porges will be discussed in this chapter.

Women as Artists

The drama of the female artist cannot — of course — escape the problems raised by the gendered discourse of creativity. Where the drama of the male artist can be primarily concerned with that individual's self-realization (because the legitimacy of the male as artist *per se* is not in question), the drama of the female artist faces a set of initial hurdles relating to the place of woman in society before the question of artistic self-expression can even be addressed.

Mathilde Paar's (1849–99) four-act play *Helene* was published in 1882.[10] It had enjoyed some success on stage, having been a runner-up for the Mannheim *Räuber* Prize after its performance at Mannheim's court theater. *Helene* was not Paar's first piece for the theater, but had been preceded by a number of other plays and an opera libretto.[11] It is a play about female creativity, but also — and, in the end, perhaps even more importantly — about who owns a woman's body and her creative energy.

The two major women characters in the drama, Helene (the heroine) and her friend, Melitta, are both practicing artists — at least when the play opens. Helene is "herrenlos": her husband, Warbek, has divorced her because she refused to give up her career as a singer. This "Mann von Grundsätzen" sees self-determination in his wife as an unacceptable threat to his own mastery, as his son explains: "Er hatte auch den Grundsatz, daß in der Ehe der Mann vom Weibe unbedingte Unterwerfung zu fordern berechtigt sei; und da meine schöne Stiefmutter diese Ansicht nicht theilte, ließ er sich von ihr scheiden" (2). Helene's view of the marriage is significantly different; she sees Warbek as a man,

> der mich an seine Seite fesselte, um mich zu quälen — zu vernichten! [. . .] Oder nennen Sie es anders, wenn man einem Menschen verbietet, das zu sein, wozu sein innerstes Wesen ihn unwiderstehlich treibt? [. . .] Er sah in meinem Spiel und Gesang nichts weiter als eine Auflehnung in Tönen. (23–25)

Since her father, too, has cast her from the family home because she is divorced, Helene is in an unusual situation for a nineteenth-century woman: she is outside the normal patriarchal structures of marriage and family. This is also, of course a risky situation — patriarchy is protectionist, and when a woman is not subordinate or protected she is vulnerable.

Helene's first response — which preserves the element of risk, the "Herrenlosigkeit" — is to seek support from a woman friend. Her friend, Melitta, is another character who takes risks, who lives without male protection: she is single, educated, and a painter. She is adamant that only self-ownership can enable self-expression: "Künstlerinnen müssen ledig bleiben!" (31) — here she agrees, albeit from another perspective, with the biological determinists of turn-of-the-century literary criticism, and echoes the single-mindedness of Druskowitz's Dora Hellmuth.[12]

Paar's own perception of the threat posed by Melitta to the world *outside* the play, to her audience, is evident in a footnote that accompanies the character's first appearance. Melitta is so emancipated, so potentially threatening in her self-ownership and self-expression, that she might well need to be laughed at, for the sake of audience relief; but this is something her creator is keen to avoid. Paar notes for the director that her character is merely "etwas emanzipiert [. . .] muß humoristisch, aber doch sympathisch wirken, darf nicht durch Uebertreibung ins Lächerliche gezogen werden" (10).

The problem of marriage, and the subordination of one's body and energies and right to freedom of movement that it entails, is clearly at issue. Early on in the play Helene's ex-husband, Warbek, and her future husband, Lothar, discuss the boundaries that their ownership of women and of the public sphere permit them to set:

> WARBEK. Würdest Du Dir ein Weib von den Brettern nehmen?
>
> LOTHAR. Vielleicht — wenn ich sie liebte!
>
> WARBEK. Und würdest Du Dein Weib, wenn es talentvoll wäre, die Bretter betreten lassen?
>
> LOTHAR. Nie! (14–15)

While an unmarried woman may go "on show" on the stage, a married woman certainly may not: her body is now the private property of her husband. Because Warbek no longer owns Helene as his wife, he is reduced to using sheer economic power to prevent her from appearing in public: he attempts to bribe her with an offer of cash if she will only stay off the stage (15).

Warbek's crass performance of masculinity reads, at least to the modern eye, something like a masquerade. It is as if Paar were appropriating and mimicking the discourse of gender, ownership, and power with the intention of exposing its dehumanizing, objectifying impetus. For a little while it really looks as if Helene might achieve the kind of personal and artistic freedom that Melitta enjoys, albeit (like Melitta) at the cost of her exclusion from the social support structure of the family. There is an enormous effort involved in breaking free of this structure, as Helene explains: "Ich bin gleich einem Wanderer, der mit unsäglichen Anstrengungen einen steilen Berg hinangestiegen ist [. . .]. Endlich liegt der Gipfel vor mir, von dem ich einen freien, schönen Blick in das Leben erhoffe" (19). The image of the "Wanderer," loaded as it is in German literary history with connotations of (usually masculine) freedom and *Bildung*, is significant here.

But Paar has no intention of letting her heroine escape. Helene has given Warbek the slip, it is true, and her father, the other instance of patriarchal authority in her life, has died; but before she can sign the artistic contract that will take her to America — the epitome of freedom — Lothar, her second suitor, moves in to assert *his* right of ownership over her, and masterfully claims her as "mein Weib" (67). The play ends with an exchange in which it becomes quite clear that Helene is no longer a "Wanderer"; her will to freedom and *Bildung* disappears (metaphorically speaking) into a crack in the wall when her intended calmly quashes her plans for a future in the New World:

> LOTHAR. Und wir ziehen nicht nach Amerika?
>
> HELENE. Bestimme Du, wo wir leben sollen. Ich habe keinen Willen mehr, als den Deinigen! (67)

The import seems to be that where her marriage to Warbek involved enforced subordination, Helene's "true" love for Lothar produces voluntary self-subordination, which is *quite* different. In the context of the play, does Paar really expect her audience or reader to believe this?

Mary Russo has argued for the emancipatory potential of masquerade, because, she argues, "to put on femininity with a vengeance suggests the power of taking it off."[13] Masquerade "highlights that there is a performance taking place, and as such it emphasizes that gender is always a performance."[14] Helene's radical feminization at the end of Paar's play could well be read, on one level, as masquerade (although not a masquerade that will emancipate *her*). The scene is highly sentimental, and sentimentality almost invariably functions as a legitimating cover for brutality. Paar's "happy ending" provides a recognizable, culturally established form of closure to the play: she pops a large and sticky candy — romantic love — into her audience's collective mouth. Its sweetness disguises the distasteful violence that has been done, for the second time, to Helene.

Other elements in the play are less easy to swallow. I have already commented on elements of apparent masquerade, and particularly on Warbek's performance of masculinity that, in its exaggeration, seems to parody itself. Other, often tiny, details in the text offer an alternative reading alongside the conventional progress of the action. During Helene's stay in Melitta's home, for example, the latter paints her guest in the guise of Sappho; a footnote to the text tells us that, depending on the actor's type, she might also be portrayed in the painting as Gretchen. But this reads like an ironic joke, for a transformation from Sappho to Gretchen would reflect all too bitterly on the domestication, and in some senses destruction, of Helene that is imminent at this point in the play. Both Sappho and Gretchen meet violent deaths, but Sappho survives in cultural belief as an artist, woman-centered and independent, Gretchen by contrast as abject, abused, and bound entirely (as the savior of her seducer's soul) into the service of men. Another literary cross-reference pinpoints a problem just before the play's dénouement, when Helene is discovered hiding at Melitta's home. The song that betrays her where-abouts to the men who are hunting her is Mignon's, from *Wilhelm Meister*: "Heiß mich nicht reden, heiß mich schweigen" (60). The words are of course prophetic: Helene's quest for self-expression is about to be ended; she is about to be silenced for good.

Paar's literary hints are a classic example of "writing between the lines" — the technique of offering two different readings for different kinds of reader.[15] Despite (or perhaps because of) its "happy ending," her play is not optimistic: what we see performed or reiterated on stage is the conventional notion that was propagated by the likes of Ella Mensch,[16] namely that creative women either (like Melitta) exclude themselves from the protective institutions of marriage and the family, or (like Helene) surrender their creativity when they surrender ownership of their bodies to a husband.

The notion that the place of the woman artist is necessarily in isolation from the comforting social institutions of marriage and the family is also a defining feature of Elsa Bernstein-Porges' play, *Wir Drei*, published under her pseudonym Ernst Rosmer in 1893. Like many women playwrights, Elsa Bernstein-Porges preceded her career as a dramatist with work as an actress. She has attracted more critical attention than any other German-language woman playwright of her generation. Not only were her plays well received by her contemporaries (despite frequent comments on her femaleness and only slightly less frequent remarks on her Jewishness),[17] but she is the only woman writer of that generation to have become the subject of a modern monograph dedicated specifically to her dramatic work.[18] Bernstein-Porges has been described as "das erste Weib [. . .] dessen dramatisches Wirken ernst genommen wird,"[19] and more recently as "the finest woman dramatist in German literature";[20] however, we should not forget that similar claims to uniqueness were made about Luise Gottsched in the eighteenth century, Charlotte Birch-Pfeiffer in the nineteenth, and Marieluise Fleisser and Gerlind Reinshagen in the twentieth.

Bernstein-Porges's most lastingly known piece is the libretto she wrote for *Königskinder*, first performed in 1897 with an accompanying opera score by Engelbert Humperdinck (it is Humperdinck's name and not Bernstein-Porges's that is generally associated with this opera). But she wrote at least twenty other plays between 1891 and 1930; of these, the best known are those which appeared in the 1890s and early 1900s, which include *Wir Drei*.[21]

The threesome of the title, *Wir Drei*, are Sascha, a successful writer; Richard, her friend and a second-rate author; and Agnes, Richard's wife. Sascha shows striking resemblances to Bernstein-Porges herself. She is a dramatist, and the author of a piece called *Königskinder* (Bernstein-Porges's libretto of that name was first published in 1894, and she may well have been working on it at the same time as she was writing *Wir Drei*). Another point of contact between the character and her creator are the reviews Sascha receives of her work. Elsa Bernstein-Porges was criticized for her free use of language ("man hat der Rosmer ihre Vorliebe für die unverfälschte Eindeutigkeit ihrer Ausdrücke vielfach verübelt. 'Wie kann eine Dame so etwas schreiben?!'"),[22] and Sascha is exposed to similar accusations of unladylike style.

Like Melitta and Helene at the end of Paar's play, the two women in *Wir Drei* represent two poles: the artistic and the domestic. In Paar's play, however, Melitta is never party to the abjection and domestication of Helene. Bernstein-Porges's Sascha, by contrast, extends or underlines her creative "masculinity" when she takes a masculine role in subordinating Agnes. Agnes's husband Richard, we learn, is or has been in love with Sascha, and to preserve her own freedom Sascha has brought him Agnes as a wife, offering the body of the other woman in place of her own: "Herb und heiß und süß," Sascha assures us, "Der Richard kann sich die Finger ablecken" (22). In this way she lives wifehood and domesticity vicariously, through Agnes, while continuing her activity as an artist.

But the action of the play will show that even Sascha's ingenious solution to the problem of combining womanhood and creativity — escaping the consequences of her own female corporeality by substituting another woman's body for hers — is impracticable. Agnes, jointly owned as she is by Sascha and Richard, is shown in the play's opening scenes in a state of miserable married subservience. She only becomes active after Richard has made a declaration of love to Sascha: at this point Agnes starts divorce proceedings. While the crisis is precipitated by Richard's infidelity, Agnes's change in character — from passivity to activity — springs from knowing that she is pregnant, something which radically changes her sense of her self in the world. Previously, Agnes has only ever been owned; now she becomes an owner. She describes the unborn baby as "mein Eigentum. Mein erstes Eigentum, seit ich lebe" (83). Her power over a fetus that is potentially a child, another human being, somehow confers personhood on her.

Agnes's empowerment as an owner is short-lived. She leaves Richard only to find herself again under the control of Sascha, who decides first to take her in, and then secretly to allow Richard into the house. This enables him to hear the birth of the child, during which he celebrates his proprietorship of Agnes: "Mein Weib! Mein Weib!" (101). But the baby escapes all three of its waiting would-be owners: it is stillborn.

In terms of the drama, the stillbirth is necessary so that Richard can complete the process of *Bildung* — acquiring life experience and achieving adulthood — in which he is engaged (the same process that was radically cut off for Paar's Helene, when she was acquired as wife-to-be by Lothar). At the moment of the baby's birth Richard believes himself adult, but he is in fact still immature, because he has not yet fully accepted the responsibilities of the *Familienvater*: fidelity and breadwinning, and bourgeois solidity. Richard, too, will have to give up his pretensions to an artistic career. The child's death is the stimulus necessary to help him complete the process of growing up — the next time we see him on stage, in the last act, his graying hair testifies to this. In dramatic terms, then, Agnes's baby dies so that Richard can become a fully socialized man; and this, as the gender rule of complementarity demands, forces Agnes back into a more passive and feminine role. She, who was rational, purposeful, and articulate when arranging her divorce, loses all will and is silenced by the death of her child.

When her dead baby disqualifies her from the position of owner, Agnes returns to her old status, as merely owned. As before, Sascha decides what is to be done with her: she gives her back to Richard, so that he can impose his will on this wife who is resisting him. He responds to her single demand after the baby's death — namely that he be quiet, "es soll still sein" (109) — with long speeches, so that her speech act is rendered failed or infelicitous, her linguistic position abject.

Agnes is finally reintegrated into the family structure by the mystical word: "Vater." Ignoring her requests for quiet, Richard asserts his position in that structure with reference to his stillborn child: "verstohlen bin ich hingeschlichen [. . .] zu meinem verstoßenen Kind — sein Vater" (109–10). Evincing the first sign of life she has shown in this scene, Agnes repeats the word: "Va — ter" (110). Remarkably, a rapprochement is thus made possible: the name of the father restores order in the family and in the dramatic world.

Part of this order is the exclusion of Sascha from the family unit. Adult socialized families do not comprise three adults, and "wir drei" from now on will be the more acceptable, conventional threesome of father, mother, and (projected, living) child. The focus here, as at the play's beginning, is not on Agnes, but on Richard and Sascha and their respective sacrifices: his determination to give up both Sascha and his artistic ambitions in order to be a father, and her voluntary withdrawal from the threesome. What is interesting here is Bernstein-Porges's insistence that domesticity and creativity are not compatible for women *or* men, and that it is a man (Richard) who finally treads the domestic path, while a woman, Sascha, returns to her creative career at the cost of familial, and hence social, outsiderdom.

One reading of this would be to see Agnes and Sascha as two possible sides of womanhood, the creative and the procreative — together, therefore, as one "whole" woman — and the play as a study of a failed experiment in combining those two sides; as "proof" that such "wholeness" cannot exist. The same is true for Richard, the man, but finally Bernstein-Porges casts the creative woman (who, we remember, is on several occasions associated with the play's author) as the outsider.

A particularly interesting dramatic investigation of the woman artist in relation to the family, and the last I shall consider here, is *Der standhafte Zinnsoldat* by Anna Croissant-Rust (1860–1943),[23] a play that was published in 1896, but never performed. Croissant-Rust was the author of only two full-length plays: the other was a Bavarian dialect drama called *Der Bua* (1897), which tells the story of a spoiled young working-class man who first impregnates two girlfriends, then kills the foster mother who indulged him. The boy is finally stabbed to death by his foster father in retribution for the murder.

Der standhafte Zinnsoldat, on the other hand, is — like *Helene* and *Wir Drei* — a middle-class drama that deals with the subject of creative endeavor, and specifically (as in *Wir Drei*) literary endeavor. The brave tin soldier who finally makes the sacrifice in this play is a man, and the sacrifice is made for the sake of a woman's artistic freedom.

Croissant-Rust's heroine, Johanna, is a writer. At first she writes secretly, shut away in the "room of one's own" she insists she must have: "Ich hab's nötig, einmal *alleine* zu sein" (10; Croissant-Rust's emphasis). Her first novellas are accepted for publication at the same time as her fiancé, Ernst, finds the job that will give them the financial security they need to get married. But instead of being angry with her — as she expects — for her secret authorship, Ernst is delighted and supportive. In this relationship, there is none of the rhetoric of ownership that we find in Paar's and in Bernstein-Porges's play. Johanna asserts her separateness from Ernst, her autonomy as artist, even within the relationship to him:

> manchmal überfällt mich etwas mitten in unserm Glück, ein andres Glück, woran Du keinen Anteil hast, wobei ich alles um mich vergesse, — eine schmerzhafte Seligkeit, ein Taumel kommt über mich — und ein Drang, diese Trunkenheit hinaus[zu]schreien, Allen zu sagen, nicht Dir, nein, Jedem zu sagen, was ich empfinde — (48)

Outside of her private relationship with Ernst, Johanna maintains her relationship with "Allen," that is, with the public sphere in which she practices her art.

Everything augurs well for the marriage except the state of Ernst's eyesight, which by the third and final act has deteriorated so far that the couple's finances are by no means secure, and Johanna is distracted from her writing by the need to earn a wage and to care for her husband. Ernst is keenly aware of the limits this puts on her personal freedom: "Deine Natur schreit nach Freiheit und Du bist geknebelt. Meine Krankheit, ich, die Verhältnisse, all das hat Dich unfrei gemacht" (77). "Geknebelt," gagged, is an interesting choice of verb here — his worry is that Johanna has been silenced. Where silencing was an essential part of the re-socialization of both Paar's Helene and Bernstein-Porges's Agnes, it is specifically rejected as a fate for Johanna, not by Johanna herself or an emancipated woman friend like Melitta, but by the very person whom society would grant the right to dispose over her speech and silence: her husband. In Croissant-Rust's other play, *Der Bua*, the young woman Nannei refuses to be silenced by her violent lover's threats, and in fact provokes *his* silencing (at the hand of his foster father) when she shouts out that he has murdered his mother; in *Der standhafte Zinnsoldat*, Ernst ensures Johanna's freedom of expression by silencing himself — by shutting himself quietly in his room and suffocating himself with chloroform.

Croissant-Rust turns gender roles upside-down when she envisages a male protagonist who sacrifices himself for the sake of a woman's artistic freedom. The sacrifice of a man's life for the sake of a woman's writing can only be seen as extremely problematic in the late nineteenth century. Johanna is a novella writer, not a dramatist, but prejudices regarding women's abilities in any genre were widespread, and even where talent was recognized it was generally measured on a specifically female scale of ability, separate from and unquestionably less than what might be expected of a man. A contemporary audience would (had the play been performed) inevitably have been troubled by the question whether Ernst's self-sacrifice was really worthwhile — for the sake of a woman's writing. So Croissant-Rust doubly prepares the ground for this question, first in an exchange between Ernst (whose surname is Griese) and Johanna's friend Frau von Bornheim:

> FRAU VON BORNHEIM. Wenn ein Weib bedeutender ist als ein Mann, muß da nicht der Mann — nein, so geht's nicht. Wenn Jemand [*sic*] geopfert werden muß, soll da nicht der weniger Bedeutende das Opfer bringen?
>
> GRIESE *(reicht Johanna die Hand, die sie kurze Zeit hält, sehr erstaunt, etwas unsicher)*. Ja, meine Gnädige, — ich meine allerdings, es wird mehr die Bedeutung als das Geschlecht entscheiden — (64)

Later we hear Johanna's account of a dream, in which Ernst appears as a Christ-like figure:

> Plötzlich standest Du vor mir. Du warst gekleidet wie ein Priester [. . .] Da legtest Du mir leise die Hände auf [. . .] Deine Worte klangen wie ein Schwur und aus Deinem Herzen sickerten Blutstropfen. Da stand ich auf und küßte Deine Wunde, Du nahmst mich bei der Hand und wir schritten still durch den schönen Garten. Deine Wunde blutete fort und fort — (48)

The pragmatic basis for Ernst's decision to sacrifice himself is delivered, from his own lips, in the conversation with von Bornheim; but the profound meaningfulness and rightness of his act, in case we should doubt it, is signaled in the most persuasive metaphorical terms available in Western culture, through its association with the sacrifice of Christ.

The most striking similarity between *Der standhafte Zinnsoldat* and Paar's and Bernstein-Porges's plays of the female artist is that Johanna, like the other two practicing women artists Melitta and Sascha, finishes up in isolation. After Ernst's death we hear that Johanna will survive; but she will have to do it alone: "Laß sie nur allein, sie wird fertig damit werden, (nickend) sie *muß* fertig werden, (wieder nickend) *allein*" (94; Croissant-Rust's emphasis). Once again the price of artistic activity is exclusion from the normal social support structures. The upshot of Ernst's heroic self-sacrifice is that Johanna, when the play ends, is a single woman, as we have come to expect of one engaged in non-procreative creativity.

Contemporary critical responses to the play were mixed. They were also limited: despite the prediction of the influential Otto Julius Bierbaum ("Dieses Drama wird, denke ich, aufgeführt werden"),[24] the *Zinnsoldat* was not performed. Bierbaum praises Croissant-Rust's characterization, but, like some other reviewers, he complains about her choice of material. The essence of the recurring complaint is that this piece is not dramatic, but epic. Gustav Morgenstern in *Die Gesellschaft* "fragt sich, ob wir am 'Zinnsoldaten' nicht einen guten Roman verloren haben,"[25] Paul Bornheim in *Das litterarische Echo* calls the play "eine dialogisierte Novelle,"[26] and even Bierbaum laments "warum just Stoffe wählen, die verbieten, alle Register des Dramatischen zu ziehen? Warum Coulissen aufbieten für Novellen? Es ist das: es fehlt der Sinn für die Masse."[27] Whether or not we agree that there are "right" and "wrong" materials for drama, or that Croissant-Rust's piece is "undramatic," the critics' will to re-categorize is interesting. In the cases of Mataja, Bernstein-Porges, and Ebner-Eschenbach, as we saw above, women playwrights were re-categorized as "masculine" writers. Here we see the re-categorization of the work rather than the writer — Croissant-Rust's play is shifted towards the more "feminine" genre of prose narrative. Instead of the rationalizing argument "drama is masculine, therefore this woman dramatist is masculine, too," we meet the alternative explanation "drama is masculine, therefore what this woman writes is not dramatic."

Bornheim's other major criticism of *Der standhafte Zinnsoldat* is that the play is overly subjective: "Das Ganze macht den Eindruck eines persönlichen, nicht genügend objektivierten Erlebnisses."[28] Bornheim may well be right to identify a strong personal impetus in the drama. In a short autobiographical sketch written some years later, Croissant-Rust describes her own experience of writing in terms that recall her protagonist's, Johanna's, impulse to communicate with a wider public:

> Wenn ich an die Zeit zurückdenke, da ich mich gedrängt fühlte, "zur Feder zu greifen" anders als bisher, nicht um Briefe zu schreiben, in denen ich ungeschickt und verschämt *das* niederlegte, was mich gerade bewegte und erhob, sondern um einem noch verworrenen starken Gefühl nachzugeben, das gebieterisch nach Auslösung verlangte, so will mich das nicht so verwunderlich erscheinen, vielmehr als eine Notwendigkeit, zu der ich langsam gedrängt wurde. (Croissant-Rust's emphasis)[29]

Like Johanna in her explanations to Ernst, Croissant-Rust is here describing a powerful tension between her cultural identity as a woman and her creative need for self-expression. Precisely this tension drives the dramatic action of *Der standhafte Zinnsoldat*, although that dramatic tension seems, perhaps unsurprisingly, to be inaccessible to the male reviewers who have themselves never been confronted with that dilemma. Bornheim, Morgenstern, and Bierbaum read the expression of the divided female subject as something irrelevant to their own subjectivity, and decide that it is therefore insufficiently objective ("nicht genügend objektiviert") and lacks broad appeal ("Sinn für die Masse"). All three agree that *Der Bua*, with its rebellious male central character (the "bad boy" Irgei), is the stronger of Croissant-Rust's two plays.

Clearly their reception in a male-centered literary critical economy, by critics who have never learned to perceive their own subjective interests as anything other than definitive, is one problem for these women playwrights. But another is the act of creating a play about female creativity in that same ideological environment. There is no doubt that Paar's Helene, Bernstein-Porges's Sascha, and Croissant-Rust's Johanna are creative women; but, following the notions established and reiterated in the criticism and theory of the time, all the dramas reiterate or perform the notion that it is exceptional or unnatural for women to be creative artists. As a counterbalance, we find in each of the plays the norm or the "natural": the voluntary self-subordination of women in marriage and motherhood. In *Wir Drei* this is performed by Agnes, in *Helene* by the central protagonist, at the play's close. Even in *Der standhafte Zinnsoldat*, both Johanna's initial choice to write secretly and the theoretical discussions of the Bornheims on women's creativity and marriage signal a constant background awareness of what is "proper" or the norm.

Worth noting, however, is that before achieving closure, each of the dramas has performed an alternative to the marriage-and-motherhood paradigm. Helene *almost* achieves the artistic freedom that Melitta has; Sascha *almost* has Richard for her lover as well as literary success; and Johanna *almost* has a career as a writer alongside a functioning marriage. We have to ask why each of the dramatists takes this alternative away from her protagonist at the very moment it seems to beckon most persuasively. There are a number of possible answers, such as that drama as a genre does not thrive on harmony and easy solutions; or that, in the era of Realist and Naturalist writing, a happy outcome for the protagonists would disturb the realism and credibility of the plays (this answer suggests that the playwrights did not themselves believe in the compatibility of creative activity and womanhood/wifehood); or, indeed, that the dramatists were afraid to suggest that a compatibility denied by the literary critical authorities might in fact be possible — such a notion might be received by those authorities either with aggression towards, or suppression of, the work.

Another possible answer follows from the Chodorowian interpretation of the writer-protagonist relationship offered by Judith Kegan Gardiner, when she maintains: "the hero is her author's daughter."[30] If we add to this Dörte Giebel's commandment, "du sollst es nicht besser haben, als deine Mutter,"[31] we have the basis for the notion that the dramatist denies her character what she herself cannot have: in this case, an unbroken relationship with her womanhood and her creativity.

Women Supporting Men

We find more extreme forms of the repression of women protagonists in dramas where the male artist is dominant, and women play a supportive role. Eleven years after *Wir Drei* was published, Bernstein-Porges wrote another *Künstlerdrama*, this time a play of the male artist. Looking at the title, we might even call it a drama of the male artist's father: although the central character is Albrecht Herkner, the play is called *Johannes Herkner*, after Albrecht's father.

The five-act drama was published by Fischer in 1904,[32] when its author was already an established and successful writer whose female identity had been exposed by critics, with some relish, "hinter dem starkgeistigen, starkwortigen, beinah männlichen Gehaben Rosmer'scher Dramatik."[33] For the first time the playwright's own, unmarried name (even though she had married Max Bernstein in 1890) as well as her pseudonym appeared on the work:

Johannes Herkner
Schauspiel in fünf Akten
von
Elsa Porges
(Ernst Rosmer)

Given the perspective that we find in the text, we might argue that it is Elsa rather than Ernst who should be bracketed. In *Johannes Herkner*, no obvious attempt is made to find space for female subjectivity. The orientation of the play is masculinist; it is, therefore, what Croissant-Rust's critics might have called "genügend objektiviert." Albrecht Herkner, a sculptor, has left his country home and family to find the beginnings of artistic success and a beautiful lover called Mirjam in "einer süddeutschen Kunststadt" (perhaps Munich, where Bernstein-Porges lived for most of the earlier part of her life, until she was deported to Theresienstadt in 1942). The studio in which Albrecht seduces Mirjam, and in which she works as his (nude) model, is dominated by an enormous sculpture of Lucifer; Lucifer as counter-figure to the eponymous patriarch Johannes, who is ever-present even though he never appears on stage.

In acts 1 and 2, father Herkner is alive, although visible only in the form of a letter from home that Albrecht chooses to ignore; his death and burial are structurally central in the play, and are the pivot on which Albrecht's moral fortunes turn. After his father's burial in act 3, Albrecht turns away from both his sculpting and from Mirjam, who now functions as the sign of his artistic degeneracy, but he is led back to his art by a purer muse, his sister Elisabeth. Albrecht returns to the studio, ceremoniously hands the obsolete Mirjam back to *her* brother, installs Elisabeth as his new (clothed) model and begins the task of creating the greatest sculpture of all, for his father's grave. Lucifer is cast from his pedestal.

Bernstein-Porges's play is formally well-designed and effective in its use of structural binaries (Lucifer v. the Father, Mirjam v. Elisabeth). The figure of the patriarch Herkner is central to the piece, and Albrecht is central to the action. All the women revolve around and consciously depend on these two. Frau Herkner's response to her husband's death in act 3 is to commit spiritual suttee ("an mir ist gar nichts. Ich bin nur durch ihn was gewesen," 51); we learn that Elisabeth, who is clearly gifted, never wrote except to take dictation from her father (59); and Mirjam, denied the possibility of independent artistic expression even though we are told that she is a talented musician, is desperate to be allocated a part in the creative process of Albrecht's sculpting: "ohne mich ist's nicht möglich? Sag doch, sag!" (12).

Bernstein-Porges seems determined to present all this not as part of a repressive system, but within the terms of that system as (idealized) female self-subordination, and like Paar at the conclusion of *Helene,* she is prepared to use sentimentality to cloak what might otherwise look like oppression. Mirjam, for example, discourages Albrecht in sentimental tones from commitment to her, even though her own reputation and related quality of life are at stake (they are sleeping together):

> mein Herz fühlt dich so und begreift dich so und gibt dir in Allem [*sic*] Recht [. . .]. Ich weiß ganz genau was ich will! Dich halten, so lang ich kann — und dich lassen, so bald ich muß. Das werd ich spüren, ehe du selbst es weißt, und dann geh ich so leise zur Türe hinaus, daß auch du mich nicht hörst. (47)

Mirjam is the woman who "knows what she wants" — and that is to accommodate a man in all of his whims at the expense of her own emotional and social well-being. The ideal she incorporates is rendered particularly insidious by the illusion of self-determination. Not a hint of irony disturbs the text.

Further difficulties arise when Elisabeth struggles to prove that her father, Johannes Herkner, was *right* rather than sexist in his preference for the absent son who ignored him over the dutiful daughter who was his unpaid secretary:

> Mutter — mich hat Vater lieb gehabt, aber Albrecht — den hat er ge-liebt. Nicht weil es der Mann, nicht weil es der Sohn gewesen ist, son-dern weil er diejenige Kraft verkörpert hat, die sein Geist als die höchste ansah: die schaffende. Fortsetzung und Erfüllung des eignen Wesens war er ihm. (112)

Elisabeth gets embroiled here in the male-gendered associations of power and creativity that give the lie to her own claim that Herkner's preference was not chauvinistic. There is no ironic subtext to her argument, just as there is nothing obviously ironic in Albrecht's response — dreadful to the modern reading eye — when his sister asks him whether Mirjam has not only a beautiful body, but a beautiful soul:

> Seele? Was ist einem Mann eines Weibes Seele? Hingabe, Hingabe ist sie, eine Demut, die größer ist als seine Stärke, die ihn überwindet und überwältigt und vor ihr in die Kniee wirft, nicht als einen Besiegten, als einen Erlösten — das is Mirjams Seele. (122)

Again, sentimentality and received notions of gender complementarity characterize the speech. Albrecht's grotesque disregard for Mirjam's self or subject status — he sees her exclusively in her relation to himself —

is transformed or obscured by the glorious image he conjures of a kind of redemptive Gretchen.

But the most trying melodrama is still to come: in the final act, when Albrecht confronts Mirjam's devoted brother Siegmund (undertones of the Wälsungs here? Bernstein-Porges came from a musical family, and her father Heinrich was a fanatical admirer of Wagner) to confess that they have been sleeping together. Mirjam, who opposes this revelation, is sent offstage with Elisabeth to make space for the man-to-man confrontation. When Siegmund asserts his brotherly rights of ownership, Albrecht responds with a characterization of the educated, musically gifted Mirjam that makes her sound like a Neanderthal:

SIEGMUND. So lange sie unter meinem Willen steht — so lange ich ihr Schicksal bin —

ALBRECHT. Aber du bist es nicht — du kannst es deiner ganzen Art nach nie werden! So weit wie die Erkenntnis deines Gehirns ihr voraus ist, so weit wurzelt ihr Wesen zurück in eine uralte Welt — (146)

After Albrecht's confession, Mirjam is led back on by her lover and Elisabeth to face her brother. Unlike Albrecht, who remains "kräftig," she is "tiefgebeugt" (150) in her humiliation; but no one corrects Siegmund's conventional assertion that the real shame and suffering is all his: "was man die Schande nennt — meine innere Schande als Mann ist viel größer als deine äußere als Weib. Die nehm ich auf mich. Kaput [sic] geschlagen hat's mich" (151). Bernstein-Porges directs audience attention not at Mirjam, but at the two men and their relationship: Siegmund's suffering in the face of Albrecht's betrayal (which has taken the form of theft of property, his sister), and Albrecht's renunciation, for the sake of Siegmund and masculine honor (respect of property) of the sexual pleasure he has had through Mirjam. Mirjam's complete loss of self in this scene — she has no will and no input into the action that is deciding her future — is reflected in her loss of voice. She is silent, even absent, while the men define her new status as dishonored and reduced in value; but in her physical posture, "tiefgebeugt," she embodies the definition their speech imposes on her. For Mirjam, illocutionary or perlocutionary speech acts — the kind that get results, which the men are constantly involved in — seem impossible. She asks Albrecht to decide her fate for her, and he performs a classic illocutionary act when he hands her over to Siegmund: "Hier ist sie" (152).

What is most disturbing about this scene is that its sentimental effect relies on our acceptance that there is something moving, or some emotional pleasure to be had, in watching two men decide a woman's future for her in such a way as to cause least pain to themselves. Once Mirjam has been returned, Albrecht's virginal/valuable sister, Elisabeth, is left to take Mirjam's place as model for his next project: old Herkner's gravestone. Elisabeth is sent away to change into white robes, to take on the identity required of her by the creative male: unsullied goods, to commemorate proprietorial status and perpetuate the name of the father.

It would be cheering to think that in this drama we were dealing with masquerade — with deliberately overplayed sentimentalism and gender clichés, designed to expose the oppressive human relations they normally cloak. But it is difficult to find any indication that Bernstein-Porges is making her characters perform gender as masquerade with conscious or critical intent. On a metaphorical level we can look for interesting touches: if Siegmund, for example, is a Wälsung, might we read Albrecht as Wagner's Alberich, the demon dwarf of *Rheingold* who renounces love for the sake of ultimate patriarchal power, which is nonetheless taken from him by the dominant father-figure Wotan (Johannes)? In Wagner, both Wotan and Alberich seek to exploit Erda, the "uralte Welt" with which Albrecht associates the unfortunate Mirjam.

But if we view the drama more conventionally we see Albrecht, the sculptor, as a creator of bodies. When he "creates" Mirjam and Elisabeth, his models, in his art, he takes up a position towards woman that recalls that of god to man. For a while there is a level of subversion in his studio: as long as the giant figure of Lucifer dominates and Mirjam has, as she demands, a part in the creative process, the devil can be seen to be presiding over a situation in which a woman has a share in the creation of her own body. But with the advent of Elisabeth, clad in white, and the toppling of Lucifer, Albrecht (now as St. Michael) finally returns to the "benign" patriarchal order that is symbolized in the invisible figure of Johannes Herkner.

Fortunately Bernstein-Porges's contemporary, Gertrud Prellwitz (1869–1942), demonstrates that a more stimulating alternative to this kind of reiteration of gendered norms is possible even in plays dedicated to the male artist. In her far less well-known piece *Seine Welt* of 1911, Prellwitz finds an ironic and often entertaining perspective on the world that revolves around men. A teacher, an essayist, a novelist, and especially later in her life a highly (and, given the political situation of the time, disturbingly) patriotic writer, she was also the author of a number of dramas, which include *Oedipus oder das Rätsel des Lebens* (1898), *Michel Kohlhas* (1904), *Die Tat! Drama aus den Tagen von Tauroggen* (1912),

Seine Welt (1911), *Der Kaisertraum* (1913), and *Die letzte Wala: Eine Wotanslegende* (1935).[34]

Seine Welt is dedicated to Heinrich von Kleist, whom Prellwitz admired. It is another drama of the male artist: in this case a male dramatist, who is also called Heinrich — perhaps in Kleist's honor, although Prellwitz's characterization of Heinrich will make us doubt how much honor the association conveys. The other central protagonist is Dr. Hadumoth Silcher, whose name exudes all the exoticism of the (presumably Jewish) female intellectual. Prellwitz designates the play "ein Lustspiel"; but its reader is likely to find herself constantly reassessing what is comic in this "comedy," and what is not.

Because dramatic success has so far eluded him, Heinrich teaches German in the same girls' school in which Hadumoth is a teacher. In fact, as we discover, all the other teachers in this school are women; Heinrich is there because the girls' parents believe they need a man to teach the top grade.

Hadumoth is clearly an extraordinary character. Early in act 2, a female colleague recounts an anecdote about their university days (the two of them, it transpires, were among the first German women to be allowed to attend university), and the story functions not only as "funny" social comment, but also shows us the unconventional bite of Hadumoth's intelligence. It is worth quoting at length:

> Es war damals, als die Universität sich zum ersten Male für uns Frauen öffnete. Das heißt, wir durften die Vorlesungen hören, wenn der Professor uns persönlich seine Erlaubnis dazu gab; und die mußten wir uns persönlich einholen. Da wollten Hadumoth Silcher und ich Professor Donner hören, und wir machten uns zusammen auf den Weg. Erst standen wir vor Ehrfurcht eine ganze Weile draußen: endlich faßten wir uns Mut. — Und da saß ein vornehmer, olympisch blickender Mann mit Silberlocken, und während Hadumoth unsere wohlgesetze Rede hielt, ruhte sein Auge wohlwollend prüfend bald auf ihr, bald auf mir. Und dann erklang uns seine Antwort! Und er sagte, daß er allerdings willens sei, uns unsere Bitte zu erfüllen, denn er wolle sich dem Fortschritt der Zeit nicht in den Weg stellen. Daß er aber nicht verhehlen könne, wir sehr er bedaure, die Zeit diesen Weg einschlagen zu sehen. Denn dadurch, daß das weibliche Geschlecht jetzt anfange, sich um Wisssenschaft zu bemühen, würde der Menschheit ein kostbarstes Gut: der reine Instinkt, den die unverbildete edle Frau als unverfälschte Natur noch in sich trage und bewahre, geschädigt werden und vielleicht verloren gehen. — Da fällt mein Blick auf Fräulein Silcher und fährt erschrocken zurück! Denn sie sitzt da, verloren mit großen Augen und fängt an zu stammeln, und es kommt heraus: "Ist das aber schade! —

ist das schade! — für all die jungen Leute, — all die Tausende! — wenn
die Wissenschaft Instinkte verbildet! Muß dann die Wissenschaft nicht
geändert werden?" (23–4)

The story is beautifully told, in comic style: Professor Donner's godlike
status before these young women is established across three religious
traditions, from the nordic Thor the Thunderer, through olympian
gravitas, to the venerable "Silberlocken" popularly attributed to the
Judeo-Christian God. He is a benign deity, "wohlwollend," but — and
here the comedy sharpens suddenly — his kindly insistence on received
(and sentimentalizing) notions of the "unverbildete edle Frau" is also a
reminder of the forced, not voluntary, exclusion of women from German
universities that was supported and enforced for centuries by smug co-
horts of just such benign pseudo-deities. The strength of Hadumoth's
exclamation is that it immediately exposes the falseness of Donner's
argument, and implicitly suggests that the reasons for women's exclusion
from the academy are less benign than they might appear.

Hadumoth's beloved Heinrich shows far less originality of thought
than she, even though he is the creative artist. Another teaching colleague remarks:

Ach, das ist auch einer von denen, für die es dreierlei gibt: Männer, und
vor denen hat man Achtung. Weibchen, und in denen verehrt man die
heilige Natur. Und arbeitende Frauen, das ist naturwidrig, das ist häß-
lich, — da sieht man nicht hin. (27)

It seems that there is intellectually little to choose between Heinrich and
Professor Donner. But Hadumoth greatly admires Heinrich, and sees his
efforts in the field of creative writing as proof that this field is beyond
her: "Siehst du, Mutter, wie recht ich hatte, daß ich es nicht wagte?"
(28). Prellwitz leaves it to the reader to draw her own conclusions, here
and elsewhere in the play. No obvious criticism is made when Heinrich
demands of Hadumoth that she function as speculum, allowing him to
uncover her as a mirror of his poetic self: "O ziehen Sie alle Hüllen zur
Seite! Ich bitte Sie: lassen Sie mich die reine Spiegelung schauen!" (46).
In exposing Hadumoth, what he expects and desires to see is not her,
but a reflection of himself.

Heinrich is more obviously lampooned when he mixes his new love
for Hadumoth with satisfaction in the notion that she will now do the
donkey work of teaching for him: "Hadumoth — Silcher! — — — — —
— — Und die Aufsätze kann *sie* korrigieren!" (58; Prellwitz's emphasis
and punctuation). This ought to encourage us to read the following
scene of the play critically. Here, Heinrich discourages a schoolgirl from

writing poetry, exhorting her to remain an object rather than seeking to become a creative subject: "tun Sie das nicht. Seien Sie gut und rein und schön! So dienen Sie der Poesie inniger, als wenn Sie Gedichte machen" (64). Like Professor Donner, Heinrich is simultaneously benign or "wohlwollend," and controlling and repressive of women's intellectual potential.

The significance of this in the wider social context comes into focus when we learn, soon after this episode, that Hadumoth's mother was once a poet. The frustration of giving up writing for the sake of her married duties has left her with a nervous illness; and her attempts to justify her own oppression remind us of Elisabeth justifying her father's chauvinism in *Johannes Herkner*. Frau Silcher insists "ich bin glücklich gewesen! Ich habe einen herrlichen Gatten jeden Augenblick mit Verehrung gedient" (71); but unlike Bernstein-Porges, Prellwitz introduces a countervoice here. Hadumoth, instead of responding to the conventional sentiment, responds to the real meanings of "herrlich" and "dienen" in this context — the master and servant relation of man and wife in traditional marriage: "Ganz dunkel hat es mir manchmal geahnt! Und der Vater in seinem immer nehmenden Egoismus!" (71–72). She posits a difference between herself and her mother, launching an attack on the ideal of feminine selflessness that was paraded by such characters as Bernstein-Porges's Mirjam. Hadumoth insists:

> *Ich* aber, ich bin ganz anders! Mir ist *nicht*: Sich-Selbst-Opfern das beste Glück! Auch nicht die heiligste Pflicht! Nein. Sondern: Des Lebens goldenen Wunderkelch zu reichster, zu unverletzter Entfaltung aufblühen fühlen — ist mir das beste Menschenglück und höchster Pflicht. (72; Prellwitz's emphasis)

But the similarities between Hadumoth and Mirjam are greater than this outburst might lead us to believe. It transpires in the course of the final act that "des Lebens goldener Wunderkelch" blossoms for Hadumoth in Heinrich's work, not in her own. She reassures him that when they are married she will work only if he needs the money, and defines "das gemeinsame Ziel: *dein* Schaffen" (102; my emphasis). Yet in the same breath she condemns married slavery: "Alle Frauen arbeiten für ihre Männer! Arme Mägdearbeit für seinen Gaumenreiz! für seine Tyrannenbehaglichkeit!" (102). Hadumoth Silcher is considerably more critical of conventional gender performances than Bernstein-Porges's Mirjam, but in the end she incorporates the same paradox: she is the woman who "knows what she wants," but who is trapped within a discourse that has already defined what women want, and has thereby blocked the paths that lead away from self-subordination.

Prellwitz's play is subtly and at times brilliantly witty. Her attempt to construct an ideal of female empowerment that operates within the social norms takes us far from Bernstein-Porges's more conventional portrayal of the gentle, passive woman. Hadumoth, like a German Jane Eyre, instructs Heinrich that he will marry her, and purposefully stage-manages the ensuing interview with her father, but her choice of the pompous, self-indulgent, often ridiculous poet for a husband is not a satisfying one. And Prellwitz leads us back into the safe harbor of dramatic convention when she concludes her comedy with their engagement, allowing the potentially extraordinary Hadumoth to finish as little more than a kind of ideal mother figure, whose primary interest is in the survival of her hapless child-fiancée; less hackneyed, perhaps, than the passive beloved, but nonetheless the acceptable face of female activity. We remain, in the end, within "Seine Welt."

Only the last line of the play reminds us that more might be implied in comedy than is overtly said. Heinrich has been encouraged to write comic drama, and Hadumoth's father — the same man who, "völlig gütig," forbids his wife ever to hold an opinion that differs from his own (91) — concludes the drama with the peculiar words: "Wenn ihm seine Lustspiele nur nicht aus Versehen — Mysterienspiele werden!" (109). Is Prellwitz hinting that her "Lustspiel" should be read between the lines, to uncover a hidden meaning — a "Mysterienspiel"? Comedy, after all, is often subversive, and at this point we might feel invited to go back and re-read this play as something more than simple romantic comedy; perhaps as an exposé of the covert controlling violence that is at the root of benignly paternalist gender relations. Where Elsa Bernstein-Porges's *Johannes Herkner* skirts masquerade, sentimentalizing and thereby legitimizing oppression, Prellwitz in *Seine Welt* forces her characters into a comic masquerade that exposes, even though it never actually escapes, repressive structures. Prellwitz's play was considerably less successful than Bernstein-Porges's.

All the plays discussed in this chapter reiterate gender norms as well as performing an alternative. Paar's Helene, Croissant-Rust's Johanna, and Bernstein-Porges's Sascha (*Wir Drei*) are artistically active, at least for a while; Prellwitz's Hadumoth is dominant in her relationship with Heinrich and also, it is suggested, with her father. In Bernstein-Porges's *Johannes Herkner* even Mirjam defies convention in an extramarital relationship, and claims to play a role in Albrecht's artistic creation of her body.

The status of the female body in these plays is worth considering. Helene's, Mirjam's, and (arguably) Hadumoth's bodies are owned, by fathers, brothers, or husbands. Mirjam's body is the most abject of them all; it is least of all (in Butler's words), a "body that matters,"[35] because she can simply be replaced by Elisabeth as Albrecht's model. In this context, the female body is clearly an object for use (as model or muse) by the creative male. Johanna's and Sascha's, by contrast, are not owned by any man, something which renders these two characters extraordinary in terms of the gendered social organization of bodies. It also leaves them, in the end, outside of that organization; alone, isolated, without the security of the family.

In her use of drama's corporeal potential, Elsa Bernstein-Porges is arguably the most successful of the dramatists considered in this chapter. Her deployment of real bodies, models and statues on stage in *Johannes Herkner* provides for a striking visual event. What the corporeality of drama also gives Bernstein-Porges, however, is the means of demonstrating the abjection of the female body.

It is of course difficult, when writing within a discourse as powerful and all-embracing as the discourse of gender, at the same time to articulate an alternative to that discourse, or to rebel against it. For a writer, there is a strong temptation to opt to provide audience satisfaction through sentimental reiteration of familiar norms. In *Johannes Herkner*, Bernstein-Porges succumbs to this temptation (this is not true for all her plays — *Maria Arndt* (1908), for example, is a different case). Paar, Prellwitz, and Croissant-Rust manage to play a double game, suggesting, albeit carefully, that the discourse might be changed: that it might be possible to view women as independent creative beings, and it might just be ridiculous when men try to style them otherwise. But Mathilde Paar, Gertrud Prellwitz, and Anna Croissant-Rust are less well-known names now than Elsa Bernstein-Porges: critics found their plays uninteresting and irrelevant. Once again we encounter the real dangers of investing one's creative energy in concerns pertaining to a non-dominant group.

Notes

[1] Hoppe, "Die Frau als Dramatikerin," in *Die Literatur* 10 (1929), 563–64 (564).

[2] Eduard Devrient, *Aus seinen Tagebüchern, Karlsruhe 1852–1870*, ed. by Rolf Kabel (Weimar: Böhlau, 1964), 393.

[3] Krack, "Schreibende Frauen," in *Die Zukunft* 24 (1898), 324–30 (326).

[4] Lessing, "Zwei Münchener Dichterinnen: Ernst Rosmer und Helene Böhlau," in *Die Gesellschaft* 13/III (1898), 16–28 (21).

[5] Mensch's novel, *Auf Vorposten: Roman aus meiner Züricher Studentenzeit*, was published in Leipzig in 1903.

[6] Mensch, *Die Frau in der modernen Literatur: Ein Beitrag zur Geschichte der Gefühle* (Berlin: Duncker, 1898).

[7] Mensch, "Der Misserfolg der Frau als Dramenschriftstellerin," in *Bühne und Welt* 13 (1910–11), 155–59 (157–58).

[8] Wiegand, *Die Frau in der modernen deutschen Literatur: Plaudereien* (Bremen: Schünemann, 1903), 38.

[9] Ada Christen, *Faustina: Drama in fünf Akten* (Vienna: Dirnboeck, 1871); Marie Itzerott, *Hilde Brandt: Schauspiel in 4 Aufzügen* (Strasbourg: Heitz, 1905); Mathilde Lisette Marie Paar, *Helene: Schauspiel in vier Akten* (Berlin: Luckhardt, 1882); Anna Croissant-Rust, *Der standhafte Zinnsoldat. Drama* (Berlin: Schuster & Loeffler, 1896); Gertrud Prellwitz, *Seine Welt. Ein Lustspiel in 5 Akten* (Berlin: Erkner, 1911); Ernst Rosmer [ps for Elsa Bernstein-Porges], *Wir Drei. Fünf Akte* (Munich: Albert, n.d. [1893]).

[10] A briefer consideration of this drama appears in Sarah Colvin, "Women and Drama at the Turn of the Century, or Thresholds of Gender and Genre," in *Schwellen: Germanistische Erkundungen einer Metapher*, ed. by Nicholas Saul, Daniel Steuer, Frank Möbus, and Birgit Illner (Würzburg: Königshausen & Neumann, 1999), 265–78.

[11] An extensive listing of Paar's dramatic work can be found in Susanne Kord, *Ein Blick hinter die Kulissen: Deutschsprachige Dramatikerinnen im 18. und 19. Jahrhundert* (Stuttgart: Metzler, 1992), 413.

[12] See chapter 1.

[13] Russo, "Female Grotesques: Carnival and Theory," in *Writing on the Body: Female Embodiment and Feminist Theory*, ed. by Katie Conboy, Nadia Medina, and Sarah Stanbury (New York: Columbia UP, 1997), 318–36 (331).

[14] Julie Marney, "Performing Subjectivities: Feminism, Postmodernism and the Practice of Identity," unpublished doctoral dissertation, University of Edinburgh, 2000.

[15] For a very good example of this, see Susanne Kord, *Sich einen Namen machen: Anonymität und weibliche Autorschaft, 1700–1900* (Stuttgart: Metzler, 1996), 95–96.

[16] "Ich glaube überhaupt nicht, daß eine Frau, die glückliche Gattin und Mutter ist, der Welt noch viel als Dramenschriftstellerin zu sagen hat." Mensch, "Der Misserfolg der Frau als Dramenschriftstellerin," 158.

[17] For example, by Lessing, 21–24, and by Rudolf Lothar, who notes: "Frau Rosmer hat einen unendlich scharf entwickelten Verstand. Das ist das Rassige an ihr. Sie hat die spekulative Güte des edlen Juden." Lothar, *Das deutsche Drama der Gegenwart* (Munich: Müller, 1905), 167.

[18] Ulrike Zophoniasson-Baierl, *Elsa Bernstein alias Ernst Rosmer: Eine deutsche Dramatikerin im Spannungsfeld der literarischen Strömungen des Wilhelminischen Zeitalters* (Bern: Lang, 1985).

[19] Lothar, 164.

[20] Peter Skrine, "Elsa Bernstein and Königskinder," in *Königskinder or The Prince and the Goosegirl*, English National Opera program notes (1992). See also Skrine, "Elsa Bernstein: Germany's Major Woman Dramatist?," in *German Women Writers 1900–1933: Twelve Essays*, ed. by Brian Keith-Smith (Lampeter: Mellen, 1993), 43–63.

[21] Giesing points out that, despite Rosmer's relatively high profile, the performance history for her plays is still surprisingly bad. See Michaela Giesing, "Verhältnisse und Verhinderungen – Deutschsprachige Dramatikerinnen um die Jahrhundertwende," in *Frauen Literatur Geschichte*, ed. by Hiltrud Gnüg und Renate Möhrmann, 2nd completely revised ed. (Stuttgart: Metzler, 1999), 261–78 (265).

[22] Mensch, *Die Frau in der modernen Literatur*, 96.

[23] A consideration of this drama is also given in Colvin, "Women and Drama at the Turn of the Century."

[24] O. J. B. [= Otto Julius Bierbaum], "Anna Croissant-Rust: 'Der standhafte Zinnsoldat.' Drama in drei Acten," in *Die Zeit. Wiener Wochenschrift* 8 (1896), 158.

[25] Morgenstern, "Anna Croissant-Rust" in *Die Gesellschaft* 13/III (1897), 211–19 (218).

[26] Bornheim, "Anna Croissant-Rust" in *Das litterarische Echo* 9 (1906–7), 924–33 (926).

[27] Bierbaum, 158.

[28] Bornheim, 927.

[29] Croissant-Rust, "Rückschau," in *Die Brücke. Monatsschrift für Zeitinterpretation* 2 (1912), 4–8 (5).

[30] Gardiner, "On Female Identity and Writing by Women," in *Writing and Sexual Difference*, ed. by Elizabeth Abel (Brighton: Harvester, 1982), 177–91 (186).

[31] Giebel, "Das Ende meiner Mädchenjahre," in *Hamburger Frauen-Zeitung* 56 (1999), 32–33.

[32] Elsa Porges (= Elsa Bernstein-Porges), *Johannes Herkner: Schauspiel in fünf Akten* (Berlin: Fischer, 1904).

[33] Lessing, 21. Rosmer's identity as Elsa Bernstein-Porges was "exposed" soon after the performance of her play *Dämmerung* in 1893.

[34] For a more complete list see Kord, *Ein Blick hinter die Kulissen*, 417.

[35] Judith Butler, *Bodies That Matter: On the Discursive Limits of "Sex"* (London: Routledge, 1993).

3: Julie Kühne, Laura Marholm, Clara Viebig: Performing Subjects

I N THE PREVIOUS CHAPTER we saw dramatic characters performing both the norm of female gender and, to a greater or lesser extent, alternatives to that norm. The alternatives — independent creative activity, hand-in-hand with self-ownership or control over one's own body — take the female subject outside the structure of the patriarchal family, because they are apparently not possible within it.

In this chapter I analyze three plays that advertise their concern with a female subject in their titles and subtitles: Julie Kühne's *Elfriede Laub oder Weib und Mensch* (1873), Laura Marholm's *Karla Bühring: Ein Frauendrama* (1895), and Clara Viebig's *Barbara Holzer* (1897). These are not historically attested or notable figures like Ebner's Maria Stuart or Marie Roland: in each case, and particularly in *Elfriede Laub* and *Barbara Holzer*, the dramatist portrays an ordinary woman, whose life does not differ in its external circumstances from that of numerous other women. What makes these women remarkable is that they believe (initially at least) that they can assert an autonomous self, even in a society where femininity or femaleness is understood to be a subordinate reflection of dominant masculinity or maleness. When this belief leads them into conflict with convention and their environment, two of the three women finish up dead, and therefore outside of the social structure in a drastic sense; one finds her way back into society in a learning process that renders the play practically a *Lehrstück*.

Performing Gender

The character who survives is Elfriede, the central figure in Kühne's play, which has the full title *Elfriede Laub oder Weib und Mensch.*[1] There is no evidence to suggest that this play was ever performed; given the subject matter, it is unlikely that a theater would have accepted it.

While the play does have a distinctly dramatic narrative, it recalls at times the Reformation dialogues of the sixteenth century rather than the theater of the nineteenth — verbal interchanges often occur with the clear intention of presenting a discourse versus a counter-discourse, and (as in the Reformation dialogues) we are left in no doubt as to whose side we ought to be on. In an early conversation with her father, in which she is arguing to be allowed to continue her education, Elfriede is polemical:

> Läßt du nicht meinen Bruder Oskar auch viel lernen, damit er seine Gesichtspunkte erweitert und anders schafft als deine Arbeiter, bin ich denn weniger oder mehr als er, daß der Unterschied zwischen der Arbeit der Tochter im Hause und der Magd nur darin besteht, daß die eine befiehlt, die andere gehorcht? (7)

At this point in the play, she is still trying to equate the terms "Weib" and "Mensch" (as if "Mensch" also meant "Weib" in the way that it does "Mann"),[2] and a misunderstanding therefore arises between Elfriede and her — apparently benign — father. When Father Laub laments his forced inactivity through illness: "das Leben wird zum Vegetiren, wenn der Mensch nicht mehr streben, arbeiten und nur in seinem Schaffen genießen kann!" Elfriede is encouraged to respond: "Auch ich möchte streben, arbeiten und in meinem Schaffen genießen können!" (6). Laub, however, is quick to suppress the hubris that led his daughter to equate herself with "der Mensch." He imposes a more confining definition on her — "du bist Laub's [sic] Tochter!" (6) — and eventually betrays a violent wish for her suppression that belies his paternal kindliness: "Du bist [. . .] so eigenwillig und eigenköpfig, daß vielleicht erst Schicksalsschläge dich gefügig machen werden!" (9). Here Laub anticipates Elfriede's later mother-in-law, who will advise her son: "Sie muß gebrochen werden, willst du glücklich sein!" (84); in both cases the vocabulary used, "Schläge," "gefügig," and "brechen" betrays the violence in the process of subordinating women who aspire to be "Menschen."

In Gertrud Prellwitz's *Seine Welt*, we saw how women are expected to fulfil the function of mirrors of the male. Kühne's play makes this point, too: father Laub unconsciously confesses to his wife that the privileged position of the patriarch depends on women's complementary subalterity: "ohne dich wäre ich nie ein Mann geworden" (40). All the men in *Elfriede Laub* enjoy the right to define themselves and the world when they speak, while the women listen and are defined (for example, when Laub tells Elfriede that her significance in the world derives from her paternity: she is "Laub's Tochter"). Where Ebner-Eschenbach gave protagonists such as Marie Roland and Sarah Hochburg ample linguistic space in which to assert themselves — their speeches are proportionately dominant in the plays — Julie Kühne shows us men's speech as dominant, in a way that more nearly reflects recent studies conducted on the dynamics of male/female conversation.

In her book *The Writing or the Sex?*, Dale Spender (writing in 1989) cites some analyses of the speech space occupied by women and men respectively. According to Spender, women lay claim to between 8% and 42% of conversational space; and both men and women may perceive an 8% (female) to 92% (male) contribution as a fair division, while a 42% female share might be experienced as unfair, because it is perceived to be too much.[3] We can compare this with Kühne's dramatic presentation of speech space in 1873. In the first scene of Kühne's play, between Laub and his wife (I, iii), he speaks 25 lines to her 16 (i.e. a 61% to 39% division in his favor); in the important family scene (II, iv), in which Laub, Frau Laub, Elfriede, and her brother Oskar are present, the division is 17 lines (Frau Laub), 28 (Oskar), 31 (Elfriede), to Laub's whopping 120; and in another crucial scene, in which Elfriede agrees to marry (III, vi), she manages 14 lines to her suitor's, Dr. Russek's, 40 — meaning that he commandeers 74% of the available conversational space.

How conversational space is acquired and used is another consideration. Interruption is the most common method of acquiring space and is, according to results cited by Spender, practiced far more frequently by men than by women.[4] In an almost comical scene (I, vii), Kühne shows us Elfriede unable to even finish speaking the name of her first suitor, Barkesleben:

ELFRIEDE.   Herr Bark —

BARKESLEBEN. Sehen Sie nicht so strenge, Fräulein. [. . .]

ELFRIEDE.   Herr Bark —

BARKESLEBEN. Was meinen Sie, Fräulein. [. . .]

ELFRIEDE.   Verzeihung, Herr Bark —

BARKESLEBEN. Erlauben Sie, daß ich [. . .] mich Ihnen empfehle.

(20–1)

Elfriede's linguistic situation in the scene with her second suitor, Russek, whom she marries, is even more extreme. Elfriede gets engaged through her silence, which Dr. Russek defines for her, as consent: "Du schweigst — schweige weiter und du willigst ein. O, meine Elfriede, so bist nun mein, für heut und immer mein! So habe ich denn ein Recht auf dich" (58). Russek's assertion of ownership comes immediately, without a pause, after his definition of the meaning of her silence as an illocutionary speech act — it is no wonder that, in relating events to her mother, Elfriede can only describe passivity or non-action on her part:

FRAU LAUB.   [. . .] Was hast du gethan?

ELFRIEDE.   Gethan! So eigentlich Nichts [*sic*]. Die Liebe, die mir
               ein edler Mann entgegentrug, ich habe sie nicht
               zurückgewiesen. (59)

Nonetheless, Elfriede is aware of a link between language and action. At
this stage in the play she does not fully appreciate what that link is; later
she will come to recognize that linguistic dominance, like rape, is an
assertion of power rather than love. For the moment she is enthused, but
her expression of trust in Russek's speech — "Wie spricht er schön! Wie
muß er handeln können!" (61) — loses credibility for an audience when
the last thing he does in act 3 is to pressure her, against her expressed
will, to have sex with him.

As a dramatic character, Elfriede's second chance comes because
Kühne breaks radically with convention by placing her "happy ending" — the engagement — at the end of the third act, with two acts of
the play still to run. Kühne, rather than merely hinting at problems to
come after the curtain has closed on a conventional joyous union,[5] actually shows us the reality. The fourth act opens five years later, on a miserable scene of domestic tyranny. Dr. Russek, now Elfriede's husband, is
still talking at her, but now chiefly to deliver commonplaces about his
rights and expectations in that role.

It is here that the character of the play as *Lehrstück* really begins to
make itself felt. The dialogue between Elfriede and Russek is an exposé
of commonplace and convention: Russek speaks of educating Elfriede,
using the verb "erziehen" (commonly applied to children and newly-
married women in nineteenth-century discourse), and he underlines the
infantilizing force of the word when he chooses to call his wife "Kind"
(67). Reminded by Elfriede of her adulthood — "Ich bin kein Kind
mehr" — Russek sulks: "Du bist in diesem Augenblick weder schön
noch weiblich" (67). To be rewarded as feminine, it seems that women
must accept juvenile or even infantile status.

Kühne gives Elfriede an analytical intelligence that enables her to expose Russek's commonplaces for what they are. When Russek postures:
"Hier nur beim Weibe fühle ich mich als Mann und frei!" Elfriede
counters: "Einseitige Freiheit nennt man Tyrannei!" (67). It is all the
more striking that Elfriede, although Russek's intellectual superior, is
disadvantaged in their discursive battle because her husband is not arguing from the position of an individual, but within the secure context of
an established masculinist discourse: that is, a discourse that provides him
with automatic authority, an automatically superior status. Russek gener-

alizes masterfully: "Die Frauen sind immer ungereimt. Sie können niemals folgern. Es ist schwer zu unterscheiden, was verdrießlicher und vergeblicher ist, Lichter zu putzen, oder Weiber mit Gründen zu bekehren, sagt schon Börne" (75).

While Kühne's methods here have some similarities with Gertrud Prellwitz's in *Seine Welt* — Kühne, too, is helping this discourse to expose itself for the hackneyed, chauvinistic thing it is — we do not find the humor, the inclination to laugh at masculine self-importance, that we found in Prellwitz's play. Where Hadumoth's premarital situation could be seen as amusing, Elfriede's postmarital condition is not in the least bit funny. Marriage has automatically given Russek control of his wife's money, and he refuses to give her a penny; she is housed but otherwise destitute, and — as he reminds her — almost completely without rights. Russek justifies his refusal to give Elfriede money or freedom with the borrowed eloquence of an established discourse of gender, as if he were reading from a book: "wenn Ihr Frauen uns bestimmen wollt, Euch eine Herrschaft anmaßen, die von Gottes und Rechts wegen uns nur zukommt und wir geben nach, so schaffen wir uns selber eine Ruthe" (70). The woman who in the first act of the play still equated herself with "der Mensch" is now forced to recognize her real status: she is "ein Nichts" (83).

The all-important realization that this status has little to do with the individual self, and everything to do with the concrete legal system that governs social organization and the institution of marriage, comes to Elfriede in the final act. Act 5 reads like a practical lesson in nineteenth-century marriage law. It opens after another time gap, during which Elfriede has left her husband and started seeking advice on divorce from a family lawyer. When the solicitor asks whether Russek betrayed her, she is quick to insist that he did: "um Alles was ich war, gedacht, gefühlt" (88). For Elfriede, the moral position is clear. However, she has yet to learn about the distinction between "justice" and the legal position of married women, and about a law that might recognize physical violence done to a wife, but never "solche systematische Mißachtung und Mißhandlung — ihres Seins" (90). She has still to discover that her children, too, are regarded as principally the property of her husband, and that she has no legal recourse to reclaim her own inheritance back from Russek. Kühne is far from taking a comic approach here; on the contrary, Elfriede is impelled to recognize the female heterosexual condition as tragic:

> die reiche Frau, sei sie an Geld, an Fähigkeiten oder Charakter reich, darf nicht lieben, denn sie verliert durch die Ehe Alles [*sic*] — sie ist gleich Lear, der sein Königreich für Liebesworte weggegeben. (91)

Neither Elfriede nor her mother — who is also present in this scene — knew the legal situation when they were married; neither had been educated to understand it. The didactic message of Kühne's "Lehrstück" is here directed not only at its characters, but at its female readers or audience.

At the play's outset, it was Elfriede Laub's intention to learn to develop her own humanity, as "Weib und Mensch." What she in fact learns in the course of this drama is a more practical lesson, namely to distinguish between the status of "Weib" and "Mensch" — to know masculinist society and its discourse. In the process, she regains some of the self-determination that was taken from her when she (to use Beauvoir's words) "became a woman"; she can survive because she understands. Rather than performing womanhood uncritically and practically unconsciously (as do most of the other women in the play), Elfriede can perform it *consciously* — she has grasped the terms of the gender contract. This gives her a head start on Russek, who is still performing masculinity unquestioningly, and is therefore trapped. His behavior is ruled by the fear of being seen as "unverständlich, unmännlich" (102). The difference in their situations is that Elfriede has acquired through her experience the "schielender Blick"[6] of those who stand outside the "norm" of humanity — who are "Weiber," not "Menschen" — and has therefore gained an insight that to some extent counterbalances the discursive power of the male.

A long dialogue, in which she regulates their marital affairs, illustrates Elfriede's new control of discourse. Not only does she occupy noticeably more linguistic space that Russek in this conversation — Elfriede dominates with more than 60% — but her speech acts are almost invariably felicitous; she takes gendered discourse by the scruff of the neck and uses it for her own purposes. By reminding Russek that he defined her as financially incompetent, Elfriede doubles the allowance he gives her; by appealing to his authority when he said she was not fit to keep house, she acquires the right to a housekeeper. And when he protests that she must do at least some of the work, she invokes the gendered order against him: "Du sprichst ja, wie ich vor Kurzem! Ich will gern, wie du oft gesprochen, dich für mich arbeiten und mich von deinen starken Armen durch's Leben tragen lassen" (105). At this point Russek starts to lose his nerve: "Elfriede, ich bitte dich, höre auf. Dein Geist, deine theure Liebenswürdigkeit wird fürchterlich" (105). There is potential for comedy here, but the aftertaste is bitter. Elfriede conjures an image that powerfully concludes the discussion:

In langen Schaaren sehe ich die bleichen Gestalten der Frauen erschei-
nen, die Unnatur und Egoismus der Menschenwürde beraubt, nur
Weiber sein läßt und fühle nur Haß gegen den Wahn, der dies Leben
über sie verhängt. (106)

Kühne's play closes with a second "happy ending": Russek and Elfriede are reunited. But the audience, or better, the reader by now knows
enough about nineteenth-century family law to be aware that this is a
necessity for Elfriede if she wants to retain access to her children and her
inherited capital — both now the property of her husband. Elfriede's
mother has the last word: she concludes the play with a piece of maternal
advice in a paternalistic world, namely that all girls, before they even
think of getting married, should ensure they get a proper education, so
that they are in a position to retain their rights and self-sufficiency.

Elfriede Laub oder Weib und Mensch could very well be described not
only as *Lehrstück* — a piece of instruction for its (female) audience — but
also as a *Bildungsdrama*. Where the male protagonist of the traditional
Bildungsroman seeks and finds a path to self-sufficiency and self-
expression in the world, Elfriede Laub seeks self-sufficiency and self-
expression, but finds a world in which these things do not exist for
women. She subsequently learns how to become an agent through the
manipulation of masculinist language and law. This is not so much a
happy ending as a compromise driven by necessity. The final ray of hope
is that Elfriede and Russek agree to live together as equal partners and
friends, abandoning the ideal of romantic love that functions as kitsch
camouflage for gendered inequality.[7]

Julie Kühne is consciously or unconsciously placing her work at the
edges of literary tradition when she makes a female character the subject
of a "Bildungsdrama." All that is of importance in this drama happens to
a woman and is viewed from her perspective; but, as the discursive
framework of the piece makes clear to us, women are not supposed to
exist except in the eyes and imaginations of men, and it would therefore
be possible to conclude, from the masculinist perspective, that nothing
of importance happens in this drama at all.

There is no performance record for Kühne's play. It tests notions of
humanness and the unconscious assumption (which has not entirely
disappeared more than a century later) that "Mensch" and "Mann"
mean roughly the same thing. "Weib" is a supplemental notion. As a
dramatist, she provides one answer to the question how far the writer can
direct or control how gender and humanness are performed. The world
of Elfriede Laub is no utopia; it is a stage replica of the chauvinistic,
discriminatory society Kühne herself was familiar with. The play is a "real

life" portrayal of the theoretical notions that were articulated by writers of non-fiction, such as Louise Dittmar, whose *Das Wesen der Ehe* of 1849 contains an analysis of married relations similar to that we see on stage in *Elfriede Laub*. Dittmar writes of

> Der Mangel an Einfluß, die Nichtachtung, die Beeinträchtigung jedes [*sic*] Willens, die Rücksichtslosigkeit des Mannes, die Unmöglichkeit, sich nach Neigung und Geschick sich auszubilden, sich geistig zu entwickeln, die *unbedingte* Hingabe an den Mann, die daraus folgende Mißehe [. . .].

She describes a female self, "das seiner Freiheit, seiner Menschenwürde beraubt durch die Selbstsucht derer, denen es Weihrauch streut."[8] In this context, which is also the context of Kühne's play, Elfriede does what is possible: she learns to perform her gender in a way that both works within the rules of that society, and eases the burden gender places on her. The change is from an unconscious, forced performance to a conscious performance on her own terms. This seems to be, in Kühne's view, as emancipatory as real life, and real life drama, gets.

Performing Womanhood

The question of a woman's self is equally central, if quite differently handled, in Laura Marholm's play, *Karla Bühring*.[9] "Laura Marholm" is a pseudonym: the playwright was born Laura Mohr in 1854 and married Ola Hansson in 1889. She grew up in Riga, in modern-day Latvia (then Russia), and only moved to Germany after she was married; she died (like Helene Druskowitz) in a psychiatric clinic, diagnosed as paranoic, in 1905.[10] Marholm is one of the few women dramatists in the later nineteenth century to use a *female* pseudonym. Given the male gender of drama, it is hard to see what benefit is to be had from changing one's name if one retains a female identity.[11] She in fact wrote her — very impressive — first drama, *Johann Reinhold Patkul* (in two parts, *Gertrud Lindenstern*, 1878 and *Patkul's Tod*, 1880) under the male pseudonym Leonard Marholm. Her reason for publishing her later work as Laura, rather than Leonard, may well have been that she was soon better known as a cultural theorist than as a playwright: the authority of her own womanhood was an essential (in every sense) basis for works such as *Das Buch der Frauen* (1895), *Wir Frauen und unsere Dichter* (1895), and *Zur Psychologie der Frau* (2 vols., 1897 and 1903). Marholm's theories underpin the popular notion of the "complementarity" of the sexes, and emphasize the essential incompleteness of woman without man (jokes about fish and bicycles were not common currency at the turn of the nineteenth century).

Although *Karla Bühring* is also a drama of the woman artist (Karla is a concert violinist), I include it in this chapter because its focus of interest is very different from that of Paar's *Helene*, Croissant-Rust's *Zinnsoldat*, or Bernstein's *Wir drei*. In those plays, the uneasy relationship between women's confinement within marriage and women's creative freedom was explored; in Marholm's piece, attention is concentrated not so much on the external structures of marriage and the family, as on women's internal needs and how these are misrecognized in male-organized society. Art itself (Karla's music) is here secondary, or even metaphorical — a sign or symptom of her sexual needs rather than a thing-in-itself. There is a similarity with *Helene* in that Marholm never engages in her drama with the subject of women who create art, but only with the more acceptable idea of women who interpret it. We might remind ourselves of Schlenther's notion of acting, which in his view appealed to "das Geschmeidige der Frau, ihre große Fähigkeit, sich in ein fremdes Wesen zu versenken, sich einem fremden Wesen zu unterwerfen."[12]

This "fremde Wesen," we understand, is gendered male: in *Das Buch der Frauen*, Marholm herself contends, with a depressing lack of original thought: "Das Weib — ja das Weib ist, seelisch und physiologisch, eine Kapsel über eine Leere, die erst der Mann kommen muß zu füllen."[13] When the dramatic character Karla Bühring performs, the (male-authored) music she plays evokes the man whom she lacks: "Ich spiele meine Sehnsucht, meine Sehnsucht, meine Sehnsucht. *(Ganz einfach sprechend.)* Das ist das Geheimnis meiner unbegriffenen Wirkung" (53–54). She is aware that the men who observe her playing (we never hear of women's responses) react narcissistically to this spectacle of possession and desire: "Ich spiele ihre schlaffen Lüste wach, daß sie zittern und brennen und kitzeln. Das ist, was sie von mir verstehen" (54). Karla's performance figures as a kind of pornographic peepshow. We might remind ourselves of Hans Pauli's slavering reading of work by women, as an invitation to keyhole-peeking, a peeping Tom's appreciation of "der reizvollen Art, wie sich eine Autorin mit Bewusstsein selber offenbart oder unbewusst selber verräth."[14]

But Marholm's approach is not critical of such responses: on the contrary, the men are shown to be interpreting Karla's performance correctly. We understand that, for Karla, her art is ersatz, and springs from the gap created by the lack of a male sexual partner; if she were to find a husband, her "Sehnsucht" would disappear, and with it, presumably, her will to play. Not for nothing is she perceived as "Sancta Cäcilia mit der Violine" (51), the virgin-martyr. In the terms of the play, her public performance of desire is problematic only because it exposes her to the proprietorial claims of the *wrong* sort of men: specifically of Siegfried Collander, the Jewish villain of Marholm's piece.[15] The sexual association between Karla and her violin is spelled out and turned around when Collander confronts her with his reading of their physical intercourse: "Sie fühlten, wie die Saiten Ihrer Seele und Ihres Leibes unter den Griffen meiner Finger zucken und klingen" (93). He has responded to Karla Bühring's recital by assuming his right to violate the privacy of any woman who enters the public arena in this way — Collander enters her house at night, to tell her: "Ich habe lange nach Ihnen gelechzt . . . seit jenem ersten Abend, wo ich Sie spielen hörte . . . Ihre wilde, heiße, frische Sehnsucht hinausspielen hörte" (68; Marholm's punctuation). Marholm's criticism is not of the response in itself — after all, the playwright has already signaled that all men react to Karla's playing in this way, and rightly — but of the fact that Collander, married and a Jew, gets to Karla first.

To understand this properly, we need to understand Marholm's views on the essential needs of women and the essential nature of Jewishness. In both sets of notions she is heavily influenced by popular discourse. In her *Buch der Frauen*, she described the life and art of the actress, Eleonora Duse, and her characterization of Duse is strongly reminiscent of her portrayal of the fictional Karla Bühring. Both are enervated by their art and by their unmarried state:

> Eleonora Duse [. . .] wird reisen und reisen, und spielen und spielen, wie alle Virtuosinnen vor ihr. Sie wird es müde werden, unsäglich müde — man sieht es ihr jetzt schon an — aber sie wird es nicht sein lassen können. Und sie wird Virtuosin werden, wie alle die anderen.[16]

Like Karla's, Eleonora Duse's art springs in Marholm's view from a particular kind of genius that, in women, is their (unfulfilled) sex drive:

> Was ist Genie? [. . .] Das Genie war eine männliche Eigenschaft [. . .]. Es giebt allerdings auch eine Art von weiblichem Genie, aber wo das Weib Genie ist, das ist es dem Mann am allerunähnlichsten und am meisten Weib, denn da ist es produktiv aus erster Hand, aus seiner Weibheit heraus, aus seiner durchseelten Sinnlichkeit.[17]

It is not simply unsatisfied sensuality, however, that leads to the emptiness or lack that is woman's essence: it is for Marholm (as for many of her sexologist contemporaries, such as Ellen Key [1849–1926] or Magnus Hirschfeld [1868–1935]) the impulse to motherhood. It is the frustrated impulse to motherhood that renders Karla's relationship with

Collander so destructive for her. Collander is, to abuse turn-of-the-century terminology, an *homme fatal*: he embodies sex and death. Karla's exclamation when they first meet is as significant as it is impolite: "Gott was Sie eigentlich für eine Bocksphysiognomie haben, Herr Collander" (38). His response puts us in the picture:

> *(streicht sich den spitzen Bart und fährt fort sie mit dem konzentrierten, greifenden Blick anzusehen).* Pan war auch nur ein Bock, gnädigstes Fräulein. Und die schnellfüßigen Nymphen ließen sich nicht von blonden, selbstzufriedenen Griechenbengeln, sondern von bocksbeinigen Satyren entführen — (38)

Collander, then, is a satyr, a pre-Christian sex fiend who is strongly associated with death. His arrival at Karla's home on the night of their sexual encounter coincides with a conversation between Karla and her younger friend, Lilli, about death — on seeing his figure in the doorway, Lilli is "tötlich [*sic*] erschrocken." She later describes a visit of his to her own house, when she was able to make him leave: "Aber als er weg war, da überfiel mich eine große Angst [. . .] nicht anders, als wäre der Tod dagewesen" (111).

For Otto von Wetterberg, the Germanic hero of the piece, the Jew Collander is a kind of fungus or bacteria, both dangerous and functional: "Er ist in seiner Weise ein höchst nützlicher Gärungspilz. Er zersetzt und befördert den Zerfall. Freilich auch ein sehr giftiger. Wo er sich einbohrt, da bringt er auch einen gesunden Organismus zum faulen" (77). Wetterberg's unconscious use of phallic imagery recalls Marholm's notion of the "filling" of woman by man — something for which Collander, who causes decay where he penetrates, is not a suitable candidate. Because he is destructive rather than productive, his seed (or spores, if we are going to stick with the mushroom imagery) bring death, not life — he fails to see sex as a path to procreation. Unlike the two other men in the play, Wetterberg and the German merchant Eschenmeyer, Collander does not see women primarily as potential mothers, because his view of sex is entirely sensual. He destroys women by offering them sex without the will to inseminate, and without proper patriarchal domination: Collander insists on being enjoyed *by* women, and glories in the passive role he claims to have played in his encounter with Karla:

> haben nicht Ihre Arme mich zu sich niedergerissen und schlug es mir nicht aus Ihnen entgegen wie eine heiße, rote, saugende Welle, in die ich hineinsank, bewußtlos, sinnlos, blind, mit einem rieselnden heiß-kalten Schauder von Ihnen genossen zu werden — (93)

Robertson has observed the parallel thinking that characterizes theories of Jewishness and womanhood toward the end of the nineteenth century (for example, in the work of Nietzsche and Weininger). Jewish men are perceived as in many respects more like women than like Christian men: "The male Jew could be imagined as unmanly, as located between the masculine and the feminine."[18] In *Karla Bühring*, Marholm shows herself familiar with this discourse. Eschenmeyer describes Collander in disparaging terms as "eine Art Übergangsglied und Zwischenformation — um mich wissenschaftlich auszudrücken — zwischen unsereinem und dem Weibe" (107). Karla's sexual encounter with him is therefore to be regarded as pseudo-lesbian and non-reproductive. Worse than this, it will prevent her from becoming the mother of Wetterberg's Germanic children — Wetterberg cannot possibly procreate via a receptacle that has already held another man's seed. Because Collander is not a "real" man, sex with him cannot fill Karla's female emptiness or compensate for her lack; instead it destroys her, because it renders her unfit to bear another man's children.

The question arises why this anti-Semitic and antifeminist play is worth analysis, except perhaps as a sociohistorical document. Interesting about the drama in the context of this study are its contradictions regarding the "woman question."[19] In *Wir Frauen und unsere Dichter*, Marholm considered men's writing about women, beginning with what appears to be a justifiably critical observation — that these women are constructions of the masculine imagination, not reality — but going on to suggest that it is not only right and acceptable for men to create a notion of woman, but that women should strive to *become* as men imagine them:

> Doch ist alle Mannesdichtung über das Weib: Vorstellung des Mannes vom Weib und Bedürfniß [*sic*] des Mannes nach dem Weibe, so ist das, was das Weib über sich geschrieben liest, Richtschnur für das Weib zu werden, wie der Mann es sich denkt. Es ist des Weibes Natur, sich in eine Form zu prägen und nach einer Form zu verlangen, in die es sich prägen könne.[20]

This is, to borrow Kay Goodman's terminology, "cross-eyed" thinking.[21] Cross-eyed thinking can be understood as the non-emancipatory version of Weigel's "schielender Blick": one eye recognizes the mechanisms of oppression while the other re-interprets what has been seen in such a way as to fit and flatter oppressive structures.

Karla Bühring can be read as a cross-eyed drama, in the sense that Marholm is on the one hand exposing the social oppression of women, and on the other, accepting and even furthering their subordination. For example: we are left in no doubt that the society we are observing is riddled with double standards. Karla complains of the different sexual rules for men and women, whereby premarital sex is practically obligatory for the former, forbidden for the latter (122); but at the same time she accepts completely and with conviction that she can never be the mother of Wetterberg's children because she has slept with Collander. Her friend Lilli Bloom, who, as her name suggests, is still in possession of the "flower" of her virginity, is posited as the ideal woman — the future mother — who in her purity goes unrecognized by the sexually sated men. She is, according to Karla, "noch heil und ganz [. . .] ein einfaches Lied, auf einer einzigen Oktave gespielt . . . kein raffiniertes Orchesterstück mit Schluchzen und Jauchzen und dem Zusammenklang von zwanzig Instrumenten" (121; Marholm's punctuation). But there is something disingenuous in this idealizing portrayal of Lilli. Karla characterizes herself as complex and passionate, Lilli as simple and limited; anyone with half a brain would prefer the former to the latter. So at the same time as pushing the notion that Lilli is the ideal, Marholm is undermining that notion. It is perfectly clear where her own authorial interests lie: the play is, after all, called *Karla Bühring*, and not *Lilli Bloom*.

In her introduction to the drama, Marholm notes that the women characters she portrays are "typisch für das, was die gegenwärtige Zeitbrechung aus dem Weibe macht" (5). She describes the essence of her protagonist as she sees it: "in der Hauptperson habe ich des Weibes Lebensdrang bis in seine Lebenswurzel selbst hineinverfolgt, wo er wieder eins wird mit des Weibes Intaktheit als Weib" (5). Given that Karla represents "des Weibes Lebensdrang" as well as "Intaktheit," and feels forced to commit suicide at the end of the play, we must assume that there is something wrong with what "die gegenwärtige Zeitbrechung" has done to women. None of the four women who play a role in the action is content or stable. Lilli Bloom, for all Karla's praise of her, is a nervous, unhappy character who hides in corners and is prone to tiny frustrated outbursts. Collander's wife, Hildegard, is thoroughly miserable and depraved; her only diversion comes from spying on her husband's affairs and torturing his mistresses with her knowledge. Frau Eschenmeyer, one of those mistresses, is described by her husband as "ein Huhn, das seine Bestimmung verfehlt hat! Ein lesendes Huhn, ein Litteraturhuhn . . . mit ungesunden Affinitäten für literarische Göckel" (98; Marholm's punctuation).

Given her obvious anti-Semitism, Marholm's portrayal of the Collanders and the Eschenmeyers, too, is curious. Even though Collander features as the "feminine" Jew and Eschenmeyer as the "masculine" German, it is Hildegard Collander and not Annette Eschenmeyer who has children. And Eschenmeyer does not emerge particularly well out of his conflict with the man who has cuckolded him: his insistent use of the chicken-yard metaphor — "Herr Collander, ich erlaube mir zu fragen, was Sie in meinen [*sic*] Hühnerhof zu suchen haben?" (98) — quickly becomes ridiculous. With his startling alibi, that he spent the night in question not with Frau Eschenmeyer, but with Karla Bühring, Collander silences his accuser and finishes their encounter "achselzuckend, mit einem frechen, selbstgefälligen Lächeln" (102). His triumph would be complete were it not for Wetterberg, who saves the day for Germanic masculinity when he steps forward to insult and assault Collander before he leaves the stage.

There is even a certain parallel between the married relationships of the Eschenmeyers and the Collanders. Hildegard has been trained by Collander in sexual depravity and driven to hysteria; her words when she describes this are "er machte mich zu dem, was ich jetzt bin" (90). When accused by her husband of infidelity, Frau Eschenmeyer responds in very similar terms: "Ich bin, wozu du mich gemacht hast" (98). Eschenmeyer, who is clearly no longer interested in having a sexual relationship with his wife (he complains, "ich fange an [. . .] mir einen anderen Collander zu wünschen. Man hat dann doch seine Bettruhe," 105) has failed as a husband as much as the overly sensual Collander.

It would be possible to explain Marholm's motivation here both with her racist assumptions, which lead her to set up a comparison that is intended to put Eschenmeyer to shame — he is seen to be as bad as, or nearly as bad as, a Jew — and with her sexist assumptions, which render Eschenmeyer culpable, because he has failed to show himself a "real man." Her conception of the "real man" is formulated at the conclusion of *Wir Frauen und unsere Dichter*, and is not entirely helpful:

> Was haben wir Frauen von den Männern zu fordern [. . .]? Wir haben zu fordern, daß sie *Männer* seien; weiter gar nichts. Je echtere Männer sie sind, je echtere Frauen werden wir sein, [. . .] nur der *ganze* Mann löst das *ganze* Weib im Weibe aus. (Marholm's emphasis)[22]

We may also consider the possibility that the contradictions that are rife in all of Marholm's texts are an indication of something more complex: of a sense of a basic conflict between her own existence as an active, creative woman, and her simultaneous acceptance of the belief that women were, intellectually, essentially non-creative. Marholm herself preaches the notion that procreation, not artistic or intellectual creation, is the apex of a woman's existence. To put this in context: Laura Marholm worked not only with her husband, Ola Hansson, but with Strindberg, Richard Dehmel (1863–1920), Edvard Munch, Max Dauthendey, and Julius Bierbaum, among other prominent male writers and artists of the time.[23] As someone who was already treading a risky path as a woman writer, she may also have feared losing their approval and support if she did not embrace current gendered conceptions of creative activity.

Marholm's contemporary, the feminist Hedwig Dohm, is unsympathetic, however, and accuses her fellow writer of slipperiness — "Sie ist ein Aal, und sollten in der Zoologie schlaue Aale vorkommen, würde ich sagen: ein schlauer Aal. Will man sie an der einen Stelle greifen, schon ist sie an eine andere entschlüpft."[24] But there are times when the eel-like contortions in Marholm's writing give way to the downright bizarre. *Zur Psychologie der Frau* closes with a "Schlußwort" that provides an insight into Marholm's own psychology:

> Ich sehe sie nicht, aber ich fühle sie — die Hände, die sich an mich klammern möchten.
>
> Nachts im Schlaf greifen sie nach mir mit den verlängerten Fingern der Angst.
>
> Sie suchen sich festzuhängen an meine Seele wie mit zitternden Tentakeln. Sie wecken mich auf mit ihrem Tasten, und ich fühle den keuchenden Athem der Bessessenen in meiner Nähe.
>
> Immer sind sie da, wenn die Nacht gekommen und die Stille, und umkreisen mich. [. . .]
>
> Sie suchen ihr Leben in mir, wie der Vampyr das Blut der Lebendigen sucht. Ihr Leben ist an mir festgebunden durch die scheuen Werke der Nacht. [. . .]
>
> Mit ihren langen gespenstischen Fingern über Meilen ausgestreckt rühren sie an mich.
>
> Jene von den Meinen, die ihnen verfielen, bringen sie mit sich, damit sie zu mir reden mit den bekannten Stimmen der Entmuthigung und mit dem öden Lächeln der Ueberhebung.
>
> Sie kommen und sagen: "Nimm dich nicht aus; du gehörst uns." [. . .]
>
> Sie greifen nach mir mit den Händen der Meinen, die nun todt sind, aber sie erreichen mich nicht.[25]

Written on All Souls' Day (2 November) in 1903, this seems to be a nocturnal vision of the damned. But a concern with and fear of death is a feature of Marholm's earlier, fictional writing — it characterizes two of the figures who seem to come closest to Marholm herself: Karla Bühring, and the central character in the semi-autobiographical novel *Frau Lilly als Jungfrau, Gattin und Mutter*.[26] In a scene that is structurally central to *Karla Bühring*, late at night in Karla's home, Karla subjects Lilli Bloom to an outburst of intense anxiety that is also fear of death:

> So, wenn das Licht ausgelöscht ist und alles ist schwarz um einen herum — und still . . . dann kommt es auf einmal [. . .] *(mit dem Ausbruch der äußersten Verzweiflung)*. Alles . . . alles . . . alles wird leben [. . .] nur *mein* Leben nicht . . . ich bin nicht mehr mit . . . ich weiß nicht mehr von mir . . . keiner weiß von mir . . . ich bin nicht! Und habe nie gehabt, worin ich voll und ganz und gegenwärtig wär . . . ! (59–60; Marholm's emphasis and punctuation)

One might argue that Karla's fear of her own mortality springs from the fact that she is single and childless and therefore, in the terms of Marholm's theories, not "ganz und gegenwärtig" as a woman. However, this theory collapses when we compare her with another figure who fears death, Frau Lilly, who has a beloved and devoted husband and a baby son, and yet is subject to similar nocturnal terror attacks. She explains unwillingly, in response to her husband's questioning:

> Das Aufhören ist es . . . das *Nichtmehrsein*. Sieh, Karl: wenn es so ganz still wird in der Nacht, ganz still, still, und der Mond unter ist und der Morgen noch nicht gekommen . . . Dann steht es im Nu ganz deutlich vor einem: [. . .] Du, die ist, wird nicht mehr sein: *ich werde nicht mehr sein*. (Marholm's emphasis and punctuation)[27]

A specific fear links outbursts from *Karla Bühring* and *Frau Lilly*: the fear of the loss of conscious subject status, the loss of the conscious self. The female self — the "Weib-Ich" (*Karla Bühring*, 51) — is one of Marholm's major concerns in all her writing. It is something constantly under threat or under external pressure, as Karla explains to Lilly in passionate words:

> jedes Mädchen, das sich als Weib fühlt . . . jede, jede hat das gefühlt . . . daß — daß — daß ihr bestes Weibsein, ihr drängendstes Weibempfinden, geknebelt, getreten, gehöhnt und verachtet wurde, bis etwas in ihr zersprang oder verstümmelt war. Dann war sie zugerichtet für's Leben! [. . .] Dann durfte sie Gattin, Mutter, Geliebte, Ehebrecherin, Dirne werden — und alles ward ihr vergeben. Und alles wurde an ihr bewun-

dert. Nur sie — sie selbst — so wie sie war, als sie zum Weib erwachte — das durfte sie nicht sein, das wurde nicht an ihr geduldet — das, das, was ihr Ich war — ihr Weib-Ich. (50–51)

Elfriede Laub could not have put it more passionately. Given the battle described here that women face in gaining access to their selves, their subjectivity, their identity, it is no wonder that the extinguishing of their subject status in death figures, for Marholm, as the most fearful of threats. If men are accorded a being or materiality in their existence that women are denied (as Judith Butler would argue is still the case),[28] then it may be harder for women to accept their mortality, because it is the end of an existence-as-subject that they have never actually had — as Karla mourns, "ich bin nicht mehr [. . .]. Und habe nie gehabt, worin ich voll und ganz und gegenwärtig wäre" (60). It is doubly hard to be shown the door before one has even begun to achieve what one came for.

Marholm, as she makes clear in her introduction to the piece, intended *Karla Bühring* to be performed. In fact the play was never staged,[29] and the reaction to the published drama was unenthusiastic: Marholm was accused of bad taste, and her frank treatment of sexual and family relations in the play was taken to render it unperformable.[30] That a woman was the author of such a text presumably only intensified the moral outrage of its readers (we are reminded of the reproaches leveled at Elsa Bernstein and her fictional character, Sascha, of *Wir Drei*).

Karla Bühring shares the problem we observed in *Elfriede Laub* and other plays by women, namely that the perspective on events is female — despite Marholm's glorification of the role of the Germanic male, the play remains *Ein Frauendrama*. We view events from the perspective of the character with whom we are most encouraged to sympathize: in this case, Karla. The irrelevance of such a perspective for the viewing male finds expression in reviews of *Karla Bühring* such as that by Fritz Mauthner. The review is titled "Poesie des Weibchens,"[31] and the diminutive is a clear enough expression of his scorn. In *Karla Bühring*, we are once again faced with a play which is of interest (to borrow Julie Kühne's terms) to "Weiber" rather than to "Menschen."

Saying "I": Clara Viebig

The third and final dramatist to assess the specific conflicts and problems in women's existence whose work we shall consider here is Clara Viebig. Viebig's *Barbara Holzer* (1897)[32] differs from *Elfriede Laub* and *Karla Bühring* in that it takes us out of the middle-class and into the working-class sphere: the problems faced by Barbara Holzer are different from those encountered by her bourgeois sisters. But Viebig's play also revolves around women's ability (or failure) to assert their selves — that is, their needs and humanity — in male-run society. Across the social classes, the women characters in these plays are all involved in the fight for an identity as subject, in the struggle to say "I."

Clara Viebig(-Cohn) (1860–1952), whose name these days is familiar only among literary specialists, was nonetheless one of the best-known writers in Germany at the turn of the nineteenth century. She was particularly successful as a short story writer.[33] Possibly because of her reputation as a prose writer, Viebig's performance record for her dramas is comparatively good: *Barbara Holzer* played in Munich, and later on Berlin's *Volksbühne*, while her next play, *Pharisäer* (1899) was performed in Bremen under Erdmann-Jenitzer, "mit Erfolg." Three plays from the four-part cycle *Kampf um den Mann* premiered in Amsterdam in 1905; the play that was left out, *Die Bäuerin*, was in fact the most successful of the four, and played several hundred times in various theaters into the late 1920s. A later piece, *Das letzte Glück* (a slightly revised version of *Das letzte Lied*, 1908), premiered on 23 April 1909 in Frankfurt under the direction of Karl Heine, in a performance described as "erfolgslos,"[34] but the play had more success when it opened in Amsterdam, in a Dutch translation.[35] Viebig also wrote libretti for the operas *Nacht der Seelen* (after 1903),[36] and *Die Môra* (after 1906), set to music by her son, Ernst Viebig.

The play *Barbara Holzer*, which premiered at the *Deutsches Schauspielhaus* in Munich, was Viebig's first piece for the stage. Like others of her dramas, it was based on one of her short stories, *Die Schuldige*, a tale in which a farm maid gets pregnant by the farmer's son.

Barbara Holzer is — as Viebig's women protagonists tend to be — a powerful personality, with an inner strength that stands out sharply against the spinelessness of her lover, Lorenz. The rebelliousness of her character is betrayed by the "widerspenstige Haarsträhne" (10) that refuses to be smoothed back from her forehead. As individuals, all the men in the piece are weak; but they work together in a way that brings about Barbara's downfall. Viebig's Barbara is the prisoner of her woman's body that conceives a child, but more importantly she is the victim of a system whose double standards help men to deny paternity for economic reasons, while condemning the woman whose maternity cannot be concealed.

The idealizing notions of maternity so prevalent in the late nineteenth and early twentieth centuries (for example in the work of Laura

Marholm) are ironized or turned around in Viebig's play. Barbara's body can be understood as a site where the playwright tests and exposes as false certain ideas about motherhood. In the drama, local superstition attaches St. Genevieve (Genoveva, patron saint of women)[37] to the ruins where Barbara, homeless and desperate, hides with her baby. When a group of children spot her there, their report to the village not only turns her into Genoveva, but into a kind of Madonna figure: "On se waor e su schien, wie ons liew Moddergöddesche, mer konnt se net ankucken, ihr Gesicht waor wie de Sonn — " ("Und sie war so schön wie unsere liebe Mutter Gottes, wir konnten sie nicht ansehen, ihr Gesicht war wie die Sonne," S. C.; 58). The transformation is ironic. In this image, Viebig is by no means idealizing Barbara Holzer's experience as a single mother in late nineteenth-century Germany. What she is showing us here are the superstitions and religious beliefs that still exist side-by-side in rural communities, and function, like sentimentality, as a camouflage for social realities. Such beliefs allow elderly destitute women like Barbara's aunt (her only living relation) to be cursed as witches, and obscure the real misery of poverty and illegitimate motherhood. It is no coincidence within the play's structure that the children's starry-eyed account of the "vision" in the ruins is brutally interrupted — by the news of Lorenz's murder, perpetrated there by Barbara.

When a second attempt to transfigure the central character is made, motherhood is again the point of reference. Where the children constructed a vision using ecclesiastical and Marian material, linking Barbara with a divine ideal of womanhood, the magistrate who deals with the murder of Lorenz draws on notions of the order of nature, and characterizes her as a kind of tigress who strikes out to protect her young (67–68). Like the children's, this idea depends on its abstraction from real events. When Barbara provides the gory details of her crime, the same magistrate recoils from her depiction of her desperate violence. Glorified motherhood is, as Laura Marholm discovered, possibly the only valorizing self-image available to adult women; but idealized commonplaces about gendered behavior, Viebig seems to suggest, do not stand the test of reality.

Lorenz's death is significant within what we might call the feminist semiotics of the drama. It is announced on stage at the moment when Lorenz's father is perjuring himself for the umpteenth time in the cause of patriarchal economics, swearing to the community that his son and Barbara Holzer have had no carnal dealings, so that Lorenz remains free to profit from the marriage market. Lorenz, we know, is party to the lie and colluding in it. The news of his death at this precise moment must be read as a sign of punishment, for Lorenz and for his bereaved father, who is simultaneously robbed of his son and of the means (via a wealthy daughter-in-law) to pay off his debts. Viebig is signaling a kind of alternative moral frame, whereby *men* are punished for their double-dealings and sexual hypocrisy, rather than just women for the results.

However, Lorenz is no great villain, and his death is probably not worth the price Barbara will pay for it. Like the bourgeois Agnes in Bernstein's *Wir Drei*, Barbara Holzer experiences her baby as the only thing she has ever owned — regardless of their class, it seems, women have little real part in the capitalist system of property. Like Agnes, Barbara loses interest in the outside world once her baby is gone; her attention refocuses, destructively, on herself. Interesting in the context of this chapter is her sudden willingness and ability, in self-accusation, to speak the word "I," and thus assert a notion of herself in the world at the same time as she plans to leave it: "Ech sein verflucht, ech haon et gedahn, ech haon et gedahn! [. . .] ech — ech — ech! Sie, [. . .] schreiwen Se't uf, ech — ech, — ech haon et gedahn — on nau maacht mech dud" ("Ich bin verflucht, ich habe es getan, ich habe es getan! [. . .] ich — ich — ich! Sie, [. . .] schreiben Sie es auf, ich — ich, — ich habe es getan — und nun macht mich tot," S. C.; 81). Repeating the word "ich" nine times, Barbara creates a kind of subject status for herself, defying the stereotype "nur eine Mutter" (67) imposed on her by the magistrate, but also that of witch, "Hex" (80) imposed by the mob. Barbara Holzer is here performing a powerful speech act: she is well aware that this confession will lead to her death by execution.

Barbara is not the only one of Viebig's characters to assert her self in the face of coercion. In the second of the four short plays that comprise *Der Kampf um den Mann*, called *Eine Zuflucht*,[38] social class and the right to define oneself in speech are critical. *Eine Zuflucht* plays in a women's correction home in Berlin, and an opening exchange between an inmate of the home and its supervisor, Kubizke, already foregrounds the question of the right to speech: "Halt de [*sic*] Schnauze!" scolds Kubizke, "Hier wird nicht jeredt!" (44). Kubizke, although portrayed as a fairly sympathetic character, prescribes silence for all her charges, and makes clear that the right to speak is absolutely linked to status:

> Ruhe, Ruhe! Wollt ihr wohl stille sein! Hier wird nich jeredt! Maul halten, wie oft soll ick euch det einbläun? Det wer' noch scheenter, wenn jeder hier reden dürfte, wer wollte. Hier rede ick blos. Janz muckstill, det is in de Hausordnung. (46)

Unsurprisingly, then, Kubizke's own linguistic authority is overshadowed when the home is visited by the local pastor and two patrician ladies. In the presence of these three she loses much of her confident ownership of speech space; the change is signaled in her attempt to elevate her speaking style: *"bemüht sich fein zu reden"* (49). For Christine Müller, the inmate whom the ladies have come to see, the effect is much more extreme. Over seven pages of dialogue regarding her person and her future, Müller herself speaks just four words — and these are only murmured (54). At one point she shakes her head in response to a question, a minor act of self-expression which is, nonetheless, immediately picked up by Kubizke as excessive: "Nanu, man nich so dreiste!" (60).

The turning point comes for Christine Müller, as it did for Barbara Holzer, when she is pushed beyond the limits of passive endurance. Her bourgeois benefactors are determined to make her leave Berlin; they ignore her clear wish to stay and overrule her right to self-determination — "man muß," they agree, "den Menschen auch gegen seinen Willen glücklich machen" (63). This is the straw that breaks the camel's back, and Christine Müller's bottled-up personhood begins to release itself into language, heralded by the physical expulsion of air through the mouth — *"seufzt laut und zittrig auf"* (64). The sigh is followed by a lengthy first person narrative — Müller's life story — in which the word "ich" is reiterated with increasing frequency, until the moment when she describes her entry into prostitution. At this point she changes pronoun, to the less personal "man" or "wir" (65–66), a change which seems to reflect the young woman's alienation from herself as a prostitute. Nonetheless, once Christine Müller has begun to speak, not even Kubizke can restrain her. In the face of the beneficent ladies who would control her future, she finally explodes: "ich wer' nich mehr stille sein! Die sollen mir lassen, se sollen mir janz in Ruhe lassen, ich will ihre Wohltat nich! [. . .] Eure Wohltat is mich 'ne Last! Ich schmeiße se euch vor die Füße — da!" (71).

Barbara Holzer's first clear expression of self was linked to a deathwish following the loss of her baby, and Christine Müller's is no more positively laden: it is closely tied to a will to self-abnegation, specifically to her relationship with a man outside the home. Christine's "ich" is stirred into activity by the threat of separation from the man who, in her view, owns her. In Viebig's stage directions, she stands poised to run, like a dog, at the sound of his whistle. And Viebig leaves us under no illusions, for the worldly-wise Kubizke has already commented on the abusive nature of such liaisons: "Da is keen Loskommen mehr, da sind se rein wie jebannt. Abjebunden, anjekettet, fester wie anjetraut. Un wenn er sie auch niederträchtig behandelt, bei ihn bleiben tun se doch"

(70). For Barbara and for Christine, the expression of self is not the expression of a free self. Both women assert their identities in a context that is self-destructive.

Self-assertion once again comes dangerously close to self-annihilation when the farmer's wife of *Die Bäuerin*[39] (the first short drama in Viebig's *Kampf um den Mann* quartet) is praying for her husband's death:

> Maria, Benedeite, schwarz wer' ich um ihn tragen mein Lebenlang. En Kreuze laß ich ihm setzen von Marmorstein. Blumen tu' ich drum pflanzen lassen, Messen laß' ich lesen für seine Seel' [. . .] Da wer' ich liegen an seiner Seit', ich, die Mitte-Lange-Bäuerin, ich, bis in Ewigkeit — ich — Amen. (27)

Yet, even though "ich" is reiterated no less than eight times in this speech, the "Mitte-Lange-Bäuerin" (as she designates herself) is praying here for a subject status that depends entirely on the continued association of herself with her dying husband. For this to be possible, she needs him dead; for this is another abusive relationship, and her husband has betrayed her in an affair with a girl from the village. Only his death can protect her status as his wife: the only woman with whom he is retrospectively associated. So the "ich" of the Mitte-Lange-Bäuerin (who has no other name in the play) depends entirely on the Mitte-Lange-Bauer, just as Christine Müller's rebelliously self-articulating "ich" depends on the presence of a man outside the gates of the corrective institution.

Women in Viebig's dramas seem primarily able to say "I" in the context of a relationship with a man. Barbara Holzer is the exception, because her self emerges in response to the death of her baby, but in all cases violent emotion provokes the eruption of the repressed "ich." In the slightly later play, *Pharisäer*,[40] Viebig's heroine, Helene Thielman, finds the will to pit her own subjectivity against her dominant mother's because she is in love. This is euphemistic: what Helene understands under "love" is that ownership of her self is now transferred from her parents to the man concerned:

HELENE.   Ich —

FRAU THIELMAN. Still! Kein Wort, keinen Eklat!

HELENE.   Laß mich! Ich —

FRAU THIELMAN. *(hält ihr den Mund zu).* Still doch, sage ich! Komm!

HELENE.   Ich will nicht. Ich gehe nicht mit dir. Mögen's alle hören: *(stark)* Ich liebe ihn! Ich bin sein! (63)

The need to associate her subject status with his (or subordinate her self under his) drives her to disregard the constraints put upon her speech and self-expression.

"Der Mut zum Ich" is a factor in Viebig's work that is picked out for particular consideration by G. Scheuffler, the author of an early monograph dedicated to her work: his *Clara Viebig: Zeit und Jahrhundert* was published in 1927.[41] Scheuffler begins by noting, in terms that recall the opening scenes of Kühne's *Elfriede Laub:* "Das Ich [. . .] will leben, blühen und sich ausdehnen" (213); he then observes the conflicts and constraints in the relationship between this space-seeking ("sich ausdehnen[d]") self and society, and praises Viebig for doing the same: "Clara Viebig sieht die krankenden Beziehungen zwischen Ich und Wir äußerst scharf" (214). Only later in his account does Scheuffler note the gendered nature of the "Ich" in Viebig's writing:

> Am schärfsten zeigt sich bei Clara Viebig der Mut zum Ich dann, wenn der Geschlechts-oder der Muttertrieb um sein Recht und seine Auswirkung kämpft. Da ist alles elementar [. . .]. Clara Viebig ist nicht zu übertreffen in der Gestaltung dieser Elementarmenschen, die in ihrer Unbewußtheit und Entschiedenheit nur unter den Frauen vertreten sind. (216)

The accuracy or otherwise of Scheuffler's last statement — which is clearly fuelled by turn-of-the-century essentialist theories — need not concern us here. What is interesting is that Scheuffler notices that, in Viebig's work, women's subject status is only expressible in the context of their relationship with men or children — and both of these relationships conventionally involve the subjugation of women's subjectivity, their "selflessness" or sacrifice of self for others. We can agree with him that either maternal or sexual impulses fuel the emergence of self in speech for Barbara Holzer, for Christine Müller, for Helene of *Pharisäer,* and for a number of others of Viebig's women protagonists, notably the two women in *Mutter,*[42] and Sus Endenich in *Das letzte Lied.*[43] But his characterization of such impulses as "elementar" invites skepticism. Scheuffler, in fact, gives the game away when he gets more specific about the nature of female "instinct" ("Trieb"): he writes of "das Weib, das bereit ist, ihrer Liebe alles zu schenken, den Ruf und die wirtschaftliche Sicherheit, und kompromißlos das auf Liebe gestimmte Ich zu behaupten" (217). This "auf Liebe gestimmte Ich" is imagined femininity à la Marlene Dietrich, whose fictive "Ich" was "von Kopf bis Fuß auf Liebe eingestellt," and it reeks of nineteenth-century notions of women's "Beruf" or "Bestimmung," which can be summed up as the positive will to self-abnegation in the service of patriarchal structures. Is this, then, what characters like Christine Müller and Helene display: a "Mut zum Ich" that is (in Scheuffler's words) an "Ich-Kampf um den Mann" (218) — and therefore a contradiction in terms? The emergence of such an "ich" would be purely for the purpose of resubjugation of the self, voluntarily, under the dominant subjectivity of a male partner.

Such an interpretation does not do justice to the subversive drive in much of Viebig's work. Viebig takes on contemporary social issues, and makes clear through her writing that these are simultaneously, and sometimes primarily, women's issues. *Eine Zuflucht* lampoons the society at the turn of the nineteenth century that expected semi-educated bourgeois women, excluded as they were from public life, to successfully practice "Wohltätigkeit" in working-class circles. *Die Bäuerin* and *Fräulein Freschbolzen* (the third play in the same quartet)[44] depict unorthodox partnerships, between older, economically powerful women and younger men; and in almost all the dramas women are shown to be the stronger partners in marriage, within the confines of a social credo that asserts the opposite. Not only the bourgeoisie are targeted: working-class men appear — in *Freschbolzen*, *Mutter*, and *Das letzte Lied*, for example — as parasites on the backs of working-class women, whether as lovers, husbands, or sons. Women's biology, too, is shown to be part of their burdensome destiny in a hypocritical, masculinist society. The "Muttertrieb" idealized by the likes of Scheuffler is also, in Viebig's world view, a biological burden that this society allows to drive women into destitution (*Mutter*), desperation (*Das letzte Lied*), and death (*Barbara Holzer*).

Elisabeth Lenk has written of "die sich selbst verdoppelnde Frau":[45] the woman who develops a dual or double position, because she is both *inside* culture and society, as a participant, and *outside* it or forced to its edges by the "othering" masculinist gaze. Julie Kühne's *Elfriede Laub* shows two overt instances of doubling before we even start reading the play: in the title, which is both divided into two by "oder," and hints at a problematic duality in the phrase "Weib und Mensch"; and in the authorial pseudonym, "Thure und Dierenow," under which Kühne chose to write, splitting herself as writer into two. Her heroine, too, finally resorts to doubling: Elfriede Laub exists both as herself (as we knew her at the beginning of the play, when she still believed that she was simply "ein Mensch" because she had not yet "become a woman"), and as the female-gendered persona she learns to perform in order to survive in the world.

Laura Marholm is, to use Dohm's term, "ein Aal," and slips back and forth between her positions as on the one hand a gender-endorsing masculinist, and on the other as a creative woman writer and therefore a misfit in the masculinist order of gender. Her character, Karla Bühring, echoes this duality when she speaks her admiration of the Lilli Bloom type, but embodies a far more attractive, vital idea — even if it is her very vitality that to some extent pre-programs her death. For Clara Viebig's characters, too, the expression of self is a double-edged sword. In every case, the word "ich" is finally torn from the woman character's mouth in emotional extremis, and self-affirmation always also involves a level of self-annihilation.

An interesting feature of Viebig's plays is the dialect spoken by many of her characters. Dialect is conventionally perceived as low-status language, signaling class rather than gender status. In a play like *Eine Zuflucht*, which has an almost all-women cast, the order of class (signaled in dialect use) at times replaces the order of gender. Christine Müller and Elfriede Laub are characters at opposite ends of the class spectrum, and the difficulties they experience in asserting and expressing themselves are not identical. There are similarities, however: Kühne is at pains to show us that Elfriede, once she is married, is de facto destitute and socially powerless; and Viebig in *Pharisäer* portrays a middle-class woman, Helene, who is just as keen as the working-class Christine to subsume her own subjectivity under that of the man she loves. Such overlaps between the hierarchies of class and gender will concern us particularly in the next chapter.

Notes

[1] *Elfriede Laub oder Weib und Mensch. Drama in 5 Aufzügen von Thure und Dierenow* (alias of Julie Kühne) (Leipzig: Mutze, n.d. [1873]). All references are to this edition of the text. A briefer consideration of the play also appears in Sarah Colvin, "The Power in the Text: Reading Women Writing Drama," in *Gendering German Studies*, ed. by Margaret Littler (Oxford: Blackwell, 1997), 67–81.

[2] For an analysis of these terms from the linguist's perspective, see Luise Pusch, "Von Menschen und Frauen," in Pusch, *Das Deutsche als Männersprache* (Frankfurt: Suhrkamp, 1984), 15–19.

[3] Dale Spender, *The Writing or the Sex? Or Why You Don't Have to Read Women's Writing to Know It's No Good* (New York: Pergamon, 1989).

[4] The results are from a study conducted by Don Zimmermann and Candace West. See Dale Spender, *Man Made Language*, 2nd ed. (London: Pandora, 1985), 43.

[5] This, as Susanne Kord has noted, is the more usual method of women dramatists. See Kord, *Ein Blick hinter die Kulissen: Deutschsprachige Dramatikerinnen im 18. und 19. Jahrhundert* (Stuttgart: Metzler, 1992), 44.

[6] The term is Sigrid Weigel's. See Weigel, "Der schielende Blick: Thesen zur Geschichte weiblicher Schreibpraxis," in *Die verborgene Frau: Sechs Beiträge zu einer feministischen Literaturwissenschaft*, ed. by Inge Stefan and Sigrid Weigel (Berlin: Argument, 1988).

[7] A similar result — a friendship contract — forms the "happy ending" in Ebner-Eschenbach's short comedy *Ohne Liebe* (1891).

[8] Dittmar, *Das Wesen der Ehe. Nebst einigen Aufsätzen über die soziale Reform der Frauen* (Leipzig 1849). Reprinted in *Frauenemanzipation im deutschen Vormärz: Texte und Dokumente*, ed. by Renate Möhrmann (Stuttgart: Reclam, 1978), 63–64.

[9] Marholm, *Karla Bühring: Ein Frauendrama in vier Acten* (Paris: Langen, 1895). All references are to this edition of the text.

[10] On Marholm's biography and writing see Marilyn Scott-Jones, "Laura Marholm and the Question of Female 'Nature,'" in *Beyond the Eternal Feminine: Critical Essays on Women and German Literature*, ed. by Susan L. Cocalis and Kay Goodman (Stuttgart: Heinz, 1982), 203–23.

[11] On the interesting ramifications of gender and pseudonymity, see Susanne Kord, *Sich einen Namen machen: Anonymität und weibliche Autorschaft 1700–1900* (Stuttgart: Metzler, 1996).

[12] Paul Schlenther, "Frauenarbeit im Theater," in *Die Frau* 1 (1893–4), 150–55 (155).

[13] Laura Marholm, *Das Buch der Frauen: Zeitpsychologische Portraits*, 4th ed. (Paris: Langen, 1896), 4.

[14] Pauli, "Frauen-Litteratur," in *Neue Deutsche Rundschau* 7 (1896), 276–81 (276).

[15] Marholm's racism and anti-Semitism are further documented in *Zur Psychologie der Frau*, where she objects to "Racenkreuzung," and states that she finds the slavic/germanic ("Deutschrussen") mix "ganz erbärmlich." She also condemns Jewish/German marriages. *Zur Psychologie der Frau*, 2 vols, 2nd ed. (Berlin: Duncker, 1903; 1st ed. 1897), II, 157–58.

[16] Marholm, *Das Buch der Frauen*, 99.

[17] Marholm, *Das Buch der Frauen*, 100–102.

[18] See Ritchie Robertson, "Historicizing Weininger: The Nineteenth-Century German Image of the Feminized Jew," in *Modernity, Culture and "the Jew,"* ed. by Bryan Chevette and Laura Marcus (Oxford: Polity, 1998), 23–39 (24).

[19] Marilyn Scott-Jones observed in 1978 that "one difficulty in assessing Marholm and her writing is that her methods appear to contradict her main arguments [. . .] Marholm constantly contradicts herself." Scott-Jones, 204–205.

[20] Marholm, *Wir Frauen und unsere Dichter*, 2nd ed. (Berlin: Duncker, 1896), 131–32.

[21] Goodman, "Motherhood and Work: The Concept of the Misuse of Women's Energy, 1895–1905," in *German Women in the Eighteenth and Nineteenth Centuries: A Social and Literary History*, ed. by Ruth-Ellen B. Joeres and Mary Jo Maynes (Bloomington, IN.: Indiana UP, 1986), 110–27 (112).

[22] Marholm, *Wir Frauen und unsere Dichter*, 292.

[23] Scott-Jones, 212.

[24] Dohm, *Die Antifeministen: Ein Buch der Verteidigung* (Berlin: Dümmler, 1902), 87. Dohm is referring to Marholm's argumentation in *Das Buch der Frauen*.

[25] Marholm, *Zur Psychologie der Frau*, II, 231–32.

[26] Marholm, *Frau Lilly als Jungfrau, Gattin und Mutter* (Berlin: Duncker, 1897).

[27] *Frühläuten: Eine häusliche Szene*, in Marholm, *Frau Lilly als Jungfrau, Gattin und Mutter*, 181.

[28] Butler, *Bodies that Matter: On the Discursive Limits of "Sex"* (London: Routledge, 1993), 53 et passim.

[29] Her husband, Ola Hansson, translated the drama into Swedish, and the British playwright George Egerton (ps. for Mary Chavelita Dunne, who was one of the women who featured in Marholm's *Buch der Frauen*) into English. Only the German version found a publisher. See Susan Carol Brantly, "The life and writings of Laura Marholm," unpublished doctoral thesis, Yale University 1987.

[30] Brantly, 163. See also Karl von Thaler, "Neue Romane und Novellen," in *Neue Freie Presse* (7 March 1896); Fritz Mauthner, "Poesie des Weibchens," in *Berliner Tageblatt* (11 December 1895); "Parvus," "Ein Frauendrama und eine Frauenphilosophie," in *Die Neue Zeit* 14, II (1895–96), 58.

[31] See Mauthner, 'Poesie des Weibchens.'

[32] Viebig, *Barbara Holzer. Schauspiel in drei Akten* (Berlin: Fontane, 1897). All references are to this edition of the text. A briefer consideration of this play appears in Sarah Colvin, "Women and Drama at the Turn of the Century, or Thresholds of Gender and Genre," in *Schwellen: Germanistische Erkundungen einer Metapher*, ed. By Nicholas Saul, Daniel Steuer, Frank Möbus and Birgit Illner (Würzburg: Königshausen & Neumann, 1999), 265–78.

[33] On Viebig's biography and writing, see Urzula Michalska, *Clara Viebig: Versuch einer Monographie* (Poznań: Uniwersyset im. Adama Mickiewicza, 1968).

[34] See G. Scheuffler, *Clara Viebig: Zeit und Jahrhundert* (Erfurt: Beute, 1927), 182–90.

[35] Michalska, 25.

[36] Her source for this was René Morax's drama *La Nuit des Quatre-Temps* (1901). See Scheuffler, 190.

[37] The German folk legend of this saint is independent of the legend of St. Genevieve of Paris, and tells the story of Genoveva, who was banished with her son Schmerzensreich and given sustenance by a doe in a forest.

[38] In Viebig, *Der Kampf um den Mann* (Berlin: Fleischel, 1905). *Eine Zuflucht* is also reprinted in Reclam's *Einakter des Naturalismus*, ed. by Wolfgang Rothe (Stuttgart: Reclam, 1973), 179–200.

[39] In Viebig, *Der Kampf um den Mann*, 3–37. All references are to this edition of the text. The play was also published separately in *Bühne und Welt* 6 (1903–4), 365–73.

[40] Viebig, *Pharisäer* (Berlin: Fleischel, 1903 [1899]).

[41] See Scheuffler, *Clara Viebig*.

[42] In Viebig, *Der Kampf um den Mann,* 121–60.

[43] Viebig, *Das letzte Lied* (Berlin: Fleischel, 1908).

[44] In Viebig, *Der Kampf um den Mann,* 77–120.

[45] Cited in Sigrid Weigel, "Der schielende Blick: Thesen zur Geschichte weiblicher Schreibpraxis," in *Die verborgene Frau: Sechs Beiträge zu einer feministischen Literaturwissenschaft,* ed. Inge Stefan and Sigrid Weigel (Berlin: Argument, 1988), 83–132 (106).

4: Marie Eugenie delle Grazie, Lu Märten, Berta Lask: Political Subjects

JULIE KÜHNE, LAURA MARHOLM, AND CLARA VIEBIG were dramatists who concerned themselves overtly with sexual politics. For Viebig in particular, the politics of gender overlapped with the politics of class. This brings Viebig closest to the writers this chapter will consider: Marie Eugenie delle Grazie (1864–1931), Lu Märten (1879–1970), and Berta Lask (1878–1967). Even more than Viebig, these three make class injustice their theme; Lask and Märten even move right out of bourgeois theater to write specifically for workers and the Marxist revolutionary cause.

Interesting in this study is, first, how far these three dramatists are prepared to sideline ideas about women's subjectivity and emancipation to portray the emancipation of the (primarily male) worker; second, their reception as dramatists writing within (delle Grazie) and outside of (Märten, Lask) the bourgeois literary economy. We shall consider the possibility that women might be perceived as more interesting writers if their concerns are party political rather than gender political.

So far this study has assessed how far playwrights who are also women can assert their subject status in the context of a discourse that tends to deny women both subjectivity-in-the-world (the position of being the subject who sees, interprets, and names) and creative intellectual ability (particularly the capacity to write drama). Here we shall take the opportunity to observe what happens when the focus is not on womanhood or on personal creative endeavor, but on class injustice and revolution, in the turn-of-the-century Socialist cause. The plays for discussion are delle Grazie's *Schlagende Wetter* (1898) and Lu Märten's *Bergarbeiter* (written in 1908),[1] both of which deal with the sufferings and political self-organization of the mineworkers; and Berta Lask's *Leuna 1921* (1927),[2] a play focusing on the historical factory workers' strike at Leuna and its brutal consequences.

Delle Grazie and Lask were both prolific dramatists, although their development as writers took them in different directions. Where delle Grazie stayed within the bounds and explored the scope of bourgeois theater, Lask (who was writing around a quarter-century later) quickly invested her energies in creating theater for the working-class revolutionary cause. Delle Grazie followed her first drama, *Saul* (1885),[3] with two overtly political pieces: the one-act satire *Moralische Walpurgisnacht* of 1896,[4] and, two years later, *Schlagende Wetter*. Her political engagement finds theoretical expression in a handwritten tract with the title "Zur Arbeiterbewegung." In this she maintains optimistically: "Ein Zweifel an der Richtigkeit des socialistischen Staatsideals ist heute niemandem möglich";[5] and her political optimism shines through again in the *Walpurgisnacht*: in its closing scene an army of workers appears on stage, led by a writer (!), to celebrate the victory of socialist truth over bourgeois hypocrisy.

Schlagende Wetter was delle Grazie's first performed play. It premièred on 27 October 1900 at Vienna's *Deutsches Volkstheater*, and was generally well received: reviewers compared it to works by Ibsen, and to Hauptmann's naturalist drama about poverty-stricken Silesian weavers, *Die Weber* (1892). Although she is these days less well known than Clara Viebig, delle Grazie was in her day considered a writer of timeless genius.[6] Yet, like Viebig, her area of real achievement is positioned by critics on the side of the epic, rather than the drama. "Fräulein delle Grazie ist keine Dramatikerin," Rudolf Lothar assures us: her strengths, in his view, lie in "den lyrischen Höhepunkten ihrer epischen Schilderungen."[7] He blithely overlooks the fact that her symbolist drama *Der Schatten* had played at the Burgtheater in 1901 — a rare honor for a woman playwright — and the favorable reviews of her dramatic cycle *Zu Spät* (1903; comprising *Vinetta, Mutter, Donauwellen,* and *Sphinx*).[8]

Lask's dramatic development took a different path. She joined the German Communist Party, the KPD, in 1923, and had her first major literary success with *Die Toten rufen* (1923), a dramatic poem on the deaths of Rosa Luxemburg and Karl Liebknecht that was performed (by a proletarian choir) more than 30 times in and around Berlin. Later, Lask claimed that the First World War was the crucial moment that converted her to socialism.[9] Her earliest drama, *Senta* (1921), depicts a female odyssey; it is a stylized, lyrical piece, and details the path of the woman Senta from girlhood to death, which occurs at a moment of complete emancipation.[10] Rather than experimenting further with bourgeois playwriting, however, Lask — inspired by the socialist producer and director Erwin Piscator[11] — turned to revolutionary theater, producing plays such as the highly politicized *Thomas Münzer* (1925), a play written to celebrate the 400th anniversary of the German peasants' revolt lead by Thomas Müntzer in 1525; *Die Befreiung* (1925), a series of tableaux depicting the lives of German and Russian women during the First World War; *Leuna 1921*; and *Giftgasnebel über Sowjetrussland* (1927), a warning call to Communists following the occupation of Nanking by General Chiang Kai-shek (1887–1975). All have enormous cast-lists, and are clearly designed to involve as many workers as possible in their performance. They were produced not at bourgeois theaters (the texts were banned and confiscated by the censors), but at the political rallies of the later 1920s. *Die Befreiung* was staged by Piscator's Workers' Theater Group; we also find Piscatoresque devices, such as projections and placards, in *Leuna 1921*.

Begun in 1926, *Leuna 1921* was written in direct response to a request by workers, namely those who had survived the armed strike at the BASF-owned ammoniac factory at Leuna in 1921.[12] They had seen Lask's *Thomas Münzer* performed during a communist rally in Eisleben, and were inspired to ask to have their own experience recorded. Rather than illustrating general working conditions, as delle Grazie's and Märten's plays do, *Leuna 1921* is intended as a testament to one specific historical event, the workers' uprising at the Leuna factory near Merseburg in 1921, and as a reminder of the status of such events in the teleology of world socialism. It was to be performed in the *Mercedespalast* cinema in Berlin's Neukölln in 1927, but the Social Democratic chief of police, Karl Zörgiebel, banned the performance on the less-than-watertight grounds that plays may not be staged in film theaters. In the same year, the published play was censored and confiscated by the *Reichsgericht*. Thereafter, *Leuna 1921* was performed, in secret, by revolutionary workers' groups.[13] After that first publication by the *Vereinigung Internationaler Verlagsanstalten*, the piece was not reprinted until 1961, in an edition by the publisher Dietz, and then again by the *Verlag Kommunistische Texte* in 1973.

Lu Märten is, so to speak, the joker in the pack: her preferred form was not drama at all, but the journalistic or intellectual theoretical essay. She also wrote political poetry, including a piece on the death of Lenin, published in 1924.[14] She was active in both the workers' and the women's movements, and in contact with some of the most influential Socialists on the German cultural scene, including the Marxist theorist and leader of the Social Democratic party Karl Kautsky (1854–1938), the radical journalist and historian Franz Mehring (1846–1919), and the Socialist feminists Clara Zetkin (1857–1933) and Wally Zepler (1865–?). One stimulus for the composition of *Bergarbeiter* almost certainly came from Zetkin. *Bergarbeiter* was Märten's only published play,[15] and, like Lask's later dramas, it was designed for performance in working-class circles; it was performed in Cologne in 1911, and translated into Japanese for performances in Tokyo and around Japan in the 1920s, then into Chinese for performance in Shanghai. The play was banned by the Chinese government in 1932.[16] Märten wrote *Bergarbeiter* as the first play in a trilogy she never completed; a follow-up drama called *Jugend der Revolution*, due to appear with the Berlin publishing house Fischer, was rejected in the light of the negative official reactions to *Bergarbeiter*.

Schlagende Wetter and *Bergarbeiter*: Mutiny in the Mines

Delle Grazie's *Schlagende Wetter*, in its timing and content, falls within the scope of literary Naturalism. I suggested in chapter 2 that Naturalism, in the context of a society in which womanhood and the domestic sphere were seen as inevitably intertwined, created a certain space in theater for women dramatists. So it may be no coincidence that delle Grazie's first performed play was also her first (and only) full-length drama that was identifiably Naturalist. It is possible that she was perceived to be writing within her proper sphere, and this may have smoothed the way to a first production.

The opening scene of *Schlagende Wetter* is peculiarly intimate and feminine: it is a domestic scene between a young woman called Leni, and Annerl, the tubercular child who lives with her grandfather in the mining community. Annerl is thanking Leni, who has just finished repairing her rag doll:

> LENI *(hat ihre Arbeit vollendet und hebt sich mit raschem Ruck von ihrem Stuhl am Kopfende des Bettes, wobei sie die Puppe lachend der kleinen Anna entgegenhält)*. Gelt? G'rad wie neu schaut s' wieder her, die Gredl!
>
> ANNERL *(bewundernd)*. Was du aber auch all's kannst, Leni!
>
> LENI *(legt dem Kind die Puppe in den Arm)*. Na, schau' nur dazu, daß d'wieder g'sund wirst, und größer, dann trifft's vielleicht g'rad a so!
>
> ANNERL *(noch immer die Puppe bewundernd)*. Und lauter Fetzen — meiner Seel'!
>
> LENI *(neckend)*. Was die wieder plauscht! (3–4)

The dialect — one of the most distinctive features of Naturalist writing — works to enhance the simple, homey feel of the scene. We might contrast the intimacy of this scene with the opening scene of Lask's

Leuna, which is situated outside, evoking large-scale industry and the world of work:

> Lichtbild, Frontansicht des Leunawerkes mit den dreizehn Schornsteinen. Auf der Bühne vor der Leinwand steht der Heizer mit zerfurchtem Gesicht, dem man schwere Leidensjahre ansieht. Leunaarbeiter in Arbeitskleidung gehen einzeln und in Gruppen in einiger Entfernung am Heizer vorüber. (11)

In Märten's *Bergarbeiter* the curtain also rises on the interior of a family home, but the play begins with a conversation between the miner Burger and his daughter, Gretje, about the current strike. Gretje's first words: "Vater, heute sind es doch neun Wochen, daß der Ausstand währt?" (5) catapult us straight out of the domestic and into the public sphere of work and political struggle. It is worth noting that neither Märten's nor Lask's plays are written in dialect (we shall return to this).

Delle Grazie herself grew up in a mining community in Drencova in southern Hungary (now Romania). She dedicated *Schlagende Wetter* to the memory of her father, who, as mining director, held an administrative, intermediary post between the workers in the mine and its owners — something like the character Baselli of the play. The phenomenon of *schlagende Wetter*, which gives the play its title, was well-known and feared in such communities. In German, the term "schlagende Wetter" or "Schlagwetter" describes what an English-speaking miner would have called "firedamp." This highly combustible gas, consisting chiefly of methane, is given off by coal and was the too-frequent cause of explosions in the mines, which for the miners often meant death; for the mine owner, the result was loss of income, because the shaft was destroyed. Public interest in the issue is reflected in an essay entitled "Schlagende Wetter: Zur Aufklärung und Belehrung für nicht-Bergleute," printed in the journal *Die Gesellschaft* of 1894. The piece was written in response to the latest in a series of fatal mine accidents, this time in the Czech region of Karvina, and its author provides both practical information and a metaphysical interpretation:

> Die Schlagwetter-Katastrophe in den Steinkohlengruben von Karwin hat neuerdings wiederum das Interesse einem unheimlichen Feinde der menschlichen Kultur zugewendet, der dem vordringenden Bergmanne in der Tiefe der Erde entgegentritt und uns von Zeit zu Zeit ins Gedächtnis ruft, daß alle menschliche Kraft und Geschicklichkeit, all unser Können und Wissen nur ein ohnmächtiges Ringen ist mit der Allgewalt der Naturkräfte.[17]

With her play, then, delle Grazie was tackling a subject that was then of interest outside of, as well as in, mining communities, and would therefore be likely to appeal to the bourgeois city audiences for which it was intended.

The play is classic Naturalist theater in form and content: from the working class milieu to the illness and decrepitude suffered by its characters, and from the dialect they speak to the exhaustive detail of its stage directions. What is interesting, because more unusual, is that delle Grazie gives us both the workers' and the bourgeois perspective on events. The young mine owner is not demonized: his "speaking" name is Liebmann, and he is married to Marie, a young woman from one of the mining families. He is not, then, entirely separate from the workers' community, even though he and Marie occupy a different space from the miners, in town. Marie is the interface between the two locations of the play: the dark miner's cottage where her grandfather lives, which already feels like a passage into the still-darker mine; and the light, bright bourgeois residence which she occupies with her husband. In the dark cottage, Marie's little sister is dying of tuberculosis; in the bright town house, her baby son is thriving. Marie herself took an active decision to move into privileged space: to marry Liebmann, she left a young miner called Georg. Delle Grazie does not encourage us to blame her for that. Working-class partnership — Marie's fate, had she married Georg — is not romanticized, but described in the bitter terms of shared drudgery: "Da heißt's Gaul neben Gaul sein [. . .] immer brav Schritt halten — und fest anziehn, wenn's andre nimmer kann, daß die Peitschen nit gar zu hart niedersaust" (17).

Delle Grazie, then, shows us a separation of society into two worlds — capitalists and workers. In the course of the play, she proves to us that such a division is flawed. The "proof" is Marie: her example demonstrates that such a separation at worst precludes, at best interferes with, human(e) relations. Marie's grandfather, old Gruber, suggests that her new baby will lead her to exploit others — to take advantage of her capitalist rights, "soviele Hundert verderben zu dürfen, um ein *Einzig's* froh und reich und glücklich zu machen!" (35; delle Grazie's emphasis). The disassociation of personal interests between the classes has tangible consequences in the world of work: a story told by the Liebmann's nanny signals the importance of communication between these two worlds, of owners and workers. This time the blame is shared by the worker — the nanny's father — who caused his employer's death and serious injury to himself by failing to report a faulty machine:

Jeder hat gleich viel Schuld g'habt! [. . .] Was hätt's denn mein' Vatter
'kost't, das Wörtl zu sagen? Oder den Andern — nit immer so aufzu-
fahr'n? [. . .] Das Geld und der Hunger und der Stolz, die hab'n zu viel
aufgebaut zwischen ihnen, und so kommen s' nie dazu, das Wörtl aus-
zusprechen! (71–72)

This nanny is not merely the stock figure of a domestic servant, who "licks
the hand that feeds her" when she defends the employer and blames the
worker. Her interpretation of events contributes to the development of a
central notion in the play: namely how profound, and ultimately fatal, are
the disturbances produced by the capitalist class rift — for those on *both*
sides of it. Initially it might appear that the miners are trapped ("Gaul
neben Gaul") while the owner is free, but delle Grazie shows us Liebmann
suffering the same fate as the capitalist factory owner of the nanny's story:
he is trapped and destroyed by his property, his mine, because he fails to
communicate with the workers, who actually understand something which
he merely owns. Liebmann sees his fate in the burning mine as a personal
one, and its significance as specific to himself: "alles, was ich besessen habe,
wird ein Brand [. . .] ein einziger, fürchterlicher, der gerade mich einholt"
(132–33). But Georg — trapped down the mine with his employer —
interprets differently, universalizing events in the context of a capitalist
system:

Was da unt'n g'schehn is' — kann sein, 's g'schieht in nit allz'langer
Zeit ach ob'n — wenn einmal 's Tote soviel Macht g'wonnen hat über
die Lebenden, daß s' nimmer aus noch ein wissen aus dem Schlund von
Sünd' und Schand', der ihnen's Geld 'rausg'spien hat, und immer wie-
der nur's Geld! Und dann wird eine große Türe [*sic*] zufall'n, und viel
Irrtum in Brand aufgehn. (133)

Delle Grazie's political optimism rings a little unconvincingly in the
mouth of a miner who is about to be engulfed by burning gases. But
Georg's dramatic function here is deictic: he points us away from his own
and Liebmann's personal fates to the notion of unstoppable progress that
is contained in the image of the fire.[18] It is, however, progress that will
always be impeded by human greed and corruption: the one prominent
survivor of the catastrophe in the mine is Voltz, the corrupt engineer
who encouraged Liebmann to send his men down an unsafe shaft.

Some critics of the play complained about the "unnecessary" number
of on-stage deaths: Annerl's (of tuberculosis), and Georg's, and Liebmann's. Max Burckhardt dubs it a "Bühnenrührstück,"[19] and N. Germani
complains: "all dies sind Einzelheiten, die nicht der Rührseligkeit, wohl
aber der wahren Tragik bar sind."[20] Both find that the social/political

question is not posed clearly enough in delle Grazie's play, and both have the same view of what that question should have been: "ist der Bergwerksbesitzer berechtigt, seine Leute zwangsweise einer Todesgefahr [. . .] auszusetzen?"²¹ But Germani and Burkhardt put this question — their own question, not delle Grazie's — within the context of an unchallenged hierarchy: that is, within the context of capitalist patriarchy. They assume, as the best case scenario within this system, that the mine owner must consider his fatherly responsibilities towards "his" workers ("seine Leute"). Theirs is not, therefore, a revolutionary question — more a stimulating moral challenge for the chattering classes than a profound inquiry. Whether or not delle Grazie's piece should be described as a "Rührstück" (a tendentiously feminine category, used here as a catch-all for the various weaknesses of the piece), the political questions it raises are probably more profound than those asked by her critics. Delle Grazie questions the system itself, rather than just the symptoms it produces. Tragic catastrophes at work are, in her view, the *inevitable* result of hierarchical capitalist structures, "die in der bestehenden Gesellschaftsordnung durch den Lohnvertrag herbeigeführte Aufhebung unaufhebbarer Rechte."²²

Delle Grazie, then, sees problems arising through the capitalist employment system as a whole. In her play, the paternalist, protectionist values that "soften" that system (as they — notionally at least — "softened" the feudal economy that preceded it) are also at issue. Fathers are important in this drama: old Gruber is a father; Marie is married to Liebmann because of the death of her father down the mine, for which Liebmann's father felt a responsibility that led him to provide a replacement *pater familias* in the person of her husband, his son; and young Liebmann has himself just become a father (he and Marie have a baby son). The play is dedicated to delle Grazie's own father, and its mining director, the character Baselli, recalls him. Baselli is a positive paternal figure, who pleads for the workers and then dies with them down the mine; he is the type of father who sacrifices himself for the welfare of his children, while Liebmann, the negative patriarch, exploits them for his own gain. Liebmann and Baselli wrangle (rather like the critics Burkhardt and Germani) over the "proper" practice of paternalistic relations between employer and employees. But if the depiction of kindly, responsible paternal relations were delle Grazie's aim in this play, then Liebmann might well return to the surface at the end, having learned how to be a "good" father to his workers, instead of perishing down the mine. What we in fact see underground in the final act, between Liebmann and Georg, is patriarchal hierarchy itself defeated, by the power of a natural catastrophe. In the context of the mine, Georg as miner carries more authority than his employer, and Liebmann must beg for information and help. Georg chooses not to exploit his new position: in the face of death (the "great equalizer"), hierarchy gives way to egalitarianism. Unlike Märten, as we shall see, delle Grazie does not use the figure of a socialist hero to make her point. In *Schlagende Wetter*, no single figure dominates: grandfather Gruber, Marie, Baselli, Liebmann, Georg, Annerl, and Leni are all important characters. The final showdown in the mine between Georg and Liebmann is not so much an indication of their predominance in the play, as a means of establishing equality between the two spheres of human existence that capitalism has artificially created: owners and workers. In the context of bourgeois theater, delle Grazie provides us with a play that asks more profound questions than its critics (and possibly its audience) realized. We may read the opacity of its implications either as a weakness in the drama, or, in feminist critical terminology, as another example of "writing between the lines." In the terms of the play, it is not enough to be a "good father" within the capitalist patriarchal system; delle Grazie invokes social Darwinian argumentation to suggest that society's "natural development" is away from paternalist hierarchies.

Where *Schlagende Wetter* could still be read as straightforward Naturalist drama, the portrayal of trouble down the mines we find in Lu Märten's *Bergarbeiter* is overtly revolutionary. The play was, in fact, soon declared unperformable in bourgeois circles. Clara Zetkin called it, approvingly, "ein Stück proletarischer Wirklichkeit," and added: "wir [glauben], daß das Schauspiel trotz seines künstlerischen Wertes kaum auf ein bürgerliches Theater, vor bürgerlichen Zuschauern zur Aufführung kommen wird."[23] Franz Mehring, a basically sympathetic socialist commentator, agreed with Zetkin on both counts: *Bergarbeiter* was, in his view, "eine ergreifende und erschütternde Szene aus dem Leben der Bergarbeiter"; but, he notes, "einem bürgerlichen Publikum hat sie freilich nichts zu sagen, und so werden ihr die öffentlichen Theater verschlossen bleiben."[24]

Märten has been described as a writer who, in her personal background, falls "zwischen den Klassen":[25] somewhere, that is, between the middle and the working classes. She was a city child with first-hand experience of the difficult living conditions in working-class Berlin; her father had been a minor official for the Prussian railway, whose death left the family with very little money. In a small damp Berlin flat, Märten's two older siblings, Margarete and Walter, shared the fate of many working-class children when they died of tuberculosis. It is no accident, then, that in her early novel, *Torso* (1907), which tells the story of a tubercular child, as well as in *Bergarbeiter*, Märten underlines the social causes of that illness, and particularly the effects of cramped, damp accommodation. The brother and sister who head the cast of *Bergarbeiter*, Gretje and Hermann, are tubercular, and both die before the play is over.

Unlike *Schlagende Wetter*, *Bergarbeiter* avoids the detailed settings characteristic of Naturalist dramas. In Märten's play, simplicity is both practiced and idealized — in her brief introductory "Anmerkungen zu dem Milieu," she sets the stage for a portrayal of austere poverty: "Das Zimmer ist einfach, fast ärmlich unter auffallender Vermeidung üblicher kleinbürgerlicher oder proletarischer geschmackloser Zierrate" (one might of course argue that the sensitivity to matters of taste betrayed here is in itself bourgeois). The language of the piece is simple and presumably aspires to be universal; unlike delle Grazie, Märten does not use dialect.

Schlagende Wetter showed us class war primarily from the domestic perspective — we saw the tensions, internal to the family, caused by a cross-class marriage, and the crass contrast between workers' and owners' living conditions. *Bergarbeiter*, by contrast, even though it plays entirely inside a miner's home, is primarily concerned with events *outside* of the domestic sphere. As we might expect, this shifts the focus of attention to male characters. In delle Grazie's play, our sympathies and active interest were as much engaged for Marie, torn between loyalties to her old life and to her new husband and son, and for the child Annerl (who is intimidated and unsettled by the passions of the adult world) as they were for old Gruber, Georg, or Fritz Liebmann; in Märten's piece, by contrast, we think and feel almost exclusively with the men. *Bergarbeiter* has only one female character of any significance — Gretje — and her role is passive and supportive. That said, Gretje at least (passively) backs the revolution; Mother Wilke, a minor character, functions as a negative example because she is rendered potentially counterrevolutionary by her protectiveness and selfish love of her son. The only other appearance of women onstage is in a stage direction: "Das Zimmer füllt sich mit Leuten, auch [!] Frauen" (40).

Most disturbing, however, is the way Märten has Gretje play down her own significance as an individual, by comparison with her brother, Hermann. Both siblings are tubercular, and will die; but Gretje suggests that her death is nothing to her brother's, because he is so much more important a human being than she: "Dass Hermann überhaupt fort muss, das ist das Schreckliche [. . .]. Denn er ist ein ganz Besonderer. Was könnte *der* sein!" (9; Märten's emphasis), and again: "mit Hermann ist es ja schlimmer als mit mir, denn er kann so viel!" (10). All this is said by Gretje to her father, in the first scene, and its function is to prepare us, the audience/reader, for the arrival of the paragon (Hermann) at the beginning of scene 2. By the time

Hermann enters, heading the striking miners, we have been primed by Gretje to transfer our attention entirely to him; her only other significant action in the piece is to die. Even this she does unspectacularly, somewhere in the last third of the play, by contrast with Hermann's — dramatically far more effective — death at the end. Where Gretje simply fades away inside the home, Hermann dies a hero's death outside, rescuing a young miner (Mother Wilke's son) from a burning shaft and giving his own life in the process. Hermann's death is, indeed, almost an apotheosis: young Wilke describes his appearance before him in the mine, "weiss und leuchtend; [. . .] als ob [. . .] ein Engel in die Grube geschickt sei zur Rettung" (39).

In fact, the character of Hermann is a weakness in Märten's drama. In her very positive review of the piece, Clara Zetkin praises Märten for portraying "das allgemeine proletarische Klassenlos," and insists: "Nicht außergewöhnliches Einzellos, selbstverständliches, natürliches Massenge-schick ist das sinnlose Jungsterbenmüssen der Bergmannskinder Her-mann und Gretje."[26] This may hold true in Gretje's case, but Hermann's death is emphatically "außergewöhnlich," and his role in the play is so dominant that attention is distracted away from the body of workers and from the "allgemeine proletarische Klassenlos." Instead, audience inter-est is focused on this polemical, self-taught young intellectual, who is — another weakness in the play — not even going to survive to lead the miners' strike.

Intellectual elitism is in evidence. Gretje, who admits that she does not read as Hermann does, nonetheless appeals to her father with reference to the family's collective intellectual superiority: "Vater, die andern, die viel dunkler sind wie [*sic*] wir, viel weniger reich in ihrem Sinnen und Denken [. . .] die brauchen dich!" (8). It is stressed that the Gruber family — Hermann and his father, with Gretje in the role of praise-singer — is *different* from others in the mining community. The Grubers are, it seems, uniquely able to follow the path from reading revolutionary texts (what Hermann calls "die Bücher"), through drawing conclusions from those texts, to translating words or theory into revolutionary praxis: "die Tat" (17). The greatest similarity between *Bergarbeiter* and delle Grazie's *Schla-gende Wetter* is the primacy accorded the communication of ideas. Where for delle Grazie this was needed between the classes, for Märten it spells hope within the working-class milieu (there is only one bourgeois charac-ter in the play: Dr. Wald the politician). Even the experience of tuberculo-sis needs to be articulated: Gretje begins the process, in her intimate conversations with her brother — "Wir Schwindsüchtigen können doch darüber reden" (8) — and Hermann, predictably, completes it, when he translates that private ability to name their disease and the death it will bring them into public agitation. This, too, is the revolutionary communicative task he gives his father:

> Jede glühende Seele, die du zu Tode bestimmt weisst, wirf sie hinein in den Chor der Dinge, die reden sollen. Sie sind stumm, Vater, du musst sie reden [sic]. Zeig' auf deine sterbenden Kinder [. . .]. O Vater, ich weiss ja deinen Schmerz und dass er fürchterlich ist. Lass ihn flammen, lass ihn zum Schmerz eines jeden werden, und zum Trotz, Vater. Zum Hass! (18–19)

Speech, for Märten, is effective in bringing about revolution, and working-class speech is particularly effective. Wald, the politician and (one assumes) an experienced orator, assures Burger:

> Niemand kann zuletzt in dieser Sache reden, als ihr, als du. [. . .] Selbst deine schwere Last, die dich verzweifelt macht, gibt dir Gewicht in den Augen derer, die auch Last haben.
> Ich könnte reden [. . .] nicht wie du. Ich bin nicht Blut von ihrem Blut, kein Bergmann. (15)

The power of words, Hermann explains, is that they are the forerunner of, and in the best case the direct stimulus to, action. Words can express suffering, and the act of articulation of suffering and oppression is the prerequisite for revolutionary action. Hermann again: "Wenn ihnen das Leid, das dumpf gehaltene aufsteigt ins Bewusstsein [. . .] wie dir und mir, Vater! [. . .] Dann könnte die Tat kommen [. . .] die blutreinigende Tat" (17). Hermann's revolutionary, violent words are cited by his father Burger at the play's end, as an instruction or incitement to a pre-revolutionary audience of workers: "Ohne dass die Welt in Blut gereinigt, wird es nicht kommen [. . .]. Ganz anders müssen wir kämpfen. Ganz anders hassen" (42). In one sense this is the opposite to what we see at the close of *Schlagende Wetter*. Delle Grazie shows us the overthrow of paternalist structures by natural revolutionary forces, but Märten shows us revolution as a paternal triumph: the son (Hermann) has restored the father's (Burger's) ability to speak, and hence reinstated the patriarchal prerogative of effective language.

The political message of *Bergarbeiter* is clear enough; Märten is aiming for clarity, not subtlety, and her play is an incitement to violent revolution. But it is also highly self-referential as a literary work: all kinds of ideas in the play refer back either to the power of revolutionary writing (of the type practiced by Lu Märten) or to the author of such writing. *Bergarbeiter*, for all it presents itself as proletarian drama, is a play about the role of the intellectual in the revolution. Hermann, its hero, is a writer and an intellectual, as well as (before his tuberculosis) a working miner. He explains the genesis of his ideas to Gretje: "es sind so Dinge, die ich weiter dachte, *von* den Büchern" (20; Märten's emphasis); that is, they evolve through a *critical* reading of what Brecht would call "die Klassiker" (Marx and Engels). Hermann develops ideas, which, as an intellectual, he is able to translate into words that stimulate the masses to revolutionary action. There is a movement from books to spoken words to deeds ("die Tat"); but the starting point is theory, not practice. Like Märten, Hermann is a political theorist.

Bizarrely, we discover that he is also a dramatist. He takes time out of the action to describe his play, the existence of which is entirely irrelevant to the dramatic progress of *Bergarbeiter*. In a kind of literary excursus, Hermann rejects bourgeois literature as trivial: its writers "schreiben und denken noch meistens über ihre Liebesnot und Eifersucht und ähnliches" (20). His own drama, he suggests, is of a different ilk:

> eine Bühne wirds nicht haben wollen, denn es ist keine Rolle darin für den Schauspieler, kein besonderer Mensch, keine Liebesgeschichte, keiner, der grösser und kleiner ist, keiner, der Schuld hat [. . .], weil alle nur eines bringen und darstellen und handeln [. . .] *den grossen, grenzenlosen, unsagbaren Schmerz.* (26; Märten's emphasis)

This is very much in the spirit of Zetkin's notion of Märten's play ("nicht außergewöhnliches Einzellos"[27]); although, in Hermann, Märten has of course created a "besonderer Mensch." The space Märten gives to Hermann's literary self-presentation is remarkable in such a short and otherwise economical play, and she has him speak some thought-provoking lines:

> Wenn einer von uns unter die Dichter geht, dann ist es ein Gesetz, dass er die Wahrheit seines Lebens darstellen muss. Und wenn einer von uns die Wahrheit seines Lebens darstellt, ist's am stärksten [. . .] der Schmerz, das Unrecht. (27)

Hermann's "wir" refers to the proletariat, and, if we are to go by pronouns, to the male proletariat. But his ideas — based as they are on a sense of outsiderdom in the literary community and the issue of authenticity that raises — resonate with the sentiments expressed by many women writers. We might well be reminded of Anna Croissant-Rust or even Laura Marholm when Hermann speaks of his need to write and his simultaneous fear of the consequences:

> Weisst du, Gretje, die Angst vor allem, was in mir ist [. . .] ich meine immer, ich dürfte gar nichts herauslassen, nicht ganz, nicht zu viel [. . .] es ist so stark in mir, immer wie ein körperlicher Schmerz. Ich habe die ganz deutliche Vorstellung, ich würde wahnsinnig, liesse ich irgend was ganz heraus. (22)

Lu Märten seems to be playing a double game here, reminiscent of Laura Marholm (the eel!) in *Karla Bühring*.[28] On the one hand, through Hermann, Märten rejects the bourgeois writing norm, positioning herself as a voluntary outsider to an economy that tends to view women as outsiders anyway; but, on the other, she borrows from that norm when she builds a dramatic hierarchy in which "her" character, Hermann, is dominant. She thereby creates a significant space for her self — as transported by Hermann — within her text. At the same time, I would suggest, she supports masculinist assumptions when, in the self-abnegating figure of Gretje, she disingenuously denies the possibility of allocating significance to a female self. *Bergarbeiter*'s tubercular twins let Märten have her cake and eat it.

It is interesting that Clara Zetkin's praise for the drama is couched in distinctly masculine terms: she reads "logische Strenge" in the play, and a "gedrängt muskulöse Knappheit und Schlichtheit."[29] At first glance, delle Grazie's mining play is clearly bourgeois, and Märten's is clearly revolutionary. But if we look at the structure of these two dramas, we see something different: where *Bergarbeiter* reproduces dramatic hierarchy and masculinist assumptions (Hermann is worth more than Gretje), *Schlagende Wetter* questions and undermines the value of hierarchy, avoids creating a central hero, and focuses audience attention on female as well as male characters. Märten both expresses female subjectivity — her own, through the idealized character Hermann — and denies its importance in Gretje. *Bergarbeiter* may be a revolutionary play, but Gretje is as self-subordinating as — for example — Elsa Bernstein's bourgeois Mirjam was in *Johannes Herkner*.

Militant Action: *Leuna 1921*

If Märten's play is a call to violent revolution, Lask's *Leuna 1921* is an account of an actual militant revolt. It is a documentary drama, based heavily on interviews conducted by Lask with the workers involved in the armed strike of March 1921. A year earlier, in March 1920, Leuna workers had played an important part in the general strike that defeated the extreme right-wing Kapp Putsch. Subsequently the USPD (the *Unabhängige Sozialdemokratische Partei Deutschlands*, which had split from the SPD in 1917) and the KPD joined forces, to become the VKPD (*Vereinigte Kommunistische Partei Deutschlands*). On 7 January 1921, the VKPD published an open letter calling all labor organizations to join the struggle for the social and political advancement of the workers. The reaction from the authorities to this potential threat was immediate and radical: they resolved a "Polizeiaktion zum Schutze der Staatsautorität."[30] This involved a large-scale mobilization of police and army forces in the Mansfeld and Merseburg (Leuna) area. On 21 March, the Leuna workers voted for a general strike, and two days later took over the factory. The strike lasted six days, at the end of which the artillery were brought in under the direction of the factory owner, Dr. Oster. Some workers were killed during the attack, and many more during the brutal court-martials that followed it. The events surrounding the end of the Leuna uprising are horrifying: around 2000 workers were herded by the military into the factory's ammoniac silo (famous across Germany for its capacity), where they were held, beaten, and shot over a period of fourteen days. Subsequently most of the surviving laborers were sacked, and those who stayed faced the loss of rights they had previously fought for, such as the eight-hour working day.

Like Märten's, Lask's play was not written for the bourgeois theater, but intended for performance by the workers, for the workers. Unlike Märten's, however, her dramatic method is extraordinarily well matched with her communist intentions: one of the remarkable things about *Leuna 1921* is how grippingly the action progresses without the need for audience identification with a central character or characters. We hear the voices of many workers in counterpoint, rather than a dominant, accompanied monody. In this, structural, sense, her play is closer to that of the bourgeois *delle Grazie* than to the revolutionary Märten's.

But we could read Lask's egalitarian mode another way. The failure of the Leuna uprising — after the great success of the general strike that ended the Kapp putsch one year before — seems to have affected the Communists in much the same way as the Fall of Constantinople, centuries earlier, affected Christians: there is an agonized question in the air, namely how the dogma which is, to its proponents, so indubitably *right*, could have been defeated by one so clearly *wrong*. For the sake of a sense of order in the world an answer is necessary, and the answer given to the Leuna question is lack of leadership. A GDR account of the strike, published (in the nick of time!) in 1989, concludes: "Es mangelte vor allem an einer einheitlichen Zielsetzung und Führung. Die Parteiführung der VKPD hatte es nicht vermocht, den Kampf mit klaren Direktiven zu leiten."[31] The same answer, in essence, is given by Lask in 1927: *Leuna 1921* shows us confusion, division, lack of leadership, and the infiltration of the striking workforce by government spies. The political force of all this is that the failure of the Leuna uprising was neither necessary nor inevitable, but brought about by specific circumstances that can be learned from, and hence avoided in the future. The words of Lask's "alter Arbeiter," who dies as the play closes, are inspiring and deictic: "ihr werdet noch einmal alle aufstehen und zusammentreten, Gewehr in der Faust [. . .]. Sollst das Feuer ausbreiten, bis alle Proleten ein Feuer in der Brust haben wie du [. . .]. Weiter tragen — als Vorhut — Brüder — Proleten —."[32]

Lask is focusing in this drama on a painful struggle that involved, and caused acute suffering to, a great many men. In a less spectacular way, it also caused suffering to a great many women. As audience or reader we are not quite allowed to forget this: the third and central act of the five-act drama begins with a striking domestic montage — five workers' kitchens next to one another on stage. In intertwining dialogues we hear the discussion between each worker and his wife about the impending armed strike. The women's responses range from determined self-interest — a will to spectate rather than participate in the armed strike ("Ostersonntag zieh' ich mein Blaues an. Da können wir rausfahren und uns erzählen lassen," 67) — to painful agreement that the men's participation is necessary: "Ich begreif' schon, um was es geht. Nur es ist so schwer, und nu kommt das Kind. Und du bist ein guter Mann. Wenn's sein muß, dann geh in den Kampf" (67).

Only one woman, Else, sees her own involvement as necessary: she is so frustrated by her husband's apathy that she takes his gun and joins the strike herself. It is a dramatic gesture, but we should be cautious: this kind of behavior in women has a long literary history, and it is unfortunately the perceived *incongruity* of determination and courage in woman that lends the idea its force. Its function, in Lask's play and elsewhere, is as a shaming spur to action for men. Else's decision to fight makes her husband a figure of shame; he is rendered abject like a beaten Mr. Punch when her parting words feminize him: "Dann bleib hier und back Osterkuchen! Ich nehm' dein Gewehr und stell' mich im Leunawerk zur Verfügung" (67). The parting shot makes it perfectly clear: feminine activity (baking) is abject and useless, masculine activity (the armed struggle) is heroic and effective.

Lask's suggestion, nonetheless, is that proletarian women can and will fight alongside proletarian men in the battle for class freedom. This is an idea developed in her other plays, especially the slightly earlier piece *Die Befreiung*, which is subtitled *Sechzehn Bilder aus dem Leben der deutschen und russischen Frauen, 1914–20*.[33] But, in *Leuna*, no consideration is given to what will happen *after* the battle is won. In the context of the play we have to assume that the women will simply return to their kitchens and go on putting the currants on the Easter cake.[34] Like Lu Märten in *Bergarbeiter*, Lask in this play is concerned almost exclusively with the male workers' revolutionary cause, and the role played by women is largely supportive.[35] One might argue with some justification that, in *Leuna 1921*, women are sold short, appearing only as wives and prostitutes (the character called "die rote Gustl"). But the piece is a historical documentation, within a socialist teleology, of events in the public sphere of men's work, and in her "Drama der Tatsachen" Lask is clearly concerned to do justice to the material survivors were able to give her. While the historical context of her documentary drama makes this understandable, it limits the space available to her for the expression of female revolutionary subjectivity, and therefore for the expression of her self as writer.

Revolutionary Politics and the Woman Writer

The dramas considered in this chapter were written for different purposes. Where delle Grazie's can be seen more as a philosophical political critique, Märten's — written after the first Russian revolution of 1905 — is hands-on Communist agitation, and Lask's, which followed the 1917 revolution and a worker's uprising in Germany, has a similar political urgency. Even though the term agitprop was not in use before the 1920s, when it emerged as an abbreviation for the Agitation and Propaganda Section of the Communist Party in the USSR, the notion of *agitatsiya propaganda* as a political strategy was developed considerably earlier. The early Marxist theorist Georgy Plekhanov (1856–1918) defined propaganda as "the promulgation of a number of ideas to an individual or small group, and agitation as the promulgation of a single idea to a large mass of people,"[36] a notion taken up by Lenin in his pamphlet *What is to be done?* of 1902. Retrospectively we might very well define Märten's, as well as Lask's, piece as an example of agitprop drama.

Schlagende Wetter remains formally the most conventional of the three, which may be because it is the earliest: the play is still very much in the style of nineteenth-century Naturalism, something Lu Märten in *Bergarbeiter* was already beginning to move away from. She jettisons Naturalistic dialect and detail in favor of clarity and brevity, even while she sticks formally to the domestic, working-class milieu. Märten, incidentally, is also the only one of the three dramatists to adhere to the unities of time, place, and action — presumably for the sake of performance simplicity.

Berta Lask's playwriting moves into a different realm: in *Leuna 1921* most of the action takes place in the workplace — the factory premises — and her wide-ranging drama in some scenes resembles film more than traditional playwriting. Of the three, Lask most consistently abandons the bourgeois norm. Her drama is not only in the documentary style, but it uses the techniques of the political and artistic avantgarde: film and photo stills, and the technique of montage popularized by the Russian director Sergei Eisenstein (1898–1948). We should not, however, overlook the fact that by 1926–27, when Lask was writing, such techniques were already part of a new communist "norm"; in this context her plays are, formally speaking, predictably rather than startlingly revolutionary. The contrapuntal, non-hierarchical arrangement of the characters remains an interesting feature, and one which Brecht (for example) hardly ever managed to emulate. There is no central hero in Lask's play; but its didactic message might be taken to be that there *ought* to have been, because it was for lack of strong leadership that the battle for Leuna was lost.

By the early twentieth century, when Märten and Lask were writing, new lines of thought were leading away from traditional notions of "art" and the "artist." In the bourgeois conception, a work of art must deny the labor process that preceded it: in her essay, *Wesen und Veränderung der Formen und Künste* (1924), Lu Märten noted that "die Kunst — nicht die Arbeit wurde heilig und göttlich."[37] Anything else would diminish the status of the artist, who is not laborer but creator; not a team-worker, but a peculiarly isolated individual. As late as 1964, Gero von Wilpert's *Sachwörterbuch der Literatur* still defined "Dichter" as "der Schöpfer von Sprachkunstwerken [. . .] d.h. der Gestalter e. von der Außenwelt abgehobenen, eigenen und in sich geschlossenen Welt." Bells start to ring for scholars of women's writing when von Wilpert hierarchizes "Dichtung" and "Schriftstellerei": "[der] Dichter," he tells us, "unterscheidet sich vom Schriftsteller [. . .] durch stärkere Genialität."[38] All but the most exceptional women writers have tended to be characterized as "Schriftstellerinnen" rather than "Dichterinnen," just as, as playwrights, they have been held to produce theater rather than drama; the perception is of a difference in level, and "genius" is the separating factor.[39] Women are laborers rather than creators, an indispensable domestic workforce in the world from which the (male) genius isolates himself. Lu Märten found herself at loggerheads with some of her socialist contemporaries when she rejected this conventional, individualistic, and separatist perception of art, even though she did not extend her line of thought to the specific situation of women writers. Gertrud Alexander countered Märten's argument with a socialist (and masculinist) take on the eternal "Wesen des Künstlers," whose "Gestaltenwollen und -müssen in einzigartigen Formen" permits him [*sic*] to find "den überzeitlichen und überindividuellen Ausdruck für Zeitliches."[40] Art again is presented as the separate and timeless creation of a superindividual, rather than as socially specific, or, like theater, as the result of a collective process.

These two conflicting notions of art offer us a good insight into the different choices made as writers by Lu Märten, Berta Lask, and Marie Eugenie delle Grazie. Where delle Grazie (writing, we must remember, earlier than the other two and hence with fewer options) allowed herself to be assimilated into the masculine cult of individual creative genius, Märten and Lask eschew *l'art pour l'art* in favor of artistic production that is functional, specific, and political. In her introduction to *Giftgasnebel über Sowjet-Rußland*, written around the same time as *Leuna 1921*, Lask is explicit on this issue:

> Das Revuedrama "Giftgasnebel über Sowjetrußland" will keine Dichtung, kein Kunstwerk sein. Es ist ein eilig hingeworfenes Gemälde der Zeit von heute und morgen, ein wahrheitsgetreuer Querschnitt durch das Leben des Proletariats und die Kräfte der Reaktion, hingeschrieben, um den Massen die Augen zu öffnen, bevor es zu spät ist.[41]

And Lu Märten insists more generally: "[es] hängt das Interesse jedes echten und starken Künstlers aufs innigste mit den ökonomischen Triebfedern und Wurzeln der Gesellschaft zusammen"[42] — a notion that could not be further from von Wilpert's "von der Außenwelt abgehobenen, eigenen und in sich geschlossenen Welt." But given that, as women writers, they were unlikely to benefit from the old, canonizing system, the choice makes sense on a personal as well as on a political level. Lu Märten and Berta Lask theorize artistic endeavor as firmly tied to everyday life and social realities; in doing so, they echo a notion of woman as bound to the tangible and the everyday, and thereby position themselves as legitimate insiders to the artistic project they define. Both Lask and Märten, interestingly, attribute significance to themselves as writers in their work: Lask in that she clearly believes she is playing a role in the achievement of the revolutionary goal by helping the workers to learn from their mistakes at Leuna, and Märten when she valorizes the capacity of the writer or theorist to articulate the workers' sufferings, and hence to provoke revolution. Delle Grazie only once does something similar — not in *Schlagende Wetter*, but in her overtly political one-act play, the *Moralische Walpurgisnacht*, in which the revolutionary procession is led by a writer.

This is not to idealize women's position as socialist writers. We should not overestimate the power of (male-driven) radical socialism to liberate female creativity. Delle Grazie, Märten, and Lask were all aware of the women's as well as the workers' movement of the late nineteenth and early twentieth centuries.[43] They were also, unavoidably, aware of themselves as women writers: the prominent gender concerns of turn-of-the-century thought, reflected in literary criticism, would scarcely have let them forget it. Their concerns as socialist playwrights inevitably meet and interact with their self-interest as (women) writers in their texts.

For all the notions of the stalwart woman to be found in workers' drama by the likes of Ernst Toller, Brecht, or Lask, the workers of the public sphere are, or at least are perceived to be, primarily and most importantly men. The stalwart woman — like Else in Lask's *Leuna 1921* — will tend to be of interest insofar as she furthers the male workers' cause, and will often set a heroic and therefore shaming example that works against the background of a basic assumption that men ought, properly speaking, to be the braver and more heroic sex.

Delle Grazie is the only writer of the three to imply in her play that women are oppressed by men as the proletariat are oppressed by the bourgeoisie. This parallel structures the relationship between Marie and Liebmann. Marie is both working class and a woman; Liebmann upper middle class and a man. In Liebmann's house, as his wife, Marie is "gebunden" and "gedämpft" (40), just as his workers in the pits are bound to him and their voices muted by the power of capital. In their dialogue, Marie's use of local dialect and her brief, fragmentary speeches — frequently interrupted by her husband — signal her doubly subordinate position. For delle Grazie, it seems, far more than for Märten and Lask, the personal is also political.

Märten, as we have seen, does not keep to the non-hierarchical communist model she developed in her theoretical writing when it comes to writing drama; instead she portrays a male hero with an abject admiring woman at his side. In the later twentieth century, linguists such as Dale Spender suggested that non-hierarchical and non-competitive modes are positive "feminine" models of communication;[44] of our three dramatists, it is not the radical Märten, but Lask and the bourgeois playwright delle Grazie who write drama that is anti-hierarchical in structure and content.

But in the context of late nineteenth-century bourgeois theater, delle Grazie — like all the other women dramatists this volume has so far considered — had to accept a perception of her as a surprisingly gifted outsider: the exception to a rule. It is notable that Lask and Märten, by contrast, have been accepted in left-wing literary history on their own terms: even though contemporary reviews of their work were not always enthusiastic,[45] both have been reprinted (specifically as socialist writers), and — most unusually — neither woman has been received as essentially flawed as a dramatist due to her sex.[46] From this we might deduce that Berta Lask and Lu Märten were taken seriously as dramatic writers outside and beyond the context of their gender. That would be a positive, upbeat take on their reception. The coincidence that both are engaged socialist writers, however, also permits a different kind of conclusion. Delle Grazie, the bourgeois writer, is remembered as a poet rather than as a dramatist, and it would be possible to argue that Lask's and Märten's reception is despite all appearances structurally related to hers (and to that of almost all the other writers considered in this study): they are remembered as socialists, not dramatists. It seems that, if one is a woman dramatist, one had better be something else, too: either a (party) political campaigner, like Märten and Lask, or perhaps a poet (like delle Grazie). This is the way to get one's work received and one's self remembered; to become visible in literary history.

Notes

[1] Marie Eugenie delle Grazie, *Schlagende Wetter: Drama in fünf Akten*, 3rd ed., in delle Grazie, *Sämtliche Werke*, vol. 7 (Leipzig: Breitkopf & Härtel, 1903). All references are to this edition of the text. Lu Märten, *Bergarbeiter: Schauspiel* (1909; 2nd ed., with slight alterations by the author, Berlin: Taifun, 1924). References are to the 1924 edition of the text. *Bergarbeiter* has since been reprinted in *Aus dem Schaffen früher sozialistischer Schriftstellerinnen*, ed. Cäcilia Friedrich (Berlin: Akademie, 1966).

[2] Berta Lask, *Leuna 1921: Drama der Tatsachen* (Berlin: Vereinigung Internat. Verlagsanstalten, 1927). All references are to this edition of the text. The play was reprinted, with slight variations (several references to film and photograph use are lost; the original division into twenty-nine scenes is replaced by a division into five acts) and with an afterword by Johannes Schellinger, as *Leuna 1921: Drama in fünf Akten* (Berlin: Dietz, 1961).

[3] *Saul* was never performed, but it was awarded the Grillparzer prize on the recommendation of Heinrich Laube.

[4] Delle Grazie, *Moralische Walpurgisnacht: Ein Satyrspiel* (Leipzig: Breitkopf & Härtel, 1896).

[5] Delle Grazie, "Zur Arbeiterbewegung." Manuscript held in Vienna's Stadtbibliothek. Cited in Maria Mayer-Flaschberger, *Marie Eugenie delle Grazie: Eine österreichische Dichterin der Jahrhundertwende: Studien zu ihrer mittleren Schaffensperiode* (Munich: Verlag des Süddeutschen Kulturwerks, 1984), 102, note 313.

[6] For example by Bernhard Münz, *Marie Eugenie delle Grazie als Dichterin und Denkerin* (Vienna: Braumüller, 1902) and Hans Widman, "Marie Eugenie delle

Grazie," in *Randglossen zur deutschen Literaturgeschichte: Der Literaturbilder 8. Bändchen* (Munich: Schweitzer, 1902). Both cited in Mayer-Flaschberger, 10–11.

[7] Lothar, *Das deutsche Drama der Gegenwart* (Munich: Müller, 1905), 259–61.

[8] See "Urteile über den Einakter-Cyklus 'Zu spät,'" printed at the close of delle Grazie, *Zu spät: Vier Einakter*, in *Sämtliche Werke* 8 (Leipzig: Breitkopf & Härtel, 1904).

[9] In her biography, *Stille und Sturm*. See Agnès Cardinal, "Berta Lask 1878–1967, [Die Befreiung] Liberation: Introduction," in *War Plays by Women: An International Anthology*, ed. by Claire M. Tylee with Elaine Turner and Agnès Cardinal (London: Routledge, 1999), 81–84 (81–82).

[10] Lask, *Senta. Eine Lebenslinie in acht Szenen* (Hannover: Steegemann, 1921).

[11] See Lask, "Erinnerungen an Piscators Proletarisches Theater," in *Die Rote Fahne* 25 January 1925, reprinted in *Deutsches Arbeitertheater 1918–1933*, vol. 1, ed. by Ludwig Hoffmann and Daniel Hoffmann-Ostwald, 2nd ed. (Berlin: Henschel, 1972), 75–76.

[12] The *Badische Analin- und Soda-Fabrik*, a major producer of chlorine gas for World War One. After the war, the Leuna factory moved into the production of fertilizers.

[13] Johannes Schellenberger, "Nachwort," in Lask, *Leuna 1921* (1961), 149.

[14] In the Vienna journal *Arbeiterliteratur*. See Chryssoula Kambas, *Die Werkstatt als Utopie: Lu Märtens literarische Arbeit und Formästhetik seit 1900* (Tübingen: Niemeyer, 1988), 2.

[15] Two other unpublished dramas are on record: *Der weiße Christus* (c.1903), and *Raffael* (c.1906). See Kambas, 78–79.

[16] See the typewritten notes by Lu Märten herself, appended to the copy of the 1924 edition of *Bergarbeiter* held by the Deutsches Literaturarchiv in Marbach.

[17] By "F. A. H.," in *Die Gesellschaft* 10 (1894), 1068–86 (1068).

[18] Here delle Grazie is in line with Karl Kautsky's Darwinian Marxism (naturally inevitable development), as laid down in the Erfurt program adopted by the SPD in 1891. See "Karl Kautsky," in *Marxism, Communism and Western Society: A Comparative Encyclopedia*, ed. by C. D. Kernig, vol. 5 (New York: Herder & Herder, 1973), 1–6.

[19] Burckhardt, "Schlagende Wetter," in *Theater: Kritiken, Vorträge und Aufsätze*, 1 (1898–1901) (Vienna: Manzsche, 1905), 182–85 (183).

[20] Germani, "Zwei neue Dramen," in *Stimmen der Gegenwart: Monatsschrift für moderne Litteratur und Kritik* 2 (1901), 114–15.

[21] Germani, "Zwei neue Dramen," 115.

[22] Delle Grazie, *Mein Lebensweg*, in delle Grazie, *Sämtliche Werke*, 9 vols. (Leipzig: Breitkopf & Härtel, 1903), vol. 9, 84.

[23] Klara Zetkin, "Ein Arbeiterdrama: 'Bergarbeiter,' Schauspiel in einem Akt von Lu Märten," in Friedrich, ed., 160–64 (161).

[24] Mehring, "Lu Märtens Bergarbeiter," in *Die neue Zeit* 27/1 (1908–9), 933–4; cited in Kambas, 93.

[25] By her friend, Otto Jensen. Cited in Kambas, 5.

[26] Zetkin, 162.

[27] Zetkin, 162.

[28] See chapter 3.

[29] Zetkin, 163.

[30] Karl-Heinz Streller and Erika Massalsky, *Geschichte des VEB Leuna-Werke "Walter Ulbricht" 1916–1945* (Leipzig: VEB deutscher Verlag für Grundstoffindustrie, 1989), 57.

[31] Streller and Massalsky, 60.

[32] Lask, *Leuna 1921*, 141.

[33] Berlin 1924. An English translation of the play is also available: "Liberation [Die Befreiung]," transl. by Agnès Cardinal, in *War Plays by Women*, 85–110.

[34] This in contradistinction to the earlier play, Senta, in which a young woman is shown freeing herself from the bounds of domesticity and the expectations placed on women.

[35] In other plays, such as *Die Befreiung,* the women, too, are portrayed as workers.

[36] See "agitprop" in the *Encyclopaedia Britannica Online* (http://www.eb.co.uk: 180/bol/topic?eu=4089&sctn=1, accessed 1 March 2000).

[37] Cited in Gerhard Plumpe, "Kunstform und Produktionspraxis im Blick auf Lu Märten," in *Arbeitsfeld: Materialistische Literaturtheorie: Beiträge zu ihrer Gegenstandsbestimmung,* ed. by Klaus-Michael Bogdal, Burkhardt Lindner, and Gerhard Plumpe (Wiesbaden: Athenaion, 1975), 193–228 (216).

[38] Gero v. Wilpert, *Sachwörterbuch der Literatur* (Stuttgart, 1964), 125; cited in Plumpe, 216.

[39] As Professor Moray McGowan (Trinity College Dublin) has pointed out to me, this fact stands alongside the tendency among German writers in the later twentieth century, starting with Enzensberger, to pour scorn on the idea of the "Dichter" and elevate the "Schriftsteller."

[40] Cited in Plumpe, 221.

[41] Lask, *Giftgasnebel über Sowjet-Rußland: Revue-Drama in 35 Scenen* (Berlin: Friedrich, 1927), 3.

[42] Märten, "Kunst, Klasse und Sozialismus. Aphorismen," in Friedrich, 165–68 (165).

[43] Lask's early concerns with feminism are documented in an "Aufruf an die Frauen," published in the SPD newspaper *Vorwärts* in 1918, "which calls upon women to eschew political parties and build a new 'Menschheitssozialismus.'" *Vorwärts* 327 (28 November 1918). See Richard Sheppard, "Straightening Long-Playing Records: The Early Politics of Berta Lask and Friedrich Wolf," in *German Life and Letters* 45 (1992), 279–87 (280).

[44] See for example, Spender, *Man Made Language*, 2nd ed. (London: Pandora, 1985), 125–29.

[45] On the contemporary reception of Lask's play see Agnes Cardinal, "Shadow Playwrights of Weimar: Berta Lask, Ilse Langner, Marieluise Fleißer," in *Women in European Theatre*, ed. Elizabeth Woodrough (Oxford: Europa, 1995), 65–73 (67–68).

[46] Märten was criticized because of her class, however: an anonymous reviewer in the *Deutsche Metallarbeiter-Zeitung* (Berlin, 1909) casts doubt on the writer's knowledge of the milieu she portrays. See Kambas, 93.

5: Else Lasker-Schüler: A Theater of the Self?

So FAR IN THIS STUDY, I have considered ways of finding space for a female subject in the traditional dramatic forms of comedy and tragedy, and for the expression of female creativity within a literary and social discourse that largely denies its existence. I have observed modes of articulating the woman's self as "I," and of defining the artistic and political project of drama in such a way that female subjectivity acquires a space. One way or another, all the playwrights considered have striven to create materiality for themselves through the medium of drama. In the final chapters I shall look at the work of two writers who have, more than any of the others in this volume, been granted materiality — space or presence — in literary history: Else Lasker-Schüler (1869–1945) and Marieluise Fleisser (1901–74).

Lasker-Schüler is better known as a poet than a playwright. Both her dramatic work (with the possible exception of *Die Wupper*) and her prose have tended to be overlooked — she is known, read, and taught primarily as a writer of poetry. Like those of so many women, her plays have been classed as "undramatic";[1] the subtext, again, is that women don't *really* write drama — not even when their oeuvre includes plays. Like so many women of letters, Lasker-Schüler has been defined as a "masculine" writer, most famously by Karl Kraus, who designated her "die einzige männliche Erscheinung der heutigen deutschen Literatur."[2] This suggestion is doubly insidious. On the one hand, it is presented as a compliment to a woman writer, and the positive status of masculinity is reiterated; on the other, Lasker-Schüler is denied female identity as a poet and functionalized to shame the "feminine" male writers who are implicitly present in Kraus's statement. Nearly fifty years later, Sigismund von Radecki could still conjure the notion that literary talent is essentially male, in his crass characterization of Lasker-Schüler: "Sie war in ihrem Genialen männlich und hatte doch ein Frauenleib."[3]

Lasker's poetry readings were artistic events: she attended to details such as lighting and modulated her voice to focus audience attention on her performance.[4] Even outside of formal readings she was a performer who incorporated her artistic creations: her self-stylization as Tino of

Baghdad (the central character of the collection *Die Nächte Tinos von Baghdad*) and, even more frequently, as Jussuf (the central character of *Der Prinz von Theben*) has become her hallmark; and around the time of the Zurich production of her play *Arthur Aronymus und seine Väter* she was signing letters to friends in the persona of her child protagonist, Arthur Aronymus.[5] Lasker-Schüler chose *not* to perform the usual separation, author — fiction; and a refusal to accept rigid binary constellations (such as male-female, Jew-Christian, and class divisions) is characteristic of her playwriting.

Her first play, *Die Wupper* (1909), has been called a "Jahrhundertärgernis" for literary critics because it has effectively resisted classification.[6] Naturalist elements have been identified and denied in the piece; it has been seen as a forerunner of Expressionist drama.[7] All this might make one wonder more about the needs of critics than about the play. Certainly *Die Wupper* combines naturalistic family scenes across the classes (blue-collar workers, white-collar workers, the owning classes) with metaphorically meaningful images (such as the fair and its carousel, which spins everyone's life out of control, or the three vagabonds or "Herumtreiber" who observe rather than participate in the action, something like a classical chorus).[8] The play premièred on 27 April 1919, in Max Reinhardt's Deutsches Theater in Berlin, directed by Heinz Herald. It played again at Berlin's Staatliches Schauspielhaus in 1927 under Jürgen Fehling, before disappearing from the repertoires — along with other plays by Jewish writers — until its next performance in Cologne in 1958.[9] A version for television was produced in 1985 by Jürgen Flimm.[10]

Arthur Aronymus und seine Väter, Lasker-Schüler's next full-length play, was written in 1932, straight after her short story *Arthur Aronymus: Die Geschichte meines Vaters*. The change in the title marks a change from epic — "die Geschichte meines Vaters" — to dramatic mode, from *histoire* to *discours*; the play is nonetheless narrative in style (far more than *Die Wupper* was), and depends on stage directions to clarify characters' interaction. *Arthur Aronymus und seine Väter* was printed as a stage script (by S. Fischer) during Lasker-Schüler's lifetime, and was published after her death by Kösel Verlag in 1951. A première was planned for 1933 at the Hessisches Theater in Darmstadt, but cancelled after the National Socialists under Hitler took power. The play in fact premièred in Zurich's Schauspielhaus on 19 December 1936, directed by Leopold Lindtberg. Even in Switzerland, though, the politics of such a performance were complicated, and *Arthur Aronymus* was dropped after only two showings.[11] It was not performed again until 1968, under Hans Bauer in Lasker-Schüler's home town, Wuppertal.

Her last major dramatic project, *IchundIch*, was written in 1940–41 during her exile in Jerusalem. She had traveled to Palestine in 1934 from Switzerland (she left Germany very suddenly in fear of the Nazis in April 1933), and had subsequently written the book *Das Hebräerland* (1937). A second journey in 1937 was in preparation for another volume on Palestine, to be called *Tiberias*. One element of this project was a play, called first *Das Höllenspiel*, then *Der bekehrte Satan*, finally *IchundIch*.[12] She had intended to write *Tiberias* in Switzerland, but when she was refused re-entry after a third trip to Palestine in 1939, she settled — temporarily, she planned — in Jerusalem. *IchundIch* had its first public reading on 20 July 1941, to the German-speaking literary circle called *Der Kraal* that Lasker-Schüler had established since being in Jerusalem. At the time of her death in 1945, the manuscript was finished although still imperfect, and she had not managed to find a theater or director to perform it.

A strange and rather complex story begins here, since a number of Lasker-Schüler's friends, notably Ernst Ginsberg and Werner Kraft, pressured the administrator of her literary estate to resist a posthumous publication of the full text, thereby also rendering performance impossible. Excerpts from the play were published in the Swiss journal *hortulus* (1960), and, later, in the *Nachlaß* volume of the collected works of Lasker-Schüler edited by Werner Kraft;[13] the choice of excerpts differs in each case. Klaus Völker directed an unauthorized performed reading with Berlin students in 1961, partly with the intention of forcing publication. In fact the complete text was eventually published in 1970, thanks to the editorial efforts of Margarete Kupper.[14] The play premièred, thirty-four years after Lasker-Schüler's death, on 10 November 1979 at Düsseldorf's Schauspielhaus, directed by Michael Gruner; four weeks later it also opened in Wuppertal, under Hermann Kleinselbeck.

The titles of two lost dramas by Lasker-Schüler have also been recorded: *Isaak* (1910) and *Joseph und seine Brüder* (1932). The latter may have been lost during Lasker-Schüler's flight into exile in 1933.[15]

Religious Structures and the Place of the Self: *Die Wupper* and *Arthur Aronymus und seine Väter*

Religious beliefs and practices are a clear frame of reference in *Arthur Aronymus* — early reviews accuse the play of showing a naïve portrait of religious toleration — and they are also of structural relevance to *Die Wupper*. In this play, Jewishness is not an issue, but Protestantism and Catholicism are, and stand opposite each other in the aptly named figures of Carl

Pius and Eduard Sonntag. Carl's vision of himself as a Protestant pastor exists next to Eduard's of himself as a monk in a Catholic order. Importantly, there is no conflict here; on the contrary, the two are friends, even love each other. Carl's anxiety to appear at his best when Eduard visits is reflected in Eduard's sadness when, at the end, Carl abandons him, to form a new threesome of vagabonds: in the final scene, the triad Carl — Lange Anna — August replaces the original threesome Lange Anna — Pendelfrederich — Gläserner Amadeus. Carl's courtship of Marta Sonntag can be seen not simply as attempted social climbing, but as a displaced expression of his love for Eduard (something like the oddly intense declaration of love for Arthur Aronymus that is made in that play by the Kaplan, whose religious vow forbids him his erotic interest in little Arthur's sister, Fanny).[16]

In *Die Wupper*, Lasker-Schüler has, as ever, no interest in upholding binary oppositions. Social class and religious beliefs separate these two young men in the social matrix, but what we see in the play is the similarity of their aspirations. Both are looking to satisfy a certain vanity (they view themselves as different from, and in some sense better than, those around them), and both are looking for a tool with which to control others. Großvatter [*sic*] Wallbrecker's sarcastic reference to Carl's "Carliäre" (= *Karriere*, 13) reminds us how inseparable Carl and his ambitions are.

That the authority that comes with the priesthood — Catholic or Protestant — flatters their vanity is something that begins to emerge in both young men's speech. In his greeting to Eduard: "*frisch, markig, primanerhaft, pathetisch*: Ich grüße Dich, Gottesmann, der Du fürlieb nimmst mit unserer Speise und Trank"[17] Carl uses a self-consciously antiquated form of language that evokes the authority of older generations of men of the church, and positions him as the heir to that authority. Eduard joins in the language game with his response, "*leuchtend schelmisch*: Friede sei Deinem Haus, mein Bruder" (51); the mischievous tone marks his recognition of the game, but still he chooses to play along.

Far less lighthearted is Eduard's flight into biblical posturing when his sister will not marry the man of his choice. In dialogue with his mother, he deliberately reverses the usual mother-son authority structure to condemn her support of Martha: "*mit biblischer Wucht*: Ich sage Dir, Weib, beflecke unser Haus nicht" (67). The speech act — a veto — is both violent (Frau Sonntag breaks down weeping) and ineffectual: Eduard may invoke the authority of the Church fathers in his rhetoric, but he is not himself a father yet (neither as priest nor as progenitor), merely a son, like Carl Pius, as his mother reminds him: "Du bist impertinent wie Carl Pius" (67). He therefore has no power to prevent Marta's marriage to Herr von Simon. Eduard's rhetorical use of the word "Weib" to apostrophize his mother is, nonetheless, significant. It echoes Carl's use of the term to Mutter Pius a little earlier in the play. Carl designates Mutter Pius's speech "Weibergeklatsch" (57), and finds expression for his frustrated interest in Marta in a verbal explosion: "Ihr Weiber stört mich!" Given that only Carl and Mutter Pius are on stage, the plural "Weiber" can be taken to refer to Pius and to the absent Marta, whose naked image Carl has just put in his wallet. The derogatory term "Weib" (which takes its derogatory impetus, at least in part, from the ecclesiastical usage that posits "Weib" as essentially subaltern to "Mann") helps Carl shore up his position vis-à-vis the two women who exert power over him: Mutter Pius as his informant and confidante, Marta Sonntag as the object of his erotic interest.

The language of fathers and sons is also of relevance in *Arthur Aronymus*. Simeon, the second of father Schüler's twenty-three (!) children, like Eduard Sonntag makes an attempt to assert his authority over that of his mother; to achieve paternal rather than filial status. He begins with an imperative, regarding the proper reward due to a casual laborer at their house: "Der Mann bekommt seinen Lohn und damit basta, Mutter" (106); but this, like Eduard's command to his mother in *Die Wupper*, is ineffectual or infelicitous — the laborer in question, Nathaniel Brennessel, has already been sent to the kitchen to receive a meal on top of his payment for carpet-beating. Like Eduard, Simeon borrows the rhetoric of paternal authority to assert himself — not the rhetoric of the church fathers this time, but words clearly taken from his own father's mouth and addressed to father Schüler, man to man: "Simeon *zum Vater*. In den Dingen der Ökonomie ist mit der Mutter nicht zu reden." By not addressing her directly, Simeon relegates his mother to the position of onlooker, of audience, while he and his father perform. An amusing touch here is that Lasker-Schüler shows us Herr Schüler embarrassed by the mirror image of himself shown him by his son: he is "etwas unangenehm [. . .] berührt" (106), and possibly even threatened by the filial power-game that is being played. In his next words he re-establishes himself as the final authority in all matters: "Im Hause wollen wir schon die *Mutter* walten lassen" (Lasker's emphasis). In one sense at least Simeon has won here: father Schüler's "wir" refers to himself and his son, and indirectly to men in general. Frau Schüler is left in the position of outsider or onlooker, spoken about but not speaking.

The voice of the father and his verbal authority is an important feature of the play. In the short story *Arthur Aronymus: Die Geschichte meines*

Vaters, which Lasker-Schüler wrote just before the drama, she also shows us the young Arthur Aronymus suffering under his father's exploitation of patriarchal speech space. When father Schüler tells the story of the pogrom, it is not the violent detail that upsets his young son, but the time he takes narrating it: "Am schwersten verdroß Arthur Aronymus [. . .] die weit über den Inhalt sich ausdehnende Schauergeschichte des sich Zeit lassenden, erzählenden Vaters."[18] In the drama, father Schüler's speech space is carefully managed and defended for him by his wife. Her tactics are described in a stage direction as "klug und liebevoll" (137): she interpellates him into language, into a position at the center of the family, using his own words (a technique that flatteringly underlines their importance): "Warum lassen der Herr Vater uns so lange harren auf das spannende Ende, wie er sich gestern auszudrücken pflegte, seines Tagebuches? Moritz!"

But Lasker-Schüler, while showing us paternal rights preserved, adds a metalevel of humor here that echoes or replaces the amusing detail of Arthur Aronymus's impatience in the short story. The notion that the tale told by Herr Schüler is "spannend" is his own, and is reproduced without personal corroboration by his wife. We might also read a double meaning in her plea: "Bitte, bitte, spanne unsere Ungeduld nicht auf die Folter, Moritz!" (137): after all, the impatience of the assembled family is focused on the end, rather than the beginning of their father's story. Herr Schüler himself is rendered harmlessly ridiculous by his use of conventional turn of phrase: "*ritterlich* Also wie meine Gattin befiehlt" — although the chivalrous modesty here hides a familiar and insidious structure, whereby men use every inch of the space available to them in patriarchal society while pretending to defer to women.

Father Schüler is determined to subject his family to a lengthy reading from his diary; Frau Schüler's task is to provide him with an elegant and effortless path into the space that is his. That she fulfils this role willingly is, for the dramatist, an indication that she is "liebevoll und klug" rather than just a collaborator in her own oppression. We might very well see her as both things: a loving, intelligent women within a conventional family dynamic that the playwright allows to expose itself, when we laugh at patriarchal self-importance and pomposity. But Lasker-Schüler also shows us how female energy is eaten up by the behavior of the perfect wife: at the end of the scene father Schüler bustles off happily to check on his livestock, and his wife's mask drops: "*Frau Schüler trocknet mit einem Tüchelchen ihre Stirne. Sie ist erledigt wie nach einer Operation. Lehnt sich zurück in ihren Sessel und schliesst die Augen*" (140).

The moment at which the reader/audience is encouraged to take the voice of the father completely seriously is when he is defending not male privilege, but Jewish identity. The Kaplan has made the suggestion that Arthur Aronymus be baptized as a Christian, as a gesture to placate the anti-Semitic Christian community. Herr Schüler rises, and when he speaks he is "zum ersten Male *wirklich* echt menschlich" (152; Lasker's emphasis). This is not to say that he is not a little ridiculous, when he tangles himself in the branches of the patriarchal family tree ("meines hochseligen Vaters hochseliger Vater und dessen Väter Väterväter"), but he nonetheless performs a highly effective linguistic act when, in response to the Kaplan's suggestion that he christen his son, he resists by pronouncing the Hebrew words "adonai jischmerenu mikol ra[r]" ("Der Herr behüte uns vor allem Bösen!").[19] The effects of this pronouncement are immediate and dramatic (in every sense): the Padersteins and Frau Schüler weep, the children stare open-mouthed at their father, and the Kaplan responds as if to physical force: "ein Geschlagener" (152).

The Hebrew sentence that triumphs here is celebrated for what it is, a felicitous speech act. Herr Paderstein congratulates Schüler with the simple recognition: "Gesprochen hast Du, Moritz, na!" (153), and Katharina notes proudly: "Des Vaters Rede hat gefruchtet" (157). To understand the significance of this event for the Jewish family, we need to remind ourselves of the German language that is used against them by the Christians in the play. This language is not only effortlessly misogynist ("Weib!"), but also effortlessly anti-Semitic, enabling compound words and phrases such as "Judenbrut" (117), "feiger Jud" (143) and "fiser [*sic*] Judenjunge" (160) in the mouths of common people. We also hear "dreister Judenjunge" (119) from the Kaplan, who is deeply shocked by where his own language has taken him: "*tief erschrocken über die ihm entfahrene Bemerkung*," although "ihm entfahren" suggests an accidental physical event, as if he had belched.

Lasker-Schüler is not interested in showing a final triumph of Hebrew over German; other, more humane ways of speaking German are also possible. This is made clear in the Christian speech act, performed by the Kaplan on behalf of the Bishop, that stands symmetrically alongside Herr Schüler's Hebrew pronouncement in the play. When the Kaplan reads the episcopal bull, he lays claim to the support of two higher authorities: the Archbishop, who issued it, and god. He responds to the sight of a gathering storm with words made deliberately audible to the assembled crowd: "Der Himmel hat sich verbündet mit Seiner Gnaden, dem Erzbischof" (161). What the Kaplan delivers is truly a performance of authority: he unrolls the bull majestically, shakes his finger and casts stern looks over the crowd, pauses for effect, and finally strides back into the church. The results — as they were after Schüler's Hebrew speech — are impressive: the crowd weeps and wails, and seems already to have been cured of anti-Semitic speech by the power of the Christian speech act.

Arthur Aronymus — the central figure of the piece — makes the most startling pronouncement; one which is qualitatively different to those that go before. When Simeon speaks, when Herr Schüler speaks, and when the Kaplan speaks, all three achieve an effect through borrowing the voice of authority: Simeon from his father, Schüler from the Torah, and the Kaplan from the Archbishop. When the young Arthur Aronymus speaks, during a Pessah dinner before the assembled family and Jewish and Christian guests, the voice is not borrowed: it *is* the voice of authority, namely the voice of the dead Rabbi, contradicting his daughter's assumption:

> FRAU SCHÜLER   Und nun ruht mein armer Vater einsam in der Erden — — —
> [. . .]
>
> ARTHUR ARONYMUS   *stark, wie aus einem Medium äussert sich aus ihm die Stimme des Rabbis:* Der Rabbuni ist nicht einsam — — — *er ist versammelt mit den Vätern.* (178; Lasker's emphasis)

Even though he is a little boy, Arthur Aronymus speaks with the voice of the father. For the first and only time in the play, he assumes the role in which he is familiar to the playwright: Aron Schüler was Else Lasker-Schüler's father, as the title of the short story reminds us.

The shift in the second half of the title from story to drama — from *Die Geschichte meines Vaters* to *und seine Väter* — suggests a shift in perspective. Where in the story we look back from the writer to her father, in the play we look back from the child-father character to *his* fathers. The plural in the play title is no accident: in the short story we saw a family relationship, one single father, but in the play we are presented with the patriarchal history of a people, a collective instance of authority that massively overshadows the authority of an individual father. Jewish history speaks briefly through the mouth of Arthur Aronymus, who will later become the father of Else Lasker-Schüler. It co-exists with German cultural history, which enables the newest member of the family, Katharina's husband Engelbrecht, to declaim the entire text of *Faust* by heart (107). Language, then, is a tool of power or authority that can support a patriarchal, sometimes violent and anti-Semitic status quo; but it is also a vehicle of cultural meaning, and can carry identity and humanity for Jews and Christians. And sometimes language is a betrayer of human weakness: the audible sign of human confusion, helplessness, and striving for self. Lasker-Schüler has been compared to Horváth or Kroetz in her portrayal of "the (in)ability of language to convey what members of the lower classes are feeling";[20] but in *Arthur Aronymus* we see that the middle classes are afflicted too.

This is clear from the language games played by Fanny and the Kaplan. When Fanny invents a message from her mother and feigns concern for her little brother in order to establish contact, the Kaplan is initially confused; but he quickly grasps the situation and plays along "im gleichen konventionellen Ton" (128). When Fanny's tone becomes "plötzlich warm" the Kaplan responds by initiating a more intimate situation — he pulls up a chair for her — and establishing contact through a gift of chocolate from the Christmas tree. The language of Christianity simultaneously expresses and denies his erotic interest: he designates Fanny "eine Braut Christi," but touches her hand while he interprets the candles on the tree: "das Licht vereinigt — *er stockt* alle Herzen" (129). The stage direction here — *"Fanny bebt vor Seligkeit"* — communicates Fanny's misunderstanding of the situation. Even though he is attracted to Fanny and cannot resist the flattery of her interest in him, the Kaplan is in control of this game, and because he cannot have her body he is looking to acquire her soul; to use the erotic energy of the moment to make a convert: not "verführen" but "überführen" (130). At this point Fanny realizes that the language game is beyond her; she is linguistically and emotionally at sea, and confesses "*nach einiger Überlegung, rührend*: Herr Kaplan, ich habe keinen Wortschatz." Paradoxically, the very straightforwardness of this defeats the Kaplan's verbal sophistry, but he takes revenge. There follows the rather bizarre exchange regarding the rowan, during which he projects his erotic self on to a tree, an act of exhibitionism that leaves Fanny distressed, confused, and finally irritated. As Krumbholz comments: "So transformiert man Wollust in Kitsch — und bleibt Kaplan."[21]

"Wollust" and "Kitsch" exist side-by-side in *Die Wupper* too. Heinrich buys the pubescent Lieschen a gingerbread heart before he has sex with her and makes her pregnant, causing disaster for himself and her; Herr von Simon addresses both the women he seduces, Berta and Marta, by the saccharin pet name "Kätzchen." The world of the *Wupper* is a harsher environment than the family world of *Arthur Aronymus*, but its structures are not dissimilar: kitsch is a tool for the manipulation of the desired (female) other. In both plays, sentimentality and false sentimentality provide a screen for violent or ruthless behavior. Carl Pius, the would-be pastor, literally twists the arm of one of his projected flock, Lange Anna (18), and advises a group of workers to commit murder: "*herablassend brutal*: Schlagt Euern Herrn tot, wie s'es in Rußland machen" (59). Heinrich threatens a terrified von Simon with violence before drunkenly mistaking Lieschen and Mutter Pius for his own sister and mother, and telling them with alcoholized sentiment: "Schlaf süß, Marze, gute Nacht, Mama Charlottchen" (45).

Violence and sentimentality are juxtaposed, as are comedy and horror. These two co-exist primarily through Lasker-Schüler's stage directions, that is, in the physical rather than verbal world of the drama: for example when von Simon, petrified, is pushed around by workers who laugh horribly (*"lachen furchtbar,"* 44). August in particular, with his discolored dyer's hands and rather desperate worker's pride, has a grotesquely comic physical presence: he underlines the difference between his own and Carl's ambitions with an extravagantly subservient bow that is horribly funny (*"furchtbar komisch,"* 13), and his gesticulations are those of a furious clown (*"gebärdet sich [. . .] wie ein wütender Clown,"* 14). It is an old dramatic convention that the working classes provide comic relief; Lasker-Schüler synthesizes that convention with the Naturalist awareness of working-class misery and creates a grotesque hybrid.

She also plays with another comic tradition: drag. The portrayal of Alwine Vogelsang in *Arthur Aronymus* is probably Lasker-Schüler's most straightforward use of theatrical crossdressing. The stage directions specify that this part is to be played by a man (105); furthermore, the man must be lean and slightly bearded, and speak strong Wuppertal dialect. All this puts Alwine Vogelsang firmly in the tradition of the German comic figure or fool:[22] she is characterized as linguistically incompetent (she is unable to adapt her linguistic register to a formal situation when meeting the Schülers); and she is laughably unfeminine. Lasker-Schüler is making apparently uncritical use of a gendered comic norm: Frau Vogelsang's beard and her tendency to speak before she is spoken to ("Alwinchen plauderst wieder aus der Schule," 108) suggest a transgressive masculinity; but the potential threat in this is exploded in the relief of laughter, because she is also portrayed as an unattractive woman and therefore socially disempowered (if we accept the given that a woman's power lies in the effect of her physical appearance on men as the real powerholders). Frau Vogelsang invites audience laughter when she betrays that her husband does not want — and has never wanted — to have sex with her: "Vogelsang wollt nicht aufwachen und ich konnt doch bei seinem Schnarchen nicht einschlafen — so stört er mir immer die Ruhe seit unserer Hochzeit" (108).

Why Lasker-Schüler chose to use comic stereotypes of gender in the portrayal of this figure is unclear to me, particularly since her approach to cross-gendered performance is otherwise far less conventional. Lange Anna of *Die Wupper* is an explicitly transvestite performer, but with none of the comedy that renders Alwine Vogelsang unthreatening. Indeed, Lange Anna is a decidedly threatening figure, one of the three "Herumtreiber" or vagabonds who provide a symbolic frame for the dramatic action (they tend to appear before and after things happen), and incorporate, in a concentrated form, the sexual confusion, the exhibitionism, the violence and the vulnerability that is played out by other characters. Pendel-frederich, with his septic eye that recalls the moon and his dangling penis, figures Lieschen's and Carl's pubescent confusion as well as Heinrich's and von Simon's sexual egotism and Marta's exhibitionistic wish to be photographed naked; his sinister murmurings signal the danger sexuality poses to the individual in a narrow-minded society of Christian and patriarchal morals.

Gläserner Amadeus, who has often been linked with Lasker-Schüler herself,[23] figures the emotional vulnerability of those individuals: Carl's hurt pride when he is rejected by the class-conscious Frau Sonntag, Lieschen's desperate screams when she is taken off to a corrective institution for unmarried mothers, the inner turmoil that drives Heinrich to suicide, Eduard's sense of loss at the play's end.

Lange Anna, the transvestite, figures their physical vulnerability, and the will to both play out and subvert this vulnerability in gender games. Anna's "hohe Weiberstimme" (16) signals the helpless feminine, something which Carl Pius responds to with a show of masculine strength when he twists the tramp's arm. But Carl himself confesses to cross-gender activity: "Ich habe sogar als Knabe mit Vorliebe weibliche Hand-arbeiten selbst ausgeführt" (29), and Heinrich briefly prefigures Frau Vogelsang of the later play when he imitates a woman for comic effect: "*ulkig einen Backfisch imitierend*: Das lass ich mir nicht mehr gefallen, mir macht kein Mensch den Hof" (26). The audience are invited to laugh at his performance of an inexperienced girl's lack of sexual sophistication, something which appears less funny in the context of Heinrich's own preference for pubescent girls. Another figure also partially antici-pates Alwine Vogelsang: the giant lady of the circus in the third act has "en Bart wie en Kerl" (39), but here the effect is not so much comic as grotesque. The woman with male secondary sexual characteristics is put on show as a monster, her transgressive body contained in the cage that is her circus wagon. The threat that goes out from Lange Anna is the threat of the uncontained, the "Herumtreiber," who brings heterosexuality into confusion, notably when he suggests to Eduard that Heinrich should have had sex with him, Anna, rather than with Lieschen: "Mich hätt' Ihr Bruder lieber nehmen sollen" (71).

Mutter Pius is likewise an important, if less obviously transgressive figure. She has been seen, like Grimmelshausen's Courasche,[24] as a *Frau Welt* figure;[25] and like Courasche she has provoked allergic reactions in critics. Tyson calls her "sinister" and "evil," while Klüsener describes her in very Courasche-esque terms as "eine zynische alte Vettel."[26] Perhaps the most unnerving characteristic of Mutter Pius, which she shares with Courasche, is her tendency to perform masculine authority. Within the symmetry of the drama she stands opposite Frau Sonntag — both of them widows and independent women. Where Frau Sonntag, as factory owner, has the economic power of a man, Mutter Pius has absolute authority in her extended working-class family, which comprises the Piuses, the Wallbreckers, and the Puderbachs. Stage directions — which are of great significance in Lasker-Schüler's dramas — tell us that Mutter Pius is "herrisch" (51), that is, she displays dominant masculinity. Like a patriarch she rules her family, and assumes responsibility for the organization of sexual relations, always with an eye to social improvement — it is Mutter Pius who encourages Carl in his pursuit of Marta, and makes Lieschen available to Heinrich Sonntag.

Like so many transgressive women in literature, including Courasche, Mutter Pius figures as a witch,[27] even practices alternative medicine (51). But before we cast her as dangerous, sinister, or cynical, or believe the characters in the play when they designate her "das Karussell, wo wir All drin sitzen" (64), we need to look at the outcome of her machinations. Carl does not in fact win Marta, and Lieschen's pregnancy is a disaster because Heinrich, instead of marrying her, commits suicide. Our last view of Mutter Pius, transmitted through the report of the maid Auguste, is not of a dominant, dangerous character, but of a broken old woman whose miscalculations have done irreversible damage, and who is now — Auguste reports — revolving distractedly around Heinrich Sonntag's corpse: "De Augen standen scheel wie beim Geripp un gedreht hat se sich [. . .] um de Leichen immer rund um ohne aufzuhören, un gesungen hat sie dabei [. . .] O Du lieber Augustin Alles ist hin, hin, hin" (64). Frau Sonntag, the powerful capitalist, is far more successful in maintaining her position, even at the cost of her two sons' lives: we hear of Heinrich's suicide and Eduard's projected death. Lasker-Schüler's play is by no means the apolitical piece it has been portrayed as. It is interesting that Frau Sonntag has never struck critics as sinister, even though her behavior is ruthless in the extreme — perhaps because, unlike Mother Pius's, her gestus is never "herrisch," always ladylike.

As a working-class, single, eccentric woman, Mutter Pius has characteristics typical of the historical witch.[28] One of the major problems associated with witch figures is that they appear incongruously powerful — incongruous because power "properly" goes with maleness, economic status, family status — and are therefore feared as supernatural. In *Arthur Aronymus und seine Väter*, Jewishness is associated with witchcraft by the Christian population, who see the economic power of the Schüler family as incongruous in the context of their own relative poverty. The "world upside-down" or incongruous world that characterizes notions of witchcraft[29] is present in the "Hexenlied" that is repeatedly sung: the notional witch is told "Zieh ding [= dein] Hexenschwänzlein ein" (124), a phallic image that communicates her improper masculinity.

The gender trangression inherent in the idea of witchcraft is made visible through crossdressing, when the children play out a witch trial: Arthur Aronymus appears in drag, wearing Dora's old clothes. But Arthur Aronymus is a boy, and can leap free of the restrictive garb of femininity — "*Auf einmal springt er über alle hinweg mit einem Satz, Doras Rock verlierend, den Mönch umreissend, vom Scheiterhaufen herunter*" (169–70). In this he distinguishes himself not only from Dora (who could not escape persecution so easily and suffered terrible fear earlier in the play, before the masculine authority of the bishop released her), but also from the female children in the play, notably the Kaplan's nieces, whom we have already seen as prisoners of their clothes, by contrast with the young hero: "*Die beiden Mädchen ordnen umständlich beim Niedersetzen die weiten Röcke, um sie nicht zu verrammeln. Arthur Aronimus [sic] [. . .] [sitzt] jäh mit einem Satz [. . .] auf dem Stuhl zwischen den Mädchen am Tisch*" (117).

The witch game that the children play is watched by the Kaplan and by a laughing Bishop. His laughter denies that the game is a reflection of the real threat of violence to which the family has been exposed. It echoes the Kaplan's rather facetious response to the threatening letter received by the Schülers earlier in the play (151); despite their support for the family, neither the bishop nor the Kaplan seem prepared to face the reality of anti-Semitic violence. It is the reality of the pogrom described in father Schüler's diary reading, a story told with even more attention to violent detail in the prose version, *Die Geschichte meines Vaters*:

An den geschmückten Zweigen der hohen Tannenbäume im Rathaus-
saale, in der Aula der Schulen, hatte man kleine Judenkinder wie Konfekt aufgehängt. Zarte Händchen und blutbespritzte Füßchen lagen,
verfallenes und totes Laub auf den Gassen des Ghettos umher [. . .].
Entblößte Körper, sie eindringlicher mißhandeln zu können, bluteten
zerrissen auf Splittern der Fenstergläser gespießt, unbeachtet unter kal-
tem Himmel.[30]

The "Konfekt" that is the bodies of dead Jewish children recalls the
"Konfekt" that Arthur Aronymus takes from the Kaplan's Christmas tree
in the play, only to be designated "dreister Judenjunge" (119): the
Kaplan's words are an echo of the dreadful physical brutality against Jews
that he and his bishop avoid acknowledging. The notion that such violence is a thing of the past is contradicted, in the prose version, by a
description of Fanny's partner at dance classes, who wears a glass eye
after falling victim to a "Privatjudenhetze" (17).

In both plays, *Die Wupper* and *Arthur Aronymus*, religion is an instance of patriarchal authority. The status it conveys on the individual can
be used to satisfy men's vanity: Carl Pius and Eduard Sonntag both try to
use it to transcend their relatively low-status position as sons and achieve
the authority of fathers; the Kaplan of *Arthur Aronymus* enjoys the position his handsome face and ecclesiastical status give him among the
Schüler sisters; and his bishop verges on the ridiculous when he endlessly
extends the episcopal hand to be kissed, "aus Gewohnheit," as Lasker-
Schüler adds every time in the stage directions.

But the effects of religion as an institution are not always harmlessly
amusing. Christianity in particular is shown to have been, historically, a
transporter of violence: Carl Pius's ruthless behavior in *Die Wupper* (he
twists Lange Anna's arm and incites the workers to commit murder) is
the tip of an iceberg that begins to emerge more fully in the later play,
Arthur Aronymus. Here the motif of witch burnings recalls one of the
most violent episodes in Christianity's history. The bull read by the
Kaplan, as well as protecting the Jewish family, bears witness to the
inherent brutality of certain Christian beliefs: "Mit tausend Zungen" the
bishop threatens, "werde ich dem Himmel jedes Frevlers Sünde verkün-
den, dass seine Seele brate bis zum jüngsten Tag!" (162). The notion of
hell invoked here might be read as one explanation for the populace's
penchant for violence and burnings. But not only Christian structures
betray their inherent violence: in the patriarchally arranged Jewish
Schüler family, the burden of responsibility for upholding patriarchal
privilege — not to mention the matter of twenty-three children — nearly
finishes off Frau Schüler.[31]

All the religions that appear in the plays — Catholicism, Protestantism, Judaism — are seen to support repressive structures that are transgressed at a price. Lange Anna, the transvestite, is attacked by the would-be pastor Carl Pius; Mutter Pius offends against sexual moral codes and engenders disaster, particularly for Lieschen; Frau Sonntag attempts to hold a patriarchal position in her family and watches two of her sons die; and Frau Vogelsang, the most transgressive figure in *Arthur Aronymus*, is reported to have died along with her husband, after an oddly ruthless death wish for the two of them has been expressed by the Schülers.

The place of the writing self in all this is, typically for Lasker-Schüler, relatively explicit. We have observed that this is a writer who does not uphold the objectivist notion that would keep writers separate from the fictions and characters they create. In *Die Wupper*, the dramatist associates herself explicitly with one of the vagabond figures, Gläserner Amadeus. Lasker-Schüler wrote: "wenn ich nicht die Else Lasker-Schüler leider [. . .] geboren worden, ich stände als Amadeus, vereint mit den Kollegen, im Winkel der Nacht."[32] We have seen that Amadeus is the character who figures emotional vulnerability — his heart is made of cracked glass, and is constantly in danger of breaking. This, Parr argues convincingly, "symbolisiert [. . .] einmal das zerbrechliche Herz des Dichters [der Dichterin? S. C.], das zusammenschlägt vor Mitgefühl [. . .] zum anderen zeigt das zersprungene Herz den Riß in der "Wupper"-Welt an, die gleichsam in Scherben geht."[33] The importance of the heart for Lasker-Schüler is clear throughout her work (not least in the novel called *Mein Herz*);[34] and what *Die Wupper* shows us, transmitted via the seismographic qualities or heart of the writer, is how vulnerable human beings are, as they try to manage their individual lives in the context of the powerful social and religious systems they have built for themselves.

In *Arthur Aronymus* the central character is the father from whom the writer will descend. Arthur Aronymus, too, has seismographic qualities, as his ability to see the angel of death and to function as a medium for his dead grandfather illustrates. As the father of a writer (Lasker-Schüler), it is important that his words, or the words spoken through him, should be the most authoritative use of language in the play. In a letter, Lasker-Schüler once traced her literary family tree through the maternal, rather than the paternal, line: "Meine Mama hat früher immer mit mir gedichtet [. . .] Meine Großmutter war eine Dichterin gewesen und starb so früh, sie hieß: Johanna Kopp."[35] So it is worth asking why Lasker-Schüler chose to tell "Die Geschichte meines Vaters" rather than the story of her mother or grandmother, even if the answer can only be speculative. Considering Lasker-Schüler's performance of Joseph of Thebes (Jussuf), Mary O'Brien has suggested that "since the outer manifestation of male identity rather than any personality trait is seen as the key to acceptance, the only position open for a female speaker in search of recognition is to embrace a male sexual identity."[36] Perhaps, too, the authority Lasker-Schüler was looking for as a writer could only really come via the paternal line, since authoritative language — particularly in the religious and cultural context of *Arthur Aronymus* — can only be inherited and transported by men.

Plurality and Resistance: *IchundIch*

The most controversial and these days the most frequently discussed of Else Lasker-Schüler's dramas is *IchundIch*. Even critics who otherwise ignore Lasker-Schüler's dramatic work discuss this play.[37] The temptation may lie in the fact that *IchundIch*, with its fragmentary and intertextual form, prefigures postmodern theater,[38] and therefore lends itself rewardingly to recent critical approaches. As always one should be careful of attaching tags: Fischer-Lichte also sees the work in the tradition of epic theater, and Schalom Ben-Chorin has aligned it with the absurd theater of the 1950s.[39]

The publication history of *IchundIch* needs mention. Lasker-Schüler hoped for publication in the early 1940s, but her publisher chose instead to print the volume of poetry called *Mein blaues Klavier*.[40] After her death in 1945, Werner Kraft (editor of the first *Gesammelte Werke*)[41] and Ernst Ginsberg were extremely reluctant to see a full publication of the play: both felt that it would damage the posthumous image of Else Lasker-Schüler.[42] Kraft finally edited excerpts for the *Nachlaß* volume. Recent critics have interpreted the suppression of *IchundIch* in different ways: Klüsener explains it with reference to the messy manuscript Lasker left, which made the play look in a worse state than it was,[43] and Lorenz reads it as a misunderstanding or misreading, arguing that what *Ichund-Ich* shows is not linguistic or mental collapse, but "the breakdown of the poet's established language and symbols in the face of an unprecedented global catastrophe."[44] Hedgepeth suspects a masculinist attempt to suppress Lasker-Schüler's "écriture feminine" ("Sah man die Gattung Drama noch als Gebiet der männlich-nüchternen Aussage, in der die weiblich-subjektive Schreibweise [. . .] nur schlecht gebracht war?),[45] while Feßmann, by contrast, credits Kraft and Ginsberg with the sensitivity to recognize "die Ungeheuerlichkeit dieses Textes,"[46] the full violence of its shocking impact.

IchundIch, rather like *Die Wupper*, is a text which uses violence juxtaposed with bizarre comedy: a form of comedy that is grotesquely rather
than straightforwardly funny. Faust and Mephisto meet Hitler's National
Socialists in the realm of the devil, Hell. The Nazis' drunken yobbery at
Mephisto's table might conceivably be played as comical, when they sing
together: "Ich allein ja ich alleine bin ein Teufel comme il faut!" (201);
there is certainly entertainment value in the fact that the devil himself is
disgusted by them — "*Mephisto erhebt sich vornehm! angeekelt.*" However, one function of comedy is to defuse threat; and here, even though
we might laugh, the threat posed by Lasker's Nazis is barely diminished
by their grotesque behavior, because their lack of self-control does not
make them less dangerous. The act closes soon after with music "*von den
verwilderten heiseren Stimmen der Nacis [sic] brutal begleitet. fünfmalhunderttausend [sic] Teufel — etc.*" (202).

A more classic comic role is played by Marthe Schwertlein (Lasker-
Schüler's orthography), when she upsets the linguistic agency of the
propaganda minister. The historical Goebbels was the central propagator
of Nazi ideas through language; Lasker-Schüler has Frau Marthe render
him ineffectual, because her comic mis-hearings negate his power to
communicate. Göbbels (Lasker-Schüler's orthography) tries to describe
and glorify the Nazis, but for his word, "Wotan" (which casts Hitler as
a mighty Germanic god),[47] she hears "Truthahn" (turkey) an animal
associated with puffed-up ineffectuality. Later, when Göbbels is seeking
Mephisto's help to save the sinking Nazi troops, Frau Marthe mishears
their imminent fate — "sonst [. . .] versaufen sie" (220) — and in a kind
of Chinese whisper she reports words to Mephisto that change the message to reflect Nazi brutality: "sonst [. . .] raufen sie! Raufen sie!"
Lasker-Schüler's Marthe Schwertlein is an unintentionally subversive
figure, who renders Nazi speech acts infelicitous or failed; hence she
undermines their linguistic power and involuntarily contributes to the
process of their destruction. At the end of act 4, after the Nazi hordes
have sunk into the lava flood, the music from the end of act 2 is repeated
("Freut euch des Lebens da noch ein Lämpchen glüht"), but this time
without the violent words of the Nazis' "fünfmalhunderttausend Teufel"
song dominantly superimposed. The disappearance of the threat is confirmed, because the linguistic violence (or, in modern terminology, hate
speech) of the Nazis is removed along with the words of their song.

For all that the play uses caricature and comedy, we should not
overlook the horror of it, and its potential to shock. Else Lasker-Schüler
wrote a drama for performance (although in fact it only came to a reading) in early 1940s Jerusalem; a drama in which characters shout "Heil

Hitler" and "Juda verrecke,"[48] all-too-familiar and deeply disturbing reminders of real verbal and physical violence for the emigré Jews who were her audience. As she did in *Arthur Aronymus und seine Väter*, the dramatist puts historically "real" characters on stage (many of whom were, of course, still alive at the time of writing) — Reichsmarschall Hermann Göring; Reichsaußenminister Joachim von Ribbentrop, with the SS leader Heinrich Himmler and the Nazi Reichsleiter Alfred Rosenberg; Nazi minister for propaganda Joseph Goebbels; Hitler's deputy Rudolf Hess and the youth leader Baldur von Schirach; Adolf Hitler; the executed communist Marinus van der Lubbe and the Polish anti-Nazi Herschel Grynszpan; the theater director Max Reinhardt along with the American Ritz brothers and the Berlin actors Karl Hannemann and Aribert Wäscher; and Gershom Swet, who edited the Hebrew newspaper *Ha'aretz* ("The Country"). To these Lasker-Schüler adds Faust, Mephistopheles, and Marthe Schwerdtlein (all from Goethe's *Faust*); the Old Testament figures of King David and Baal (a graven image); a scarecrow; and "die Dichterin der Tragödie" — who is clearly related to, although not identical with, Else Lasker-Schüler.[49]

Interesting is how the central characters (whom I take to be Faust, Mephistopheles, the Dichterin, and the Nazis as a group) relate to each other in a structural sense. Our expectations of theater include distinct characters, whose individuality often leads them into conflict with one another. None of the central figures in *IchundIch* is characterized in a way that completely distinguishes her or him from all of the others. Faust and Mephistopheles, for a start, are — in the words of the director, Reinhardt — "ein Zwillingspaar! Ja, 'ein' Mensch im Grunde" (194);[50] the oneness of the pair is made visible when they combine to perform a single physical action: *"[Faust] verbirgt seinen Kopf erschüttert in Mephistos Händen"* (224) — it is more usual, of course, to hide one's head in one's own hands. But this is not a simple binary arrangement.[51] Faust is also indistinct from his author, Johann Wolfgang von Goethe, and Mephisto tends to speak to Faust as if he were the writer as well as the character, congratulating him on his poem *Wandrers Nachtlied* ("Über allen Gipfeln") and referring to Goethe's mother ("Frau Rätin") as if she were Faust's (209).

In terms of his sympathies — whose side he stands on — Faust is problematically indistinct from the Nazis. He rises to warn them of the danger that awaits them in hell, and when Mephisto holds him back, he expresses a wish to perish along with them — "Ich versänke gern dort mit dem Heere in den Tod!" (221). Faust, then, is *also* the devil who seduced him;[52] he is *also* his own author and the creator of some of the most admired texts in German literature; and he is *also* indissoluble from the most reviled criminals in German political history. Moving outside the drama, we acquire a perspective that suggests the German people, like Faust, are *also* the "devil" who, in the early 1940s, has seduced them (Nazism, Hitler). Lasker-Schüler does not exclude herself from this: she is linked both with Faust (who recites one of her poems, 193)[53] and with the Dichterin of the play, who dies at the same time the Nazis are defeated. She thereby experiences the fate Lasker's Faust wished for himself: to share in their fall. Even if you are a German Jewish writer (she seems to suggest), or even if you are Goethe (whom she admired so much), you cannot get away with portraying evil for which only the devil is responsible.

At the end of the play, the Dichterin is also the Scarecrow, who is again linked with Goethe (229). Various interpretations of the Scarecrow have been attempted: the figure has recently been read as yet another male incarnation of creativity (like Prinz Jussuf or Gläserner Amadeus), behind which the woman poet is hiding,[54] and, from another critical perspective, as André Breton's scarecrow of death.[55] Lasker-Schüler herself, in her *Zürcher Abschiedsrede*, described the German emigrés as "verscheuchte Vögel";[56] if the Dichterin of *IchundIch* is both "verscheuchter Vogel" and "Vogelscheuche," then she is not distanced from events in a binary sense (good self, bad other), but simultaneously passively affected and actively implicated as scarecrow *and* scared crow.

Her death at the end of the play is quite unlike Faust's at the end of Goethe's *Faust II*: there are no angels, no devils, no divine voices, indeed no religious trappings at all, as the scarecrow observes — "ohn [*sic*] Geistlichkeit, Raf, Scheik, Pastor" (234). Gretchen, who in Goethe's play is Mephisto's counterpart in the fight for Faust's soul, is absent; in Lasker-Schüler's drama each character is responsible for his own salvation, and Faust and the devil achieve it together: "*Es wölben sich Kronen aus Wolken um die Stirnen Mephistos und Fausts*" (225). In one sense the Dichterin takes Gretchen's place, namely as the connecting point between human being and God. After her death on stage at the end of the play she returns to answer the "Gretchenfrage":[57] "Glaubst du an Gott?" with an affirmation: "Gott ist 'da'!!" (235).[58] As if in response to Baal's dictum that without God, human beings are dead even while alive ("Was ist der Mensch doch ohne Gott? — Lebendig ist er tot!," 215), we now see the Dichterin alive even though she is dead.

Much has been written about the "Ichspaltung" in Lasker-Schüler's work, particularly with reference to this drama.[59] The title, of course, invites it: one could quickly develop the idea that we are looking here at a split or divided subject: the divided self of Sue-Ellen Case's work on women dramatists,[60] or more generally at a postmodern subject that is not identical with itself. But the title also recalls another work by a contemporary of Lasker-Schüler's, with whose writings she was familiar: Martin Buber's theological-philosophical text *Ich und Du* (1923).[61] Buber distinguishes between the "Ich-Du" and the "Ich-Es" relation, whereby the former is, roughly speaking, a subjective relation, the latter objective. Lasker-Schüler's "Ich und Ich" synthesizes these two standpoints, and suggests that the relationship both to the "Du" and to the "Es" can be held within the relationship to the plural "Ich." In the commentary to her 1970 edition of the play, Kupper establishes the proper orthography of the title (not *Ich und Ich*,[62] but more closely bound as *IchundIch*), and positions the search for the "whole" self as central to the drama: "Im Vordergrund steht die Liebe des Ich zum Ich, die Sehnsucht nach der Selbstbegegnung, der Vollendung in der ganzheitlichen Person."[63] This view can be supported with reference to the drama — the Dichterin opens the first act with a prophecy:

> auf der weiten Bühne werden wir uns finden.
> Zwischen Tugenden und Sünden,
> — Geklärt zum Schluss sich ich und ich verbinden! (188)

The fictional Dichterin also makes reference to Lasker-Schüler's earlier work; for example the passage in *Das Gebet* that recalls the story of the androgyne as the original human form: "Den Menschen aber brach [der Schöpfer], geschaffen, ins leuchtende Welteden gestellt, in zwei Hälften. Und so drängt es den Menschen, sich immer zu teilen, um sich wiederzufinden."[64] Both of these passages can be read, like the notion of the androgyne, as the expression of a binary structure in human life whose most basic form is male-female. This structure is reproduced in Goethe's *Faust*, as masculine-feminine ("das Ewig-Weibliche zieht uns(!) hinan").[65]

We should not overlook the fact that such a binary is *not* reproduced in Lasker-Schüler's play: the Dichterin of the drama may claim to have divided "in zwei Teile: IchundIch!" (188), but the arrangements Faust-Mephisto, Faust-Goethe, Faust-Goethe-Dichterin, Dichterin-Faust-Goethe-Nazis, Dichterin-Vogelscheuche, etcetera, represent not binary but *plural* structures. "IchundIch" can be "IchundIchundIch," or even "IchundIchundIchundIch." It can be read as multiplication rather than a division of the self, like the line from Lasker-Schüler's epistolary novel *Mein Herz*: "Ich, ich ich, ich kann mich kaum mehr berühren vor Süße."[66] One might profitably read this as feminine in Irigaray's sense, as an expression of the "sex which is not one,"[67] or indeed in the spirit of Elisabeth Lenk's "sich selbst verdoppelnde Frau."[68] Neither of these theoretical notions of the feminine require that what is not monolithic must be binary (that would in itself be a binary thought!): Lenk, for example, suggests that the woman who has recognized her place in masculinist culture is multiple in relation to herself, and that the doubling process is not one unique act but repeatable: "Im neuen Verhältnis der Frau zu sich ist sie Viele [. . .] die *zum ersten Mal* sich selbst verdoppelnde Frau" (my emphasis).[69]

The point of all this in the context of this volume is that Lasker-Schüler shows us a "dichterisches Selbst," a dramatic ego, that is plural; she *also* demonstrates that the acceptance of plurality (the acceptance that we are implicated even in those human events that repel us and always already persecutors as well as victims, as the Faust-Mephisto figure illustrates), is one path to resistance. Baal, the graven image, complains "daß doch der Mensch sein böses Tun dem Teufel in die Schuhe schiebt"; the significance of this emerges if we realize that Baal is structurally parallel with the other false god of the play, Hitler — described by Göbbels as "Germanias Gott" and "unser Ariergott" (204). Interestingly, Buber in *Ich und Du* warned:

> Wem aber die Nation ein Götze ist, dem er alles dienstbar machen möchte, weil er in dessen Bild das eigne erhöht, — wähnt ihr, ihr brauchtet es ihm nur zu verleiden und er schaute die Wahrheit? [. . .] Wehe dem Besessenen, der Gott zu besitzen meint![70]

Unlike in *Faust*, where evil is isolated as other and left behind when the hero is taken up to heaven, in *IchundIch* we see evil accepted as part of the self and then destroyed. The self (in the form of the Dichterin) dies with it, but only after she has supervised evil's destruction in hell — the all-embracing plurality even undemonizes the devil, accepting him as one part of the Faust-Goethe-Dichterin self and allowing him to work to destroy human evil, rather than making him responsible for it.

Hand in hand with this, however, is an anti-relativism that recognizes the extremity of the evil that the Nazis represent and is prepared to meet it with extreme measures. Here again Baal, as anti-Hitler, has a symbolic function: he stands as an Old Testament-style divinity of justice and revenge and drives the process of destruction, which (again, Old Testament-style) takes the form of a divinely ordained "natural" disaster, a lava flood. The pseudo-humane relativism of Faust, that impels him to warn the Nazi troops of what awaits them, reminds us of the tolerant Kaplan and the Bishop of *Arthur Aronymus*, who similarly failed to comprehend the enormity of the Jews' situation, laughing at a threatening letter and at the children's "burn the witch" game.

Ichundich is a play within a play, or, more precisely, a play rehearsal within a play.[71] The frame is Lasker-Schüler's contemporary Jerusalem, into which she has imported Max Reinhardt (who was in fact in exile in the USA) as the play's director. Even though it is most obvious in the prologue (where the "Dichterin des Schauspiels" is on her way to the theater with an unnamed companion) and in the final act, which plays in the garden of an optician in Jerusalem, we never in fact leave the frame behind us during the action. Because we are watching a rehearsal, rather than a polished performance, the characters of the frame — notably Reinhardt and the Dichterin — regularly intervene to comment on characterization and pronunciation, or to discuss possible cuts in the text with each other.

The framework is one of the classic techniques used by Brecht to achieve alienation — for example in *Der Kaukasische Kreidekreis*, which was written just after Lasker-Schüler's play.[72] In *IchundIch*, alienation is certainly one effect of the rehearsal within the play: the interventions remind us that the characters are not real, but are being played by actors. The particular nature of the interventions — comments made by the director and the author — makes explicit what tends to be true in theater, namely that events on stage are devised and controlled by the writer and director. Lasker-Schüler reminds us that her dramatic ego is driving the action, which plays on the "Herzensbühne" (186) of the Dichterin. So alienation here is functioning on the one hand in the Brechtian manner, confronting the audience with themselves in the theater; and on the other hand working to confront the audience with the dramatist, the Dichterin. At the same time as presenting a play dealing with political criminality of enormous import to her, Lasker-Schüler presents herself on stage, and the stage as a location where the confrontation of the self with the self is made possible:

> Wir haben, wie mein Publikum erfahren wird,
> Zu mimen ungeheuerlich Genie
> Und da vermischt im dunklen, engen Leibe nie,
> So auf der weiten Bühne werden wir uns finden. (188)

The poet who once wrote that "im Spiegel der Bäche finde ich mein Bild nicht mehr"[73] (thus anticipating Elisabeth Lenk's theoretical diagnosis: "Es kommen die Schreckensmomente, wo die Frau sich im Spiegel sucht und nicht mehr findet"),[74] finds the mirror image of her self on the stage, in drama, and reproduces that self in the self-multiplications that are her characters. This is not in itself an unusual process — every writer engages in self-multiplication and always has. What is unusual is the self-awareness that accompanies it, and the will to communicate the process to the reader/audience.

In the same year as Lasker-Schüler died, leaving *IchundIch* incomplete, Simone de Beauvoir wrote of the collective responsibility for freedom: "chacun est responsable de tout, devant tous";[75] in a similar vein, Lasker-Schüler sees the inclusion of the Nazis in her multiplications of self as an essential ingredient in enabling resistance.

The Self on the Stage

Else Lasker-Schüler — like so many women writers — was received from the start as the exception to a rule.[76] That she viewed herself as the exception to a rule, and performed outsider status in her daily life as well as investigating it in her writing, should be seen in this context. Calvin Jones notes quite rightly that critics' judgments "were often influenced [. . .] by their opinions of the groups or categories to which they assigned this author: as a modern, a Jewish, or a woman poet."[77] In 1904, Peter Hille characterized his protegée as "die jüdische Dichterin."[78] Like Kraus's remark about her literary masculinity cited above, this seems to be a compliment, but reveals its anti-Semitic edge when Hille adds: "Jüdische Dichter, schöpferische Dichter aus Judäerblut sind selten"[79] — once again, Else Lasker-Schüler is posited as the exception to a chauvinistic rule.

Robertson has shown how ideas about femininity and Jewishness are linked, especially in the early twentieth century:[80] slyness and moral weakness (among other things) are held to characterize women and Jews. This makes it all the more disturbing when later critics, observing the synthesis of fact and fiction that characterizes Lasker-Schüler's life and work, question her "schriftstellerische Redlichkeit" (whatever *that* is supposed to be) or accuse her of "Verlogenheit."[81] Lasker-Schüler was certainly creative with her biography. She changed her own birth date more than once, setting it later all the time; she regularly masqueraded in male costume and assumed male identities, especially that of her literary creation Jussuf of Thebes; she re-invented her own family history. But a newer critical vocabulary enables us to move away from morally-laden terms and describe her self-presentation as an individual and a writer as *performance*. Performance as masquerade can subvert and resist: Sieg points out that "Jussuf, the pauper-prince of Thebes [. . .] flaunted the ethnic-racial Other in images of oriental splendor."[82] But Judith Butler's notion of performance also includes the element of coercion that is always present in the social context:[83] Lasker-Schüler, we might contend, both chose a camp and orientalist gestus (she was known for her outrageous clothes and jewelry) and was coerced by gendered and anti-Semitic assumptions.

One reason, perhaps, why she was perceived as untypical among women is that Lasker-Schüler persistently took center stage — she flouted the spatial norm that positions men as performers, women as their appreciative audience. This led — as is so often the case when women take center stage — to a certain fetishization of her corporeality: the proprietorial masculinist gaze seems impelled to rest on the woman who has put herself on show. Helmut Hirsch (a Jewish Wuppertaler who later emigrated to Chicago) remembers the writer as "das schön gebaute Mädchen" who wore snippets of silk "in allen möglichen Verschlingungen und Verschleifungen um den Leib herum [. . .]. Natürlich tuschelten die Zeitgenossen";[84] and Gottfried Benn, too, focuses on her as an exotic body, in his description of her as a young woman:

> Sie war klein, damals knabenhaft schlank, hatte pechschwarze Haare, kurzgeschnitten, was zu der Zeit noch selten war, große rabenschwarze Augen [. . .]. Man konnte weder damals noch später mit ihr über die Straße gehen, ohne daß alle Welt stillstand und ihr nachsah.[85]

Lasker-Schüler inhabited what we might describe as a plural body: German and Jewish, woman and writer, and — in her performance particularly of Jussuf— male as well as female. We can read traces of the coercion to which she was exposed in the critical responses to her work over the last century. The oriental motif she adopted, but which was also imposed on her as a Jew, was picked up by a reviewer of one of her readings, who wrote: "Ihr Gesicht ist von einer orientalischen Sinnlichkeit, ihr Körper hat etwas Schlangenhaftes."[86]

O'Brien has suggested that "Lasker-Schüler's transition from a female to a male voice [Tino of Baghdad to Jussuf of Thebes, S. C.] is a narrative strategy to empower the subject, elicit recognition, and gain access to a public forum."[87] There is something in this. Lasker-Schüler on the one hand accepts the definitions of her self that are available — she plays up the Jewish oriental idea and insists that her mode of writing is femininely non-logocentric.[88] But she also adopts a masculine persona; and that not only elicits recognition in the public sphere, but confuses her reception as one distinct self. We do not need to pass moral judgment on this: it is neither an achievement nor a problem, but one part of the interest of Lasker-Schüler as a writer.

Notes

[1] For example, by Paul Fechter, in the *Deutsche Allgemeine Zeitung* of 17 October 1927; but also by Sigrid Bauschinger, *Else Lasker-Schüler: Ihr Werk und ihre Zeit* (Heidelberg: Stiehm, 1980), 235.

[2] Cited in Sigismund von Radecki, "Erinnerungen an Else Lasker-Schüler" (1950), in *Else Lasker-Schüler: Dichtungen und Dokumente*, ed. by Ernst Ginsberg (Munich: Kösel, 1951), 575–82 (578).

[3] Radecki, 576.

[4] See Markus Hallersleben, *Else Lasker-Schüler: Avantgardismus und Kunstinszenierung* (Tübingen: Francke, 2000), 12–13.

[5] Else Lasker-Schüler, *Dramen*, ed. by Georg-Michael Schulz (*Werke und Briefe: Kritische Ausgabe*, ed. by Norbert Oellers, Heinz Röllecke and Itta Shedletzky, vol. 2) (Frankfurt a. M.: Suhrkamp, 1997), 305.

[6] Martin Krumbholz, "Hölle, Jahrmarkt, Garten Eden: Zum dramatischen Werk der Else Lasker-Schüler," in *Text und Kritik* 4 (1994), 42–53 (42).

[7] Peter K. Tyson, "Else Lasker-Schüler's *Die Wupper*: Between Naturalism and Expressionism," in *AUMLA: Journal of the Australasian Universities Language and Literature Association* 64 (1985), 144–53.

[8] Sonja M. Hedgepeth, *"Überall blicke ich nach einem heimatlichen Boden aus": Exil im Werk Else Lasker-Schülers* (New York: Lang, 1994), 184.

[9] Interestingly, while the 1927 show was well received and reviewed, the Cologne audience of the late 1950s was disgusted and left the theater.

[10] See Jürgen Flimm, "Wupper-Notizen," in *Theater heute* 4 (1985), 16–17.

[11] Lasker-Schüler was certain that the reasons for this were political; Lindtberg later claims it was a direct result of an altercation between the playwright and the theater director's wife. See Hedgepeth, 187.

[12] Lasker-Schüler, *Dramen*, 349.

[13] Lasker-Schüler, *Verse und Prosa aus dem Nachlaß*, ed. by Werner Kraft (Munich: Kösel, 1961).

[14] Kupper, "*IchundIch*: Nachlaßschauspiel," in *Jahrbuch der deutschen Schillergesellschaft* 14 (1970), 24–99. Kupper also published her edition in 1980, as *Else Lasker-Schüler, Ichundich: eine theatralische Komödie* (Munich: Kösel, 1980).

[15] See Andrea Parr, *Drama als "Schreitende Lyrik": Die Dramatikerin Else Lasker-Schüler* (Frankfurt a. M.: Lang, 1988), 46. Parr also notes that a play called *Der Fakir* is mentioned in a letter to Karl Kraus of 1911 — this piece was in fact part of a varieté project planned by Lasker-Schüler, rather than a free-standing drama.

[16] *Arthur Aronymus und seine Väter*, in Else Lasker-Schüler, *Dramen*, 73–182 (152). All references are to this edition of the play.

[17] *Die Wupper*, in Else Lasker-Schüler, *Dramen*, 7–72 (51). All references are to this edition of the play.

[18] Lasker-Schüler, *Arthur Aronymus: Die Geschichte meines Vaters* (Berlin: Rowohlt, 1932), 8. An interesting detail is that Arthur Aronymus's mother has the last word in this story (this is not true for the drama).

[19] Schulz points out that the final "r" in the transliteration is an error. Lasker-Schüler, *Dramen*, 312.

[20] Sigrid Bauschinger, "Else Lasker-Schüler's *Die Wupper*," in *Thalia's Daughters: German Women Dramatists from the Eighteenth Century to the Present*, ed. by Susan L. Cocalis and Ferrel Rose (Tübingen: Francke, 1996), 161–72 (169).

[21] Krumbholz, 47.

[22] For a full discussion of this tradition see Sarah Colvin, *The Rhetorical Feminine: Gender and Orient on the German Stage, 1647–1742* (Oxford: Clarendon, 1999), 233–79.

[23] See for example Hedgepeth, 184; Parr, 55.

[24] Hans Jakob Christoph von Grimmelshausen, *Lebensbeschreibung der Erzbetrügerin und Landstörzerin Courasche*, ed. by Klaus Haberkam and Günther Weydt (Stuttgart: Reclam, 1986).

[25] Frau Welt is a medieval figure, generally portrayed as a woman who looks beautiful from the front, but reveals corruption and decay if viewed from the rear. The comparison with Mutter Pius is made by F. N. Mennemeier, *Modernes Deutsches Drama*, vol. 1, 1910–33 (Munich: Fink, 1979); cited in Parr, 61.

[26] Tyson, 149–50; Erika Klüsener, *Else Lasker-Schüler* (Reinbek bei Hamburg: Rowohlt, 1998 [1980]), 70.

[27] Compare Katrin Sieg, *Exiles, Eccentrics, Activists: Women in Contemporary German Theater* (Ann Arbor: U of Michigan P, 1994), 94.

[28] See Sigrid Brauner, *Fearless Wives and Frightened Shrews: The Construction of the Witch in Early Modern Germany*, edited with an introduction by Robert H. Brown (Amherst: U of Massachussetts P, 1995).

[29] See Stuart Clark, "Inversion, Misrule and the Meaning of Witchcraft," in *Past and Present* 87 (1980), 98–127 (104).

[30] Lasker-Schüler, *Arthur Aronymus: Die Geschichte meines Vaters*, 8–9.

[31] To put this in a context: it is perhaps worth knowing that Lasker-Schüler's historical grandmother, Rosa, died shortly after the birth of her tenth child (Aron, Lasker-Schüler's father, was her sixth); Moses Schüler, Lasker-Schüler's grandfather, married her younger sister, and the family was expanded by another seven children. Lasker-Schüler herself was the youngest of six children, and her mother, who suffered from chronic depression, died at age fifty-two, when her youngest daughter was twenty-one. The dramatist did not observe women leading long and fulfilled lives in German Jewish families.

[32] Lasker-Schüler, "Brief an Jessner," in *Gesammelte Werke*, vol. 2: *Prosa und Schauspiele*, ed. by Friedhelm Kemp (Munich: Kösel, 1962), 657–60 (657–58).

[33] Parr, 55.

[34] Lasker-Schüler, *Mein Herz: Ein Liebesroman mit Bildern und wirklich lebenden Menschen* (Munich: Bachmair, 1912).

[35] Letter to Paul Goldschneider, 3 June 1927; cited in Klüsener, 21.

[36] O'Brien,"'Ich war verkleidet als Poet . . . ich bin Poetin!!'": The Masquerade of Gender in Else Lasker-Schüler's Work," in *The German Quarterly* 65.1 (1992), 1–17 (3).

[37] For example Meike Feßmann, *Spielfiguren: Die Ich-Figurationen Else Lasker-Schülers als Spiel mit der Autorrolle: Ein Beitrag zur Poetologie des modernen Autors* (Stuttgart: M & P, 1992); Markus Hallersleben, *Else Lasker-Schüler: Avantgardismus und Kunstinszenierung* (Tübingen: Franke, 2000); Sissel Laegreid, *Nach dem Tode — oder vor dem Leben: Das poetische Projekt Else Lasker-Schülers* (Frankfurt a. M.: Lang, 1997).

[38] See Erika Fischer-Lichte, "Frauen erobern die Bühne: Dramatikerinnen im 20. Jahrhundert," in *Deutsche Literatur von Frauen*, ed. by Gisela Brinker-Gabler, vol. 2 (Munich: Beck, 1988), 379–93 (384).

[39] Fischer-Lichte, 381; Schalom Ben-Chorin, "Der Schwanengesang des schwarzen Schwans," in *Mitteilungsblatt* 4 (30 January 1981), 6.

[40] Klüsener, 120.

[41] Lasker-Schüler, *Gesammelte Werke*, ed. by Friedhelm Kemp and Werner Kraft, 3 vols. (Munich: Kösel, 1961–62).

[42] Ginsberg asked Manfred Sturmann in a letter of 2 September 1958 to persuade Kraft not to publish the play: "Denn dies Drama ist doch der Spiegel einer jammervollen Verstörung und Auflösung." Cited in Kupper, "Nachwort," in Else Lasker-Schüler, *Die Wupper und andere Dramen* (Munich: dtv, 1986), 301–309 (308).

[43] Klüsener, 120.

[44] Dagmar C. G. Lorenz, "Jewish Women Authors and the Exile Experience: Claire Goll, Veza Canetti, Else Lasker-Schüler, Nelly Sachs, Cornelia Edvardson," in *German Life and Letters* 51 (1998), 225–39 (236).

[45] Hedgepeth, 214.

[46] Feßmann, 263.

[47] Lasker-Schüler may here be making a reference to Toller's play *Der entfesselte Wotan* of 1923, in which a radically right-wing German hairdresser is parodied. I am grateful to Professor Moray McGowan (Trinity College Dublin) and Dr. Peter Davies (University of Edinburgh) for this reference.

[48] Lasker-Schüler, *IchundIch*, in *Dramen*, 183–235. All references are to this edition of the text.

[49] See also Gesa Dane, "Die Dichterin als Rabbinerin: Geschichte und Erinnerung in Else Lasker-Schüler's 'IchundIch,'" in *Text und Kritik* 4 (1994), 55–64 (57).

[50] In this play, Lasker-Schüler uses inverted commas ('ein') to signal emphasis.

[51] Margarete Kupper envisages the Dichterin, Faust, Mephisto, and the Vogelscheuche in a circular arrangement, whereby each is linked with the other. She does not, however, include the Nazis in her diagram. See Kupper, "*IchundIch*: Nachlaßschauspiel," note 32a.

[52] In Goethe's play. Here in Lasker-Schüler's drama, Baal comments critically: "das doch der Mensch sein böses Tun dem Teufel in die Schuhe schiebt," 214.

[53] Compare Dane, 58.

[54] Hedgepeth, 211.

[55] Hallersleben, 273.

[56] Lasker-Schüler, "Zürcher Abschiedsrede," reprinted in Hallersleben, 333.

[57] See Johann Wolfgang Goethe, Faust. Der Tragödie erster Teil (Stuttgart: Reclam, 1986), line 3426.

[58] A certain amount of ink has been spilt over the matter of the inverted commas. As is clear from the excellent edition of the play that appeared recently in the Jüdischer Verlag (Lasker-Schüler, Dramen) — which reproduces the original punctuation — inverted commas are used throughout to mark emphasis, much as italics are used in the modern convention. Lasker-Schüler does not use them to signal postmodern doubts or self-distancing, as a contemporary writer might.

[59] For example by Margarete Kupper, in her "Nachwort" to her 1980 edition of Lasker-Schüler's Ichundich, 80; by Sieg, 94; by Krumbholz, 51; and by almost every other commentator on the text.

[60] See Case, The Divided Home/Land: Contemporary German Women's Plays (Ann Arbor: U of Michigan P, 1992).

[61] Buber, Ich und Du (Stuttgart: Reclam, 1995). I am indebted to Dr. Mark Taplin for this reference.

[62] This orthography is still used by Heinz Thiel in 1969; see Thiel,"'Ich und Ich' — ein versperrtes Werk?," in Lasker-Schüler: Ein Buch zum 100. Geburtstag der Dichterin, ed by Michael Schmid (Wuppertal: Hammer, 1969), 123–55.

[63] Kupper, "IchundIch: Nachlaßschauspiel," 41.

[64] "Das Gebet," in Lasker-Schüler, Gesammelte Werke vol. 2, 776–84 (779–80).

[65] See Johann Wolfgang von Goethe, Faust. Der Tragödie zweiter Teil (Stuttgart: Reclam, 1986), lines 12110–11.

[66] Mein Herz: Ein Liebesroman mit Bildern und wirklich lebenden Menschen, in Lasker-Schüler, Gesammelte Werke vol. 2, 289–391 (363).

[67] Luce Irigaray, This Sex Which is Not One, transl. by Katharine Porter (Ithaca, NY: Cornell UP, 1985).

[68] Lenk, "Die sich selbst verdoppelnde Frau," in Lenk, Kritische Phantasie: Gesammelte Essays (Munich: Matthes & Seitz, 1986), 149–60.

[69] Lenk, 152; 159.

[70] Buber, 102.

[71] "Gespielt wird kein Stück, sondern eine Generalprobe." See Benjamin Korn, "Es geht um das Leben. Nur deshalb geht es um die Kunst: Zum 50. Todestag der Dichterin, der Dramatikerin Else Lasker-Schüler," in Theater heute 1 (1995), 20–23 (23).

[72] Brecht completed a first draft in 1944. He could not possibly have known Lasker-Schüler's play, however, nor she his.

[73] In the poem "Leise sagen," in Lasker-Schüler, *Gesammelte Werke* vol. 1, 163.

[74] Lenk, 158.

[75] This is the epigraph to Beauvoir's *Le sang des autres* (Paris 1945), cited in Ursula Tidd, *Simone de Beauvoir: Gender and Testimony* (Cambridge: Cambridge UP, 1999), 20. I am grateful for this reference to Dr. Susan Bainbrigge (University of Edinburgh).

[76] There is more well-meant sexism in Radecki's comment: "Sie konnte sich nicht verstellen, was doch Frauen sonst leicht vermögen." Radecki, 580.

[77] Calvin N. Jones, *The Literary Reputation of Else Lasker-Schüler: Criticism 1901–1993* (Columbia, SC: Camden House, 1994), 5.

[78] Hille, "Pastellbilder der Kunst," supplement to *Kampf 7* (March 1904).

[79] Hille, "Else Lasker-Schüler" (1904), in Schmid, 565.

[80] See Ritchie Robertson, "Historicizing Weininger: The Nineteenth-Century German Image of the Feminized Jew," in *Modernity, Culture and "the Jew,"* ed. by Bryan Chevette and Laura Marcus (Oxford: Polity, 1998), 23–39.

[81] Dieter Bänsch, *Else Lasker-Schüler: Kritik eines etablierten Bildes* (Stuttgart: Metzler, 1971) and Angelika Koch, *Die Bedeutung des Spiels bei Else Lasker-Schüler im Rahmen von Expressionismus und Manierismus* (Bonn: Bouvier, 1971), both cited in Christine Reiss-Suckow, *"Wer wird mir Schöpfer sein!!" Die Entwicklung Else Lasker-Schülers als Künstlerin* (Konstanz: Hartung-Gorre, 1997), 10.

[82] Sieg, 91–92.

[83] In her second book, *Bodies that Matter*, Butler seeks to correct the impression given to many by the first, *Gender Trouble*, that human beings choose freely how and when they perform gender. See Butler, *Gender Trouble: Feminism and the Subversion of Identity* (New York: Routledge, 1990); *Bodies That Matter: On the Discursive Limits of "Sex"* (New York: Routledge, 1993).

[84] Cited in Ulrike Müller, *Auch wider dem Verbote: Else Lasker-Schüler und ihr eigensinniger Umgang mit Weiblichkeit, Judentum und Mystik* (Frankfurt a. M.: Lang, 1997), 62–63.

[85] Benn, "Erinnerungen an Else Lasker-Schüler," in *Tagesspiegel* 26 February 1964. Cited in Müller, 63.

[86] Cited in Klüsener, 78.

[87] O'Brien, 9.

[88] Lasker-Schüler claimed to have written *Die Wupper* overnight, in a kind of dream state. See Lasker-Schüler, "Meine Wupper," in *Gesammelte Werke* vol. 2, 656.

6: Marieluise Fleisser:
A Theater of the Body

Ins Theater drang ich ein als ein frecher Wicht.
Ich gehörte da nicht hin, ich zählte ja nicht.[1]

MARIELUISE FLEISSER'S SENSE OF HERSELF as a foreign body in the world of theater is documented not only (as the above quotation illustrates) in her fiction, but in a theoretical text she wrote called "Über das dramatische Empfinden bei den Frauen":

> Gewiß haben wir vereinzelte Stücke von Frauen, die aber nicht beson-
> ders bekannt und wichtig geworden sind. [. . .] für gewöhnlich bleibt
> es denn auch bei dem einen Versuch und die Autorin biegt wieder in
> das Epische aus, weil ihr das mehr liegt.[2]

Fleisser wrote this in 1930: that is, shortly after her second play, *Pioniere in Ingolstadt*, had (with a good deal of stirring from Brecht) caused an explosion of critical hostility, and just after she had withdrawn her third drama, *Der Tiefseefisch* (which contains fairly overt criticisms of Brecht's exploitative working methods) from production at Berlin's Theater am Schiffbauerdamm. Fleisser withdrew the play on Brecht's insistence — he had been warned about its content by the Theater am Schiffbauerdamm's dramaturg, Heinrich Fischer, who was present at Fleisser's reading of the piece. After this, she did not try to write another drama for eight years; and she did not permit another performance of *Pioniere* for forty.

All this makes it less surprising that Fleisser, as a dramatist, should have distanced herself (along with women in general) from the genre of drama in "Über das dramatische Empfinden bei den Frauen." She does not except herself from the generality of writing women, who — her essay argues — are more naturally drawn to narrative prose: in 1963, she said of herself "das Erzählen liegt mir wohl mehr."[3] Whether this is a true reflection of her literary strengths, or a notion she imbibed from early twentieth-century critical theory (which helped critics such as Kurt Pinthus to read her stories as "wertvoller und dichterischer [. . .] als ihre Stücke"),[4] is a question we need to consider separately.

It is also a question that is difficult to answer without making unhelpful value judgments. In the context of this study, it is worth noting the pressure exerted on Fleisser by the literary critical discourse of the early twentieth century, which persistently reiterates the nineteenth-century notion that women do not really write drama. Albert Zimmer, writing in 1929/30, follows Pinthus when he sees in the young woman writer "eine starke epische Begabung auf lyrischer Basis," and in her plays "[eine] in äußere Dramenform gebrachte epische Entwicklung." *Fegefeuer in Ingolstadt* is, according to Zimmer, a "dramatisierte Novelle," and its figures "haben kaum dramatischen Impetus."[5] It is possible that Zimmer helped inform Fleisser's view of her own, and other women's, literary abilities, when he asserted that her short stories are "das beste Zeugnis ihrer Begabung."[6] In her autobiographical *Notizen* of 1972, which — in a dissociation of self and biography — she chose to write in the third person, Fleisser retrospectively described the feelings that informed her literary decisions in 1931: "Sie schreibt kein Theaterstück mehr, sie fühlt sich künstlerisch völlig verunsichert."[7]

All of Fleisser's plays, except one (*Karl Stuart*, 1945), exist in more than one version, and there is as yet no single volume or series in which all of the various versions are collected. *Fegefeuer in Ingolstadt* was written in 1924, in a version that is no longer extant; it premièred in a revised form on the Junge Bühne at the Deutsches Theater, Berlin, in 1926.[8] Fleisser rewrote the piece again for performance in 1970, at Wuppertal's Schauspielhaus.[9] She wrote *Pioniere in Ingolstadt* under instructions from Brecht in 1928 (the topic and the "epic" style of the drama were his ideas). Its première the same year at the Komödie in Dresden was uneventful, and this led Brecht to "pepper" the text for performance at the Theater am Schiffbauerdamm in 1929; he instructed Fleisser to add sexually risqué episodes.[10] The desired scandal resulted on the play's first night, and the text had to be cut before further performances were allowed.[11] Fleisser rewrote the play in 1968, and the new version premièred in March 1970 in Munich's Residenztheater.[12] Her third early play, *Der Tiefseefisch* — which she later considered re-naming *Ehe in Ingolstadt* — was written in 1929/30, but was not performed during her lifetime.[13] Fleisser was still rewriting the piece shortly before her death in 1974; a widely revised "vorläufige Fassung" of 1972 is reprinted in her *Gesammelte Werke*.[14] *Karl Stuart* (written 1938–45) was never performed; Fleisser's last new play was a comedy, *Der starke Stamm* (1944–45), which she revised for its Munich première in 1950 and again in 1972.[15]

In this chapter I shall concentrate on the earlier versions of the Ingolstadt plays and *Der Tiefseefisch*, which have tended to receive less critical attention than the revised versions of the late 1960s and early seventies.

Scholars assessing Fleisser's life and work have been struck not only by the absence of a monolithic body of "finished" texts, but also by the elusiveness of the writer's identity. Elke Brüns weighs the meaning of "Marieluise Fleißer: ein falscher Name und ein Werk, das durch die vielen Überarbeitungen als authentisches — im Sinne eines originären Textkorpus — schwer zu rekonstruieren ist,"[16] and others have noted related difficulties.[17] The problems begin with the name: Luise Marie Fleisser, who was calling herself Lu, was renamed Marieluise by her mentor, the well-known novelist Lion Feuchtwanger, in the early 1920s. It was Feuchtwanger who passed the text of *Fegefeuer in Ingolstadt* to Brecht, but the play, too, began life under a different name. Fleisser called it *Die Fußwaschung*; Moriz Seeler of the Junge Bühne renamed it before the première in 1926, asking the author's permission only *after* he had sent out the press release.[18]

Pioniere, the play written under instructions from Brecht, was later renamed by Rainer Werner Fassbinder, who (again, without asking Fleisser) called it *Zum Beispiel Ingolstadt* when he adapted it for his Action Theater Munich production of 1968.[19] Fleisser's apparent lack of control over or ownership of her own work is most clearly illustrated in Brecht's creation of a scandal over *Pioniere*, which had unpleasant personal consequences for Fleisser, and by his subsequent insistence that she withdraw *Der Tiefseefisch* from production at the Theater am Schiffbauerdamm. Fleisser does not appear to have resisted: in her biographical notes she writes simply: "Brecht läßt sie [. . .] wissen, daß sie das Stück zurückziehen soll, und sie tut es sofort. Sie sieht das Stück nie wieder an."[20]

In the late 1960s and early 1970s, during what Fassbinder called "der Fleißer-Boom,"[21] a group of young men — Franz Xaver Kroetz, Martin Sperr, Rainer Werner Fassbinder — collected around Fleisser and claimed her as their "geistige Mutter." Her *Gesammelte Werke* appeared in 1972 as a direct result of Kroetz's intervention and support; this already betrays a blip in the parent-child relationship suggested by the term. The "sons" exploit (Fassbinder) and protect (Kroetz) their "mother" — the notion of the spiritual mother is, then, less emancipatory or empowering in its suggested equivalence to the more traditional spiritual father than it might appear. Fleisser's relationships with men have been explored at length, even ad nauseam. The focus tends to be on her fascination with them, particularly with Brecht. But one might very well turn the idea around: men of letters such as Feuchtwanger,

Brecht, Draws-Tychsen, Fassbinder, Sperr, Kroetz, as well as men of the arts world such as the arts manager and academic Günther Rühle, the television producer Wend Kässens, and the journalist Michael Töteberg were or are all fascinated with Marieluise Fleisser. What is it about this writer that draws their interest?

The reception of Fleisser's early plays, in the late 1920s, is still informed by the nineteenth-century notions of gender and genre that have been discussed at length in this study. It seems impossible for her reviewers to see her as anything other than a *woman* dramatist, and many can only view the work through crassly gendered spectacles. The critic Paul Fechter appeals to a still-current prejudice: "Frau und Drama scheint sich nach bisherigen Erfahrungen überhaupt schlecht zu reimen,"[22] and Kurt Pinthus is quite distracted from the play by the physical presence of the woman writer: "Eine blonde, schlanke, straffe Bürgerin aus Ingolstadt ist — nicht die Heldin, sondern die Verfasserin dieses [. . .] Stücks."[23]

Pioniere, spiced as it was with Brecht's "Pfeffer," attracted comments that were just as sexist, but more aggressive: Felix Zimmermann found it "feminin raffiniert und verlogen schamhaft, also schamlos,"[24] and Paul Fechter saw the misogynist notions of drama that influenced his reception of *Fegefeuer* confirmed: "So etwas kann sich ein Kerl erlauben mit Mark in den Knochen [were Fleisser's bones hollow, in his imagination?] und Kraft des Worts und der Gestaltung, nicht ein dünnes, blasses Talentchen."[25] But there were positive responses, too: Heinrich Zerkaulen is impressed by Fleisser — "Ihren Namen wird man sich nach dieser neuen Talentprobe [. . .] zu merken haben" — and Herbert Ihering recognizes "ein schwerblütiges, wertvolles Talent."[26] Kurt Pinthus, once he has got over another flash of enthusiasm for "die blonde stramme Ingolstädterin,"[27] turns to the more relevant matter of the dialogue with real admiration: "es gibt da Gespräche [. . .], die in ihrer tastenden Sehnsucht, in ihrer schlagenden, urwüchsigen Kraft einzigartig sind in unserer Dramatik."[28]

Traces of the old, essentialist modes of reading still disturb some recent Fleisser criticism. There is, as Göttel has rightly and irritably noticed, a tendency to describe Fleisser's work as "intuitive" or "instinctive," "subjektiv" or "unbewußt":[29] all gendered adjectives in the context of literary history. Even McGowan, in his work on Fleisser, calls her *Tiefseefisch* a "subjektives Seismogramm" (suggesting both a highly personal approach and a natural response to events, like a seismograph reading earth vibrations).[30] Rühle opens his volume of *Materialien zum Leben und Schreiben der Marieluise Fleißer* with the astonishing statement: "Die Autorin hat über nichts anderes schreiben können als über

Erlebtes"[31] — as if writers ever separated their art entirely from their experience, and as if Marieluise Fleisser's texts were little more than diary entries, barely artistically transformed. It is a long-standing convention among literary critics to read women's writing as confessional (we might remember Hans Pauli in 1896, who salivated over "die reizvolle Art, wie sich eine Autorin mit Bewusstsein selber offenbart oder unbewusst selber verräth");[32] this approach avoids upsetting the gendered dichotomy men/art/intellect – women/nature/body. If women's writing is primarily autobiographical, then we scarcely need to worry about whether or not it is "art."

A Theater of the Body?

Rather than being distracted by the "autobiographical," we might usefully consider the notion of Fleisser's dramatic writing as peculiarly corporeal. It has been described as "ein Theater der Körper":[33] Olga, of *Fegefeuer in Ingolstadt*, inhabits an erotic body — a pregnant, sexualized body — by contrast with Hermine and her sister, Clementine, Brüns argues. She designates Roelle (by contrast with Pepe) anti-phallic (that is, subversive of masculine dominance);[34] but we might more accurately say that Roelle is a failed phallic male, rather than an anti-phallic male. He is clearly looking for dominance, and soon finds a traditional path: through "knowledge" of Olga's body, albeit not in the sense of sexual possession, but because he has discovered she is pregnant. This knowledge gives him the power to command, which he immediately exploits:

> ROELLE. Gehen Sie her. *(Olga geht bewußtlos.)* Noch ein
> Schrittchen, sagen Sie Ihre Lektion auf.
>
> OLGA. Sie haben eine Kolonialwarenhandlung, wo es nicht
> stinkt. (113)

Roelle fantasizes about linguistic power, the power of the phallic tongue: "Ich will sagen, beuge dein Knie, und sie wird da beugen ein Knie und wird wie eine Hörige sein vor meinem Gesicht, wie ich es mir ausdenke" (115). The biblical tone only emphasizes the borrowed authority of patriarchal tradition that Roelle would invoke in his quest for masculinity: for the ability to perform a felicitous speech act that is the sign of the phallic male.[35] (This is reminiscent of Carl Pius and Eduard Sonntag in Lasker-Schüler's *Die Wupper*.) But, like Carl and Eduard, Roelle fails, and Olga notices his failure, when his voice betrays him: "Ihnen schlägt ja die Stimme über" (115).

Roelle's failure to incorporate a phallic body is mirrored in Olga's missing femininity: this begins with her pregnancy, which — although it is a clear sign of her femaleness — offends against the convention for young unmarried women. Clementine's comment about Olga: "Von der Seite schaut sie wie ein Mann" (129), is both potentially ridiculous (if Olga's pregnancy is visible) and significant: Olga "looks like a man" because she inhabits what is to some extent a phallic body. She is carrying a child (which Freud, rightly or wrongly, identified as the mother's "phallus")[36] and she is, with her body, subverting the notions of virginity and purity that traditionally disempower young women, marking them as the property of fathers until they become the property of husbands. Berotter's infirmity underlines her unstable position: his tendency to fall over is a clear enough sign of paternal impotence.

Many of the women's bodies in Fleisser's early plays are associated with water.[37] Olga in *Fegefeuer* is carrying an embryo in the "Fruchtwasser" or amniotic fluid in her womb, and she seeks to put an end to her life and her pregnancy by drowning herself. This means of ending a woman's life, particularly a pregnant woman's life, has a long literary history.[38] Given the association of water and sex, as well as water and pregnancy,[39] it can be seen to work symbolically as a "hair of the dog" method of atonement for the sexual aberration that led to the unwanted pregnancy. If the (voluntary) punishment fits the crime, the sinner can be understood to have done penance and — crucially — to have understood and accepted the nature and structure of the order that her crime disturbed. In *Fegefeuer*, however, all this is turned on its head because Roelle, who is hydrophobic, overcomes his fear of water (which is also, as we shall see, a fear of sex and the corporeal) and pulls Olga from the river, thus upsetting the orderly process of crime and (self-)punishment.

In *Pioniere*, the pioneers are engaged throughout in building a bridge over a river; they are also engaged in seducing women they intend to abandon. The bridge, then, could be read as their capacity to dominate but also make their escape from water (qua sex, the body, women). So it is no coincidence that the bridge is present as background in the photograph Karl leaves Berta. It is dynamited as the pioneers leave town, by Fabian, another failed phallic male — Fleisser/Fabian thereby manages to explode the phallic power that the pioneers incorporate, that will from now on be limited (theoretically, at least) by command:

> Es ergeht [. . .] der Befehl, daß in der nächsten Zeit der Urlaub des gemeinen Pioniers eine wesentliche Einschränkung erleidet. Statistiken haben ergeben, daß bei dem Aufenthalt von 300 Mann in einer Stadt ca. 33 illegitime Kinder ergehen [. . .] Das ist 10%, Ihr Karnickel! Die Ziffer soll durch vorgetroffene Maßnahmen künstlich gesenkt werden. (222)

Elnis (in the later version of the play, Laurenz) of *Der Tiefseefisch* is not afraid of water; on the contrary, he asserts his right to live in it: "Ich bin ein Tiefseefisch" (17). This simultaneously signals his right to live in, through, and on the back of Ebba (later Gesine): "Ich muß doch hinuntergreifen. Durchtauchen durch dich wie durch Wasser" (55). Woman — or a specific woman, Ebba — is the "dark element" in and through which Elnis, the "Tiefseefisch," lives: she must function as a life-giving, passive, supportive element, like water.

Ebba's body and self, the "water" through which Elnis lives, are therefore not hers, but his. A lack of self characterizes the women in *Pioniere*: when Berta and Alma attempt female bonding ("BERTA. [. . .] Die Freundschaft muß bleiben. ALMA. Berta! Und ich werd dich nicht verlassen. *Reicht ihr die Hand*," 189) this is exposed as an illusion. The exchange is a failed attempt to perform a significant speech act, for Berta, soon after, is betrayed by Alma, for the sake of a pioneer. The women's bodies, we understand, are not their own to bond. Karl is skeptical when Berta describes herself as "verraten" (194); his perception tells him that only a man can betray a woman, since only a man's body is significant or material enough to make the betrayal matter. For the men in the play, controlling one's own and other bodies — even inanimate bodies — is paramount: the "Jäger" signals his phallic status to Alma by performing on a bicycle: "das Rad gehorcht seinem Herrn."[40]

For the men, control of a woman's body is not so much an end in itself as practice for a "real," masculine world in which women do not feature: the world of the military and of capitalist ownership of material goods. Father Benke taunts his son Fabian: "Nicht einmal einem Mädel wird er Herr und will einem Auto Herr werden" (202); the "nicht einmal" formulation makes it clear enough which of the two objects, the woman or the car, is of more significance. Later, Fabian's claim to be a "Würger der Frauen" is a parody of phallic power. He is appealing to the masculinist world view (widely represented in art and literature in the early twentieth century)[41] by which men achieve maleness — the status of the dominant body — by oppressing or destroying women's bodies. In a gloriously Jelinekesque exchange,[42] Fleisser temporarily debunks the notion: because Berta, as a servant, has no notion of the artistic and literary discourse Fabian is drawing on, she plunges his self-stylization into bathos:

FABIAN [. . .] Glaubst du an mich, Weib?

BERTA. Warum sagst du denn immer Weib?

FABIAN. Du bist für mich das Weib

BERTA.   Das macht die Aufregung

FABIAN.   Berta, ich bin ein Würger der Frauen, [. . .]

BERTA.   Tu mir nichts, Fabian, ich tu dir auch nichts.

Berta's reaction here, which rests on a misunderstanding of what she "ought" to say (what the fictive female victim of masculinist imagination that Fabian is attempting to conjure would say) is pure comedy. Fabian's communicative speech act fails because Berta is not familiar with the conventions it relies on, and therefore responds pragmatically, like a real woman, rather than like a female character created by a man. Her attempt to understand, even indulge Fabian ("Das macht die Aufregung") gives way to a command whose structure reflects a notion of equal power: "tu mir nichts [. . .] ich tu dir auch nichts," rather than the brutal hierarchy Fabian would like to create.

Fleisser's dramatic writing has frequently been singled out for its linguistic impact. The theater critic Michael Skasa enthuses over "die gehauene Schönheit der Fleißerischen Sprache, die visionäre Kraft ihrer dunklen Bilder";[43] McGowan sees the plays as a kind of chemical experiment in language: "Die Retorte, in der alles zusammenläuft und aus der es qualmt und spritzt, is die Sprache";[44] and Hoffmeister notes that Fleisser's characters, for all their corporeality, are "highly verbal people."[45] Fleisser's language is both stylized and impressively realistic, communicating more than the sum of the words.[46] Her characters verbalize their corporeality in self-referential speech acts that read almost like stage directions (those reminders of theater's physicality that normally punctuate a dramatic text). Roelle, for example, refers back to his own act of speaking — "Dies sage ich mit einer stillen Hartnäckigkeit" (*Fegefeuer*, 112) — and interprets his own act of looking: "Ich sehe Sie bedeutend an" (142). Ebba in *Der Tiefseefisch* similarly describes her own actions in speech: "Ich verlasse fluchtartig das Lokal. Ich ziehe mich um" (42), and Gronoff (in the later version, Tütü) does something similar: "ich beginne im Sinne meines Systems auf Sie einzuwirken [. . .] Ich schwinge die Peitsche über Sie" (69). Fleisser can again be seen to anticipate the late twentieth-century dramatic language of Elfriede Jelinek, whose grotesquely comical character Dr. Heidkliff (of *Krankheit oder moderne Frauen*) tells us: "Ich spreche jetzt [. . .] Ich zahle [. . .] Ich kaufe etwas. Ich frage nach dem Preis. Es ist mir erlaubt."[47] Because such speech acts are self-referential, they focus our attention on what the characters are performing or attempting to perform: in Roelle's and in Gronoff's (and in Dr. Heidkliff's) case, phallic dominance, and in Ebba's, invisibility or the obliteration or disguise of the self.

Where Roelle's attempts to achieve linguistic and thus corporeal dominance repeatedly fail, Gronoff's are — initially at least — successful. His linguistic mode is typically imperative: "Man behandle mich vorsichtig! Man erhalte mich bei guter Laune!" (62), backed up with a threat of violence: "Wenn ich schlechter Laune bin, zerschmeiße ich Existenzen!" (62). His first action in the play is a speech act: the sacking of Miss Orion. Gronoff's three words to his secretary, "Streichen Sie Orion" have immediate physical consequences: *"Miß Orion geht"* (63).

"Ich" is a word that occurs with noticeable frequency in Gronoff's speech, so that we are persuaded of his egoistic stance before he spells it out: "Menschen sind dazu da, um verbraucht zu werden" (65); the use of "verbraucht," rather than merely "gebraucht" is particularly harsh. What is interesting, though, is that Gronoff — like Roelle — eventually fails in his bid for complete phallic/linguistic dominance. Fleisser's dramas have been characterized approvingly (and perhaps hopefully?) as "keine Modellfälle für feministische Thesen";[48] I hope already to have demonstrated the contrary, particularly because a feature of Fleisser's dramatic writing is her will to sabotage the inevitability of male authority. In *Pioniere*, she explodes it with the bridge that represents male domination of the female element, water; in *Fegefeuer* she shows its recurring impotence in the figure of the father who keeps falling over (cannot stay erect) and in Roelle's failed attempts to achieve an authoritative status in language; and in *Der Tiefseefisch* we see the epitome of phallic control, Gronoff, finally fail. He fails, it is true, not in a confrontation with a woman, but with a man (Elnis) who perceives himself as representing Ebba.

To take a brief detour: it is clear from Fleisser's own writings, as well as from numerous critical interpretations, that Gronoff (Tütü) is a deliberate parody of Bertolt Brecht, while Ebba (Gesine) performs elements of Fleisser's experience as the ex-partner (in both the personal and the literary sense) of Brecht. Elnis (Laurenz) incorporates features of Fleisser's next partner, the poet Hellmut Draws-Tychsen.

In the play, the confrontation between Gronoff and Elnis culminates in a stand-off. Both use, as a matter of course, a mode of communication that functions via control. Because neither is prepared to give an inch, communication finally breaks down; a situation that is described by Elnis: "Dann haben wir einander nichts mehr zu sagen" (71). With these words, Elnis leaves the stage, thus rendering further communication physically impossible. For the first time, Gronoff is unsuccessful in an encounter; his meeting with Elnis is a failed bid for linguistic control. Within minutes of this first failure, he fails again: Wollank resists his command to destroy Elnis professionally, and hence renders that speech act infelicitous. Gronoff is reduced to the level of a Roelle — our final view of him in the play is of a (temporarily?) failed phallic male.

Elnis, on the other hand, has successfully resisted Gronoff's authority; he has thereby triumphed where Ebba once failed. His immediate reaction is to issue an authoritative, controlling instruction of his own, to Ebba: "Wir werden noch fünf Minuten warten, aber keine Minute länger" (73). Her response reflects his dominant linguistic status: "Um dich ist jetzt Bewegung, aber um mich ist Schweigen." Ebba is retreating from language, and she does not speak another word in the play. Fleisser here stages a linguistic failure for Gronoff/Brecht, who abused his control over her regarding the staging and rewriting of *Pioniere*, but she does not parallel it (at least not in this earlier version of the play) with a linguistic triumph for Ebba. Instead Elnis does battle and triumphs, metaphorically wearing her colors like a medieval knight.

Fleisser's characters are not only "highly verbal people," they believe in the power of language. Roelle believes that if he can force Olga to speak certain words, then he can achieve acceptability within the social group (that is, that her words will re-incorporate him). Using his knowledge of her pregnancy as the threat, he insists: "Bei uns [in the Roelle family home, S. C.] stinkt es nicht. Ich möchte, daß Sie mir das sagen" (113). It seems that this near-mystical belief in the power of spoken words is something Roelle has imbibed from authority figures, from a powerful offstage adult world. That Roelle's notion of the power of adults is misguided is illustrated in every adult figure in the play; only Berotter (Olga's father) and Roelle's mother are completely identifiable as adults, and neither wields real power. Berotter, as we shall see, fails to control Olga, and Roelle's mother can control him only for as long as he believes she can. Nonetheless, Roelle imitates (or parodies) adult authority in his own bid for status: in speaking to Olga, he borrows biblical and ecclesiastical speech patterns, casting her as the sinner and the subordinate partner in their interaction: "Ich frage Sie als Ihr Katechet: Dieses Kind Ihrer befleckten Empfängnis, ist es Ihnen ein Gegenstand der Liebe oder des Hasses? [. . .] Ich frage Sie als Ihr Katechet: Leugnen Sie, daß Sie es haben beseitigen wollen?" (115). Olga is on trial, and the pseudoreligious discourse used by Roelle renders it very nearly a witch trial. Later it is Roelle who rescues her from her self-imposed "ducking" (accused witches in early modern Britain and Germany were "ducked" in lakes and rivers to establish whether they were under the protection of the devil; if they survived and surfaced, they were presumed guilty). This is read by Olga as proof of his determination to show her guilt and punish her: "Deswegen hat er mich aus dem Wasser geholt, weil ich ihm nicht genug ausgestanden habe, [. . .] das ist alles ausgedacht mit einer Genauigkeit" (147).

Roelle also indulges in travesties of parental language and parental power. Regarding the pregnancy, he tries to admonish Olga "mit spitzem, falschen Ton": "Das hätten Sie und Herr Pepe sich vorher überlegen müssen" (115). But, just as the adults in the play fail to establish their authority, so too Roelle — their epigone — fails. In the next scene, Pepe has taken charge, linguistically and physically: he drags Roelle onstage, to force him to speak words of apology to Olga. Pepe is the phallic male who really is the father of Olga's baby, something Roelle later claims to be, for Roelle is flexible in his search for models of power — if he cannot "be" adult, he will "be" Pepe. Roelle's will to (literally) incorporate authority climaxes when, at the end of the play, he eats his confession — an act of speech/language incorporation much discussed by critics. I would choose to read this with Brüns, *both* as the ingesting of authoritarian oppression *and* as a bid on Roelle's part finally to play an active part in the system of language and control.[49]

For all his will to control bodies through language, however, Roelle cannot bring himself to speak the corporeal. When he would like to signal his will to paternalistically "manage" or control Olga's pregnancy, he founders, and can neither name her physical condition, nor spell out his plans for her:

> ich bringe es nicht über meine Lippen, weil mich das ganz verstört [. . .] das soll mir erlassen sein, *(nach Worten suchend)* wenn ich gleich-zeitig was verheiße [. . .] *(herausstoßend)*: Es ist was mit einem Land-aufenthalt. Das kann ich aber nicht so genau sagen. (121)

Roelle will never achieve phallic power because he attempts to speak what phallic discourse would suppress: the pregnant body of an unmar-ried woman. This is the involuntarily subversive element in Roelle's character as an otherwise would-be patriarchal collaborator.

Pepe, by contrast, takes the far more direct and conventional route of insisting that Olga is complicit in the silence that must surround her pregnant body: "Gib still, du warst immer meine Gescheite" (117). Her father, Berotter, does the same: in an exchange in act 1 it becomes clear that, even at this stage in the play, Berotter is aware of Olga's condition, but he insists on silence:

CLEMENTINE. Die Olga muß garnichts tun.
BEROTTER.   Wenn ihr schlecht ist.

CLEMENTINE.   Was soll das für eine Krankheit sein?
                (Olga senkt den Kopf)
BEROTTER.   Du hast zu schweigen. (111)

It is open to interpretation whether Berotter is speaking to Clementine ("you should not ask questions") or to Olga ("you should say nothing in response to such questions"); but if we understand here that Berotter already *knows* that Olga is pregnant and — like Pepe — imposes silence, then an otherwise oddly opaque speech of Pepe's near the end of the play makes sense. Shortly before the play ends, Olga announces to her father that she is pregnant: "Vater! Ich muß dir was sagen: Ich habe ein Kind" (142). If we accept that Berotter has already guessed this fact, and that Olga knows that he knows, then the emphasis here is on "sagen," and Pepe's response to the announcement: "Ich begreife, daß sich der Mann heut nicht durchsetzt" (143) therefore refers to Olga's *voicing* her physical condition. She has flouted her father's (and his, Pepe's) command to keep silence. In doing so, Olga has finally taken linguistic command of her own corporeality.

Berta, in *Pioniere in Ingolstadt*, also rebels against the rule of female silence that safeguards patriarchal double standards. Like Berotter and Pepe, Karl demands silence of women with regard to the corporeal: "Red nicht," he tells Berta, "weils sonst nichts wird" (199). Later he stops her in her tracks when she wants to talk about the decision to have sex: "Das will ich alles nicht wissen. Das Weib hat zu schweigen, wenn es genommen wird" (219). But Berta is not silent. After the event, she asks, "War das alles?" (220), and is reprimanded by Karl for breaking the (man-made) conversational rules: "Tu wenigstens so, als wenn es dir recht wäre, wie die anderen auch" (220). When Karl (like Roelle) borrows a biblical turn of phrase, to claim, "wir wissen nicht, was wir tun" (216), he is clearly lying. In a masculinist social and linguistic system, men like Karl do know what they are doing, but they do not *speak* it, least of all in the presence of women. Alma, more effectively socialized than Berta, understands this, and explains it kindly to Fabian (another would-be phallic male): "Sehen Sie, Herr Benke, die Hauptsache ist, daß man nicht so viel dabei redet" (220).

Fleisser's Berta, like Olga, is caught between accepting and resisting the system. On the one hand, she actively collaborates in linguistic falsification when she hears what she wants to hear, rather than what Karl says: "Ich hör nicht hin, was er sagt, weil er das nicht so meint" (195). We are reminded of Ebba in *Der Tiefseefisch*, who insists that Elnis means what she wants him to mean, and not what he says: "Du meinst nicht, was du sagst" (315). On the other hand, Berta challenges masculine self-stylization in language. When Karl tries to abjure responsibility for his exploitative behavior, she objects pragmatically:

> KARL. [. . .] Berta, auf mir liegt ein Fluch, daß ich die Frau quäle, die in mich verliebt ist. [. . .]
>
> BERTA. Warum ein Fluch? [. . .] Du tust's halt gern. (198–9)

The tendency of male dramatic characters who are being character-ized as peculiarly "masculine" to occupy considerably more speech space than their female counterparts — a tendency we have observed in others of the plays considered in this study — is already present in *Fegefeuer* and in *Pioniere*, but is made crassly or blindingly obvious by Fleisser in *Der Tiefseefisch*. Elnis speaks far more than Ebba does, and her speech tends to be a response to his: reactive rather than active. This has much to do with the problem already observed in the Ingolstadt plays, that men demand that women play the language game by *their* rules. Ebba cannot win, because Elnis defines her meanings for her: when she needs some of her own money, this is defined as "hetzen" or "mit dem Kopf durch die Wand" (13); on financial matters (like Olga on corporeal matters) she is forbidden to speak: "ELNIS. Ebba, wirf mir nicht vor, daß ich dein Geld verbrauche. In diesen Dingen höre ich furchtbar fein" (14). Spending all Ebba's money is precisely what Elnis does, but Ebba is not allowed to speak that state of affairs, just as Olga is not allowed to speak the fact of her pregnancy: double standards are effected through linguis-tic control. Like Karl in *Pioniere*, Elnis puts the responsibility for his exploitative behavior on his partner, while he hides behind a pseudomys-tical notion of the necessity of being how he is: "Du hast dich mir ange-lobt, du mußt die schwierigen Folgen [. . .] auf dich nehmen [. . .] Ich habe dich vor mir gewarnt" (16).

But where Olga and Berta find their voices and speak a level of re-sistance, Ebba finds it harder to rebel. This may be because Olga and Berta are subjected primarily to male control of their bodies, and when the truths communicated to them by their bodies contradict the rules laid down by father and boyfriend respectively — Olga *is* pregnant, Berta is *not* impressed by sex with Karl — they can translate these truths into language. Ebba is subjected primarily to psychological control, in such a way that the meaning and sometimes even existence of her own lan-guage is taken from her. Elnis not only reinterprets or imposes new meaning on what Ebba says; he also impels her to become a mere con-ductor of his words, when she types long letters to his dictation (secre-tarial work — the reproduction of men's language — is, of course, still regularly done by women).

There is a clear imbalance in the efficacy of Elnis's and of Ebba's speech. Like Gronoff, Elnis likes to use imperatives, especially when he is speaking to Ebba. These range from modal instructions — "Du sollst mich nicht immer ansehn. [. . .] Du sollst still sitzen. Du sollst mich nicht berühren. Du sollst nicht knistern. Du sollst bloß da sein" (31) — to straightforward commands: "Fertigmachen!" (29). Perhaps the crassest example of Elnis's linguistic, psychological, and corporeal control of Ebba is when he makes her sit down to write the dictated list of directives for her own behavior — particularly her speech:

1. Ebba soll nicht, wenn sie gefragt wird, mit Fragen antworten.
2. Ebba soll, wenn sie gefragt wird, stracks antworten.
   [. . .]
5. Ebba soll Elnis's Sätze nicht unterbrechen wollen durch eigene heftige Reden.
6. Ebba soll reden und schweigen können am richtigen Ort. (22)

When Ebba attempts imperatives, they are generally infelicitous: Elnis ignores her, for example, when she admonishes him "Sei gut!" (31). In response to his bizarre command, "Nimm die weißen Fliegen von meinen Augen" she tries to perform a complementary speech act, telling him: "Jetzt nehme ich sie weg" (31). But again she fails: communication does not occur, and Elnis reacts "als habe er etwas ganz anderes gehört." If Roelle "becomes language" when he ingests his written confession at the end of *Fegefeuer*, Elnis has done the same by the end of the first act of *Der Tiefseefisch*, in the sinister little note he writes and gives to Ebba: "Auch wenn ich nicht gut gegen dich bin, werde ich bei dir sein jeden Tag" (31).

Displaying Gendered Bodies

Fleisser has been characterized as an author who writes "only" from her own experience. This is, as I suggested earlier, in itself a fairly meaningless statement, and casts more light on the critic's notion of women's writing than it does on Fleisser's work. In Fleisser's plays we see characters in conflict with each other, fighting to assert their selves — a process we might expect to see in drama, since this is traditionally how the genre functions. Where we can begin to identify something relevant to Fleisser's own experience as a woman rather than as a man in society, is in her investigation specifically of the conflict between men and women — in her words, "immer nur etwas zwischen Männern und Frauen"[50] — and in the nature of that investigation. Rather than conforming smoothly to female gender roles (selflessness, self-subordination, fearfulness, the will to redeem men, and so on) Fleisser's women protagonists simultaneously perform and resist them. And a number of her men protagonists — Roelle, Fabian, Gronoff — occupy precarious rather than secure masculine spaces, and are constantly in danger of falling short of phallic status; they are, then, simultaneously attempting and failing to perform male gender roles, and thereby (unconsciously) helping to render subversion possible.

Fegefeuer, Sieg has noted, is "marked by the absence of [. . .] authoritarian father figures or maternal role models."[51] The gender binary as model that is usually provided by parents is missing from the children's world, and their scope to explore the meaning of their gender is therefore unusually wide. Because Roelle repeatedly fails to achieve a position of linguistic and physical authority, and therefore cannot curtail Olga's linguistic and corporeal space in the way that Pepe can with his demand that she be silent, she is able to find a relationship both with speech and with her body and hence, finally, to assert her self in the dramatic world. Olga resists the pressure to self-subordination; it is significant (as Cocalis has argued)[52] that she refuses to function as Roelle"s "redeemer," thus resisting the traditional and pernicious notion that women's ideal function is to make better men of men, abandoning the development of their own selves in the process. This is the false notion of love that is so crassly exposed in *Der Tiefseefisch*, in Elnis's childishly selfish demands that Ebba invest all her money and all her energy in making him "better." Elnis even wants Ebba's energy to flow into *his* writing; like Gronoff, he wants women to ensure his personal and professional development: "Beide Bereiche," Göttel observes, "funktionieren nur aufgrund der Disposition der Frau, sich emotional und als Arbeitskraft ausbeuten zu lassen."[53] It is worth observing that one of Fleisser's most notable and enthusiastic critics, Kurt Pinthus, manages to cast Fleisser as a "selfless" dramatist: Pinthus adjusts Goethe's (clearly self-affirming) "gab mir ein Gott zu sagen, was ich leide" to fit his own notion of feminine creativity, and sees in Fleisser someone who is "begnadet [. . .] zu sagen, nicht was sie leidet, sondern was armselige, gehemmte, junge Wesen leiden, die bisher selber niemals Worte für ihr Leid fanden."[54]

In chapter 4 we observed Lu Märten inserting her self into her drama *Bergarbeiter*, in the male character of Hermann. We can see something similar happening in the character of Roelle in Fleisser's *Fegefeuer*: not because Roelle overtly displays traits and expresses ideas that are part of the personal identity of his author (as was the case with Märten's Hermann), but because the audience gaze is directed at Olga through the desiring eyes of Roelle.[55] Roelle is also desirous of an audience, and is constantly seeking recognition, "Erkennung" or "Anerkennung"[56] — in Butler's terms, the affirmation that his is a body that matters.[57] For the other players in the piece (excluding his mother), Roelle's body only matters because it is different and disgusting: he smells and is afraid of water. They recognize him, then, only as "other," as unnatural and repellent. This, in my view, is where the Fleisser-Roelle connection is clearest: the woman dramatist, too, is an unnatural body, something disgusting or unnatural looking for recognition. One of Fleisser's most aggressive early critics, Felix Zimmermann, concluded his crassly gendered review of *Pioniere* with the terse comment: "Dem Beifall am Schluß zeigte sich die Autorin."[58] Given that his criticisms of the piece rely on notions of lacking feminine "Schamhaftigkeit," the reference to Fleisser's body, on willful show to the audience (*sich zeigen* is a verb one might use of an exhibitionist exposing his genitals), is clearly damning. The shameless female body on display is something to be rejected, because it is seeking a recognition of its status that is, in gendered thinking, unnatural. (This may also explain why Fleisser in fact so much disliked taking curtain calls, and often resisted being pulled on stage).

An interesting feature of Fleisser's reception is the prominence given to her biographical place of origin, Ingolstadt. Brüns has observed that "Ingolstadt" comes to have stronger significance for the work than Fleisser's name — "es [ist] in Fleißers Fall nicht der Autorinnenname, der für Autorposition und Werk einsteht, sondern das Wort *Ingolstadt*."[59] This is in one sense "proof" that the impossible thing — a woman dramatist — exists. Ingolstadt "hat etwas von einer Beweisführung angesichts der unbewiesenen Existenz von Dramatikerinnen: ja die Marieluise Fleißer, *die* aus *Ingolstadt*. Die damit dingfest gemacht wird [. . .], ortbar" (Brüns' emphasis). Simultaneously, Ingolstadt functions as a sign of Fleisser's position, as a woman writer, on the margins of literary culture; even as a method of reinforcing that marginality, "als Symptom einer Abwehrbewegung [. . .]. Es [= Ingolstadt, S. C.] entspräche der Festlegung auf die Provinz als dem Verweis und die Peripherie innerhalb eines Geschlechterverhältnisses."[60] It is worth noting, however, that after the scandal Brecht caused with *Pioniere*, Marieluise Fleisser was *not* unproblematically "aus Ingolstadt"; she was vehemently rejected by that community, and did not return willingly, but only after it became financially impossible for her to stay in Berlin, in 1932. Her reacceptance into the community did not even begin until she married a local man, Bepp Haindl, in 1935; although by this time her status as *persona non grata* with the National Socialist Party further complicated matters. So Fleisser, even while she was characterized primarily as "aus Ingolstadt," was not at home there — she herself was in the position her characters have been seen in, in "einer Welt, die ihnen keine Heimat bietet."[61]

I have argued elsewhere that this is a position frequently problematized by women writers — the insecure, "in-between" position of those who are not at home in the language of men.[62] It is the non-space occupied by Olga in *Fegefeuer*, who will not leave "Ingolstadt" (the representative town of the play) despite all that has happened to her there, presumably because there is no point: "For a woman, there is no place outside patriarchal ideology. Barred from hell, she is condemned to the intermediate space of purgatory."[63] Nor will Berta, in *Pioniere in Ingolstadt*, leave the place where the pioneers have been — having attempted to assert her self within a relationship, she is left behind as an episode in Karl's biography. Berta is one of many girlfriends whose space to relate to a male body has been compressed within the borders of a photograph, a remnant: neither nothing, nor anything. Ebba, of *Der Tiefseefisch*, simply retreats out of linguistic space with her final announcement "um mich herum ist Schweigen."

Even though all these characters — even Ebba, occasionally — resist the masculinist gendered order, their resistance can hardly turn into rebellion because there is no place for that rebellion to go. Elnis can rebel against Gronoff, when he takes up a rhetorical counterposition, and Karl against Willi (his lieutenant) when he exchanges insubordinate remarks with his colleagues, because these positions are recognized as existing within masculinist discourse: the angry young man and the son (or subordinate male) who defies his father (the dominant male) occupy established and accepted, even respected spaces within the hierarchical order of patriarchy. The dominant male and the rebellious (male) upstart are two sides of the same coin, so long as (as is usually the case) what the upstart aspires to is the status of dominance. In this case his impetus is merely to reposition himself in, and not to overthrow, the hierarchy. Pfister postulates:

> Der Sündenfall — das Verlassen der bürgerlichen Ordnung — kann nur für Männer in eine eigene Freiheit führen, für die Frauen jedoch führt er in eine neue Unterordnung [. . .] für die Frauen sind die Gesetze der Gegenwelt nicht eigene, sondern wiederum fremde Gesetze, ihr [*sic*] genauso aufgezwungen, wie die der bürgerlichen Welt.[64]

Fleisser's Ebba illustrates this particularly clearly: as a woman writer and — we infer — sexual *bohème*, she has already left the "bürgerliche

Ordnung" (as her difficult interaction with her landlady makes clear), but neither in the "Clique" led by Gronoff, nor in her relationship with Elnis does she experience anything but subordination, in a different kind of gendered hierarchy.

During the period of Nazi government, Marieluise Fleisser's publication possibilities were severely limited, to six articles per year.[65] But, as the incident of Brecht and *Der Tiefseefisch* illustrates, this was not the first time Fleisser found herself subject to censorship. The Fleisser-Brecht situation, rather like the fictive Ebba-Gronoff situation, exemplifies the lack of space available to creative women, outside of traditional bourgeois culture as well as inside it. In Lenk's words: "Die kulturellen Männer sind die Kultur, selbst wenn sie sie revolutionieren: uns bleibt sie ein Gegenüber."[66] And as for so many of the writers considered in this volume (Lasker-Schüler is a notable exception), there came a time when Fleisser stopped creating new drama — she wrote no more plays after 1945.

Notes

[1] Marieluise Fleisser, "Die im Dunkeln," in *Erzählungen*. (*Gesammelte Werke*, ed. by Günther Rühle (Frankfurt a. M.: Suhrkamp, 1994 [1972]), vol. 3; henceforth *Gesammelte Werke*), 270. These sentences, which open the story, are also cited as motto by Eva Pfister, in her "'Unter dem fremden Gesetz': Zu Produktionsbedingungen, Werk und Rezeption der Dramatikerin Marieluise Fleißer" (doctoral thesis, University of Vienna, 1981).

[2] Fleisser, "Über das dramatische Empfinden bei den Frauen," in Fleisser, *Aus dem Nachlaß* (*Gesammelte Werke*, vol. 4), 408–409 (408).

[3] Urs Jenny, "Gespräch mit Marieluise Fleißer," in *Materialien zum Leben und Schreiben der Marieluise Fleißer*, ed. by Günther Rühle (Frankfurt a. M.: Suhrkamp, 1973; henceforth *Materialien*), 341–43 (343).

[4] Kurt Pinthus, "Marieluise Fleißer" (Berliner Rundfunk, 18 December 1928), in *Materialien*, 365–72 (370).

[5] Zimmer, "Marieluise Fleißer" (*Die Literatur*, 1929/30), in *Materialien*, 373–77 (375).

[6] *Materialien*, 376.

[7] Fleisser, "Notizen," in *Materialien*, 411–28 (418).

[8] Under Paul Bildt and Bertolt Brecht. This version is reprinted as Marieluise Fleisser, "Fegefeuer in Ingolstadt," in *Zeit und Theater: Von der Republik zur Diktatur, 1925–33*, ed. by Günther Rühle (Berlin: Propyläen, 1972), 105–54. Unless otherwise indicated, all references are to this version and edition of the text.

[9] Under Günther Ballhausen. This version is reprinted as *Fegefeuer in Ingolstadt: Schauspiel in sechs Bildern*, in Marieluise Fleisser, *Gesammelte Werke 1: Dramen*, ed. by Günther Rühle (Frankfurt a. M.: Suhrkamp, 1994 [1972]), 61–125. This volume henceforth *Dramen*.

[10] "Pfeffer" is Fleisser's expression, recalling Brecht's instructions for additional material. See *Dramen*, 445.

[11] This production was directed officially by Jacob Geis, with plenty of interference from Brecht. The final (bowdlerized) text of 1929 is reprinted as *Pioniere in Ingolstadt: Komödie in zwölf Bildern: Fassung 1929*, in *Dramen*, 187–222. Unless otherwise indicated, all references are to this version and edition of the text.

[12] This version is reprinted as *Pioniere in Ingolstadt: Komödie in vierzehn Bildern: Fassung 1968*, in *Dramen*, 127–85. It has also appeared as *Pioniere in Ingolstadt*, ed. with an introduction, notes and vocabulary by David Horton (Manchester: Manchester UP, 1992).

[13] Nor was this version published during her lifetime. It finally appeared as *Der Tiefseefisch (1930): Schauspiel in drei Aufzügen*, in Marieluise Fleisser, *Der Tiefseefisch: Text — Fragmente — Materialien*, ed. by Wend Kässens and Michael Töteberg (Frankfurt a. M.: Suhrkamp, 1980), 11–75. Unless otherwise indicated, all references are to this version of the text.

[14] In *Dramen*, 289–356.

[15] *Karl Stuart* reprinted in *Dramen*, 357–434; *Der starke Stamm* (1972 version) reprinted in *Dramen*, 223–88.

[16] Brüns, *Außenstehend, ungelenk, kopfüber weiblich: Psychosexuelle Autorpositionen bei Marlen Haushofer, Marieluise Fleißer und Ingeborg Bachmann* (Stuttgart: Metzler, 1998), 97.

[17] See for example, Susanne Kord, "Fading out: Invisible Women in Marieluise Fleißer's Early Dramas," in *Women in German Yearbook* 5 (1989), 57–72 (57); Pfister, 36; Katrin Sieg, *Exiles, Eccentrics, Activists: Women in Contemporary German Theater* (Ann Arbor: U of Michigan, 1994), 23.

[18] See his letter to Fleisser in *Materialien*, 27.

[19] Fleisser initially opposed this production, which threatened to happen against her will, but later capitulated. Faßbinder went on to film *Pioniere* for ZDF in 1971, and directed it as a play in Bremen in January of the same year. See Annette Sabelus, "'Mir persönlich brachten sie allerhand Verdruß . . . ': Zu den Bearbeitungen von Marieluise Fleissers *Pioniere in Ingolstadt* durch Rainer Werner Fassbinder," in *Reflexive Naivität: Zum Werk Marieluise Fleißers*, ed. by Maria E. Müller and Ulrike Vedder (Berlin: Schmidt, 2000), 254–71.

[20] *Materialien*, 418.

[21] Cited in Donna L. Hoffmeister, *The Theater of Confinement: Language and Survival in the Milieu Plays of Marieluise Fleißer and Franz Xaver Kroetz* (Columbia, SC: Camden House, 1983), 22.

[22] Fechter, "Marieluise Fleißer: 'Fegefeuer in Ingolstadt'" (*Deutsche Allgemeine Zeitung*, 27 April 1926), in *Materialien*, 42–45 (44).

[23] Pinthus, "Fegefeuer in Ingolstadt" (*8-Uhr-Abendblatt*, Berlin, 26 April 1926), in *Materialien*, 45–47 (46).

[24] Zimmermann, "Pioniere in Ingolstadt" (*Dresdener Nachrichten*, 27 March 1928), in *Materialien*, 59–61 (60).

[25] Fechter, "Pioniere in Ingolstadt" (*Deutsche Allgemeine Zeitung*, 3 April 1929), in *Materialien*, 80–83 (81).

[26] Zerkaulen, "Pioniere in Ingolstadt" (*Fränkischer Kurier*, n.d.), in *Materialien*, 56–57 (57); Ihering, "Pioniere in Ingolstadt" (*Berliner Börsen-Courier*, 2 April 29), in *Materialien*, 74–7 (76).

[27] Pinthus, "Abermals ein Verbot im Theater am Schiffbauerdamm" (*8-Uhr-Abendblatt*, Berlin 2 April 1929), in *Materialien*, 86–89 (86).

[28] *Materialien*, 88.

[29] See Sabine Göttel, *"Natürlich sind es Bruchstücke": Zum Verhältnis von Biographie und literarische Produktion bei Marieluise Fleißer* (St. Ingbert: Röhrig, 1997), 17–18.

[30] Moray McGowan, *Marieluise Fleißer* (Munich: Beck, 1987), 86.

[31] Rühle, "Vorbemerkung," in *Materialien*, 7–8 (7).

[32] Pauli, "Frauen-Litteratur," in *Neue Deutsche Rundschau 7* (1896), 276–81 (276).

[33] Brüns, 119.

[34] Brüns, 104–105.

[35] Compare Ebner's Bothwell in *Maria Stuart* (chapter 1).

[36] See Sigmund Freud, "Femininity" (1933), in *The Essentials of Psycho-Analysis: The Definitive Collection of Sigmund Freud's Writing*, ed. by Anna Freud (London: Penguin, 1991 [1986]), 412–32 (426).

[37] See also Brüns, 113.

[38] For examples see Elisabeth Bronfen, *Over Her Dead Body: Death, Femininity and the Aesthetic* (New York: Routledge, 1992).

[39] The association of water and sex is testified to in the Undine myth, even before Freud linked water, sex, and intra-uterine life. See Sigmund Freud, *The Interpretation of Dreams*, transl. by James Strachey (New York: Basic Books, 1965 [1956]), 435–36.

[40] This speech is added in the later version of the play; see Fleisser, *Pioniere in Ingolstadt* (1968), 133.

[41] Examples include the (conceivably critical, but nonetheless culturally significant) paintings of Otto Dix and George Grosz with their portrayals of "Lustmörder," and of course Jack the Ripper in Wedekind's *Lulu*. I am indebted to Ingrid Sharp (Leeds University) for providing me with a copy of her unpublished paper "Dangerous Women: Female Criminality in the Weimar Republic."

[42] It is a favorite technique of Elfriede Jelinek (in works such as *Die Liebhaberinnen* [1975] or *Krankheit oder moderne Frauen* [1987]) to "help" language to parody itself; to present us with clichés that demand to be recognized in all their clichéd glory.

[43] Michael Skasa, "Das Ingolstädter Kleine Welttheater" (*Donau Kurier Ingolstadt*, 2 November 1971), in *Materialien*, 292–94 (292).

[44] Moray McGowan, "Kette und Schuß: Zur Dramatik der Marieluise Fleißer," in *Marieluise Fleißer* (Text und Kritik 64), ed. by Heinz Ludwig Arnold (Munich: Text und Kritik, 1979), 11–34 (13).

[45] Hoffmeister, 20.

[46] On Fleisser's "gestische Sprache" see Theo Buck, "Dem Kleinbürger aufs Maul geschaut: Zur gestischen Sprache der Marieluise Fleißer," in Arnold, 35–53.

[47] Jelinek, *Theaterstücke*, ed. by Ute Nyssen (Reinbek bei Hamburg: Rowohlt, 1992), 193.

[48] Wend Kässens and Michael Töteberg, "Psychodrama und Literaturbetrieb," in Marieluise Fleisser, *Der Tiefseefisch: Text — Fragmente — Materialen*, ed. by Wend Kässens and Michael Töteberg (Frankfurt a. M.: Suhrkamp, 1980), 176–86 (186).

[49] Brüns, 113.

[50] Interview with Hans Fröhlich, in *Materialien*, 349–50 (349). This is a favorite quotation with critics, and provides the title for Jutta Sauer's biographical monograph *"Etwas zwischen Männern und Frauen": Die Sehnsucht der Marieluise Fleißer* (Cologne: PapyRossa, 1991).

[51] Sieg, 27.

[52] Susan L. Cocalis, "'Weib ist Weib': Mimetische Darstellung contra emanzipatorische Tendenz in den Dramen Marieluise Fleißers," in *Die Frau als Heldin und Autorin*, ed. by Wolfgang Paulsen (Berne: Francke, 1979), 201–10 (206).

[53] Göttel, 129.

[54] Pinthus, "Marieluise Fleißer" (1928), 367–68.

[55] Compare Brüns, 117.

[56] Brüns, 120.

[57] Judith Butler, *Bodies that Matter: on the discursive limits of "sex"* (New York: Routledge, 1993).

[58] Zimmermann, 61.

[59] Brüns, 98.

[60] Brüns, 99.

[61] Angelika Döpper-Henrich, *"Entfremdung" in den dramatischen Schriften Marieluise Fleißers* (Frankfurt a. M.: Haag & Herchen, 1996), 99.

[62] See Sarah Colvin, "Regretted Absences and Insecure Spaces: Voluntary or Enforced Exile in German-language Writing by Women," in *New Readings* 4 (1998), 39–54.

[63] Sieg, 30.

[64] Pfister, 184.

[65] Kord, 58.

[66] Elisabeth Lenk, "Die sich selbst verdoppelnde Frau," in Lenk, *Kritische Phantasie: Gesammelte Essays* (Munich: Matthes & Seitz, 1986), 149–60 (154).

Conclusion

Women and German Theater:
The Self Staged, or Silenced?

> *what men dub tattle gossip women's talk*
> *is really revolutionary activity*
> *and would be taken seriously by men*
> *(and many women too)*
> *if men were doing the talking*[1]

IT IS CERTAINLY true to say, and scholarship is increasingly aware, that women *do* write drama, and did so even before the mid-twentieth century. But there is also, as this study illustrates, a pattern to many women's careers as playwrights: Ebner-Eschenbach, Druskowitz, Croissant-Rust, Marholm, delle Grazie, Märten, and Fleisser can all be shown to have had dramatic ambitions in their earlier years as writers that were never fully realized. "Die Autorin," says Fleisser, "biegt wieder in das Epische aus, weil ihr das mehr liegt."[2]

I have argued that Fleisser is wrong: that theater is by no means a genre that is in itself incongenial to women — its corporeality might even be read as a particular invitation to the sex that has been cast throughout the history of ideas as particularly corporeal. So why did so many of them abandon the genre?

The classic "comparative" answer is that many men writers did not succeed in the realm of the drama, either, and that literary misfortunes — bad timing or lack of talent — befall men and women equally. But it is clearly not as simple as that. We have observed that even women who did not give up writing serious drama (such as Viebig and Lasker-Schüler) have not been received as dramatists in literary history, but as prose writers (Viebig) and poets (Lasker). Nor do chauvinistic reviews and overpersonalized reception befall men and women equally: Fleisser was "die blonde stramme Ingolstädterin"[3] where Brecht was never (to my knowledge) dubbed "der fahle feiste Augsburger" or anything similar. In 1990, the then-new dramatist Kerstin Specht (who recently wrote a drama about

Fleisser called *Marieluise*)[4] found a keen reviewer in Peter von Becker, who enthused over her "roter Haarschopf und das Lächeln eines weiblichen Pierrots, Charme und klugen Witz in den Augen."[5] *Plus ça change, plus c'est la même chose.*

Men have, certainly, been more likely to have their plays performed, in theaters whose artistic directors and dramaturgs have also tended to be men. This is not so much a conspiracy against women writers as the inevitable result of a system of belief that posits male experience as the only experience really worth hearing about. "Bis heute," women theatre makers argued in 2001, "ist das Theater von einer ausgesprochen hierarchischen und immer noch patriarchalischen Entscheidungsstruktur geprägt."[6] Women's words, like women's bodies, tend to be perceived as immaterial (or not perceived at all): they do not *matter*. As dramatists, women interpellate themselves into discourse via the world of the stage — as creative subjects and, often, in the characters they create. Some playwrights are driven to create women characters that figure as bodies that matter, for their own sake, and not only in terms of their effects on men (Kühne's Elfriede, Croissant-Rust's Johanna, Fleisser's Berta in *Pioniere*); such plays reap confusion and sometimes aggression, or, like Kühne's, they are ignored. Other dramatists, such as Lu Märten, prefer to channel their creative selves into male characters, such as Hermann of *Bergarbeiter*. If a play can also be read from the perspective of male experience (and many women writers — Elsa Bernstein is a case in point — become expert at producing this effect), critics wonder whether the author may not "really" be a man (Bernstein is "beinah männlich," Viebig "rugged and virile"),[7] or whether — since drama is unfeminine — the play in question is not, really, undramatic.[8] The more woman-centered the drama, the more likely it is to be regarded as trivial and/or uninteresting.

I began this study with the notion that what the performance text might offer women, even within the structures of gendered discourse, is language that is quintessentially embodied. Where abstract language has been theorized as the realm of "pure" ratio and the masculine, theatrical language — because it is *discours* rather than *histoire* — is corporeal. In gendered discourse, the body has been seen as the place of the feminine. But again, things are not that simple. Drama is also a high-status genre whose implicit or latent corporeality also gives it a particular claim to materiality: drama has a potentially physical, public presence as theater. Furthermore, because the play demands witnesses (spectators, listeners), the audience is thrown into a receptive, "feminine" role vis-a-vis the "masculine" performed action. The notion that the audience position is feminine or passive vis-à-vis the text fits with the notion that the drama text is masculine or active, and reflects a structural understanding of the relation of active/male to passive/female that stands alongside, rather than conflicting with, the masculine gaze of an audience. This describes not a structural relation, but a dominant hermeneutic position: for example, a soldier can stand in a "feminine" — that is, passive — structural relation to an officer, but still retain his masculine identity and viewpoint. If, as nineteenth and some twentieth-century theories of drama and acting imply, female corporeality is only acceptable when contained or controlled by the masculine spirit, women cannot automatically be assumed to have a free hand to create their own corporeality on stage. So what space remains for a female self?

The early modern notion of the *theatrum mundi* envisaged the stage as a microcosmic world. We might develop this idea to suggest (with Judith Butler) that role-playing in theater mirrors the gendered role-play of daily life:

> gender is in no way a stable identity of locus of agency from which various acts proceed; rather, it is an identity [. . .] instituted through *a stylized repetition of acts*. [. . .] the acts by which gender is constituted bear similarities to performative acts within theatrical contexts.[9] (Butler's emphasis)

This is not just to make the banal observation that relations in theater, are, as in life, gendered relations. Rather it is to emphasize that theater is — as the notion of the *theatrum mundi* already suggests — a self-reflexive form. Human beings play human beings being human, and that is on no account a gender-neutral activity. The drama as a kind of surrogate world or society offers its creator a certain control over how humanness is to be performed,[10] albeit within the bounds of norms and their subversion.

Given that gender, although itself a "performance," is (as Butler explains in *Bodies that Matter*, the sequel to her much-misunderstood *Gender Trouble*) "*not* an artifice to be taken on or taken off at will and, hence, *not* an effect of choice" (my emphasis),[11] sex roles cannot simply be discarded on stage and replaced by a performance of utopian egalitarianism. But they can be investigated, possibly even subverted. I have argued elsewhere that, if performance is (as the dictionary suggests) the fulfillment of an agreement to deliver, then the playwright can at least determine the terms of the contract.[12] Here I would modify that and say that the playwright can at least demonstrate that she has read the small print. To expose gender as a performance of human power relations is not yet (necessarily) to redefine those relations — that is, it is not yet (necessarily) an overtly political act; but it is already a revolutionary act. It provokes the response described by Brecht in "Vergnügungstheater oder Lehrtheater?": "Das ist höchst auffällig, fast nicht zu glauben," which is just a step away from "Das muß aufhören."[13] Exposing structures and language as constructed and arbitrary, rather than natural and given, is, in the Brechtian sense, alienating.

Assessing the difficulties of articulating the feminine "other," the "sex which is not one," in a positive manner, Luce Irigaray suggests that one route open to women is mimesis:

> there is [. . .] perhaps only one "path," the one historically assigned to the feminine: that of *mimicry*. One must assume the feminine role deliberately. Which means already to convert a form of subordination into an affirmation, and thus to begin to thwart it [. . .]. To play with mimesis is thus, for a woman, to try to recover the place of her exploitation by discourse, without allowing herself to be simply reduced to it.[14]

Mimesis is profoundly associated with theater, but also with subversion, in the form of masquerade. Masquerade — the over-performance of a familiar role — is a feature of many works considered in this study, notably Paar's *Helene* (Warbek's performance of masculinity), Prellwitz's *Seine Welt* (especially Professor Donner's and Heinrich's roles), or Fleisser's *Pioniere* (Karl and Fabian) and *Der Tiefseefisch* (Elnis and Gronoff). The dramatic masquerades we have seen are always also linguistic masquerades — the element of "borrowed" performance of pre-written linguistic roles is illustrated particularly well when Fleisser's Roelle (*Fegefeuer in Ingolstadt*) and Lasker's Simeon (*Arthur Aronymus*) strive to appropriate authoritative, patriarchal language.

These are not conscious performances on the part of the characters — the element of masquerade is imposed on them by the dramatist. Interestingly, masquerades of femininity of this kind are rare. What we find instead are performances that we might read from a postmodern perspective as masquerade, but are unlikely to have been consciously imposed on characters as such (Marie Roland at the end of Ebner's play, or Mirjam in Bernstein's *Johannes Herkner*). In some cases, the intentionality of the performance is entirely debatable: Helene at the close of Paar's play and Hadumoth at the end of Prellwitz's are two cases in point. But in all cases, such performances function in dialogue with the play's projected audience, who will need to recognize the masquerade in order for it to be effective. The *discours* of the play becomes a kind of meta-speech act, dependent upon the felicity conditions of its reception.

The most deliberate performance of femininity that we meet in these plays is given by Lasker-Schüler's male character, Lange Anna; a pattern which echoes the playwright's own cross-gender performance of Prince Jussuf. There is, then, a sliding scale of self-reflexivity in the use of masquerade. At its most sophisticated, it can signal an awareness of the gendered self, and perhaps the ability to undermine or "take off" that gender costume; although the latter notion presupposes, problematically, that there is an essential something, an ungendered body, to be found underneath (precisely this is thematized in Gerlind Reinshagen's much more recent drama of roles, womanhood, and identity, *Die Clownin* of 1986).[15]

Elin Diamond has recently expressed the hope that "a feminist mimesis [. . .] would take the relation to the real as productive, not referential, geared to change, not to reproducing the same."[16] In recent years, more and more women dramatists have had their characters "put on" gender roles with what is clearly a deliberate intent to alienate (and in a way that is hence, arguably, "geared to change"). One (notorious) such is Elfriede Jelinek, whose protagonists subvert gender by performing it to the point where it becomes laughable. The two male protagonists of Jelinek's *Krankheit oder moderne Frauen* (1987), for example, come bounding on stage bursting with masculine attributes that range from Apollonian light to unbounded physical dynamism:

> Plötzlich helles, gleißendes Licht über die Landschaft. Heidkliff und Benno Hundekoffer kommen im Tennisdress und mit Tennisschlägern dynamisch-federnd herbeigetrabt [. . .]. Sie halten keinen Moment still, bersten vor Aktivität [. . .]. Vor Kraft können sie kaum gehen.[17]

The self-reflective awareness of language and cultural traditions that developed radically in the modern and postmodern twentieth century has helped women writers more consciously to perform what their predecessors (as this study shows) have always practiced: dramatic mimesis that is, simultaneously, masquerade. I do not suggest that the development of literary techniques that also carve a space for women's subjectivity has been smoothly chronological: on the contrary, where Ebner-Eschenbach is still struggling with masculinist traditions and historical female subjects in the late 1860s (*Maria Stuart, Marie Roland*), Julie Kühne in 1872 is already having her Elfriede Laub perform nineteenth-century femininity in a highly self-conscious manner. And in the early twentieth century, we find a writer like Elsa Bernstein appropriating masculine views of "what a woman wants" (Mirjam, in *Johannes Herkner*), while Gertrud Prellwitz mercilessly parodies male needs and ideals of the feminine in *Seine Welt*.

However — and this, if you like, is the essence of a "tradition" of women's playwriting in German — we do find the same techniques used again and again.[18] If the *discours* that is drama resists women as active subjects and as bodies that matter, then women will subvert (Prellwitz, Fleisser) and confuse (Kühne, Marholm) and redefine (Märten, Lask) that discourse until they have created — by sleight-of-hand, if necessary — the space that they, as writers, need.

One should on no account gloss over the difficulties women have encountered when writing for the theater, or ignore the dejection that failed or non-existent performances can cause — even to the extent that the writer finds it better to abandon the genre. But women have, again and again, found ways of interpellating themselves into the world of the drama, and if the recent spate of successful German-language dramatists at the beginning of the twenty-first century is anything to go by — for example Theresia Walser, Dea Loher, Kerstin Specht, and Gesine Danckwart in Germany; Elfriede Jelinek (as Büchner Prize winner) and Marlene Streerowitz in Austria — they will continue to do so for the foreseeable future.

Notes

[1] Astra, "Women's Talk." Cited in Dale Spender, *Man Made Language*, 2nd ed. (London: Pandora, 1985), v.

[2] Fleisser, "Über das dramatische Empfinden bei den Frauen," in Fleisser, *Aus dem Nachlaß* (*Gesammelte Werke*, ed. by Günther Rühle. Frankfurt a. M.: Suhrkamp, 1994, vol. 4), 408–409 (408).

[3] Pinthus, "Abermals ein Verbot im Theater am Schiffbauerdamm" (*8-Uhr-Abendblatt*, Berlin 2 April 1929), in *Materialen*, 86–89.

[4] Printed in *Theater heute* 9 (2001), 93–100. The play premièred on 24 November 2001 in the Ingolstadt Theatre.

[5] Peter von Becker, "Letzte Nachrichten aus dem deutschen Niemandsland — und eine neue Dramatikerin: Kerstin Specht," in *Theater heute* 1 (1990), 28–29 (28).

[6] Barbara Engelhardt and Therese Hörnigk, "Vorwort," in *TheaterFrauenTheater*, ed. Barbara Engelhardt, Theresa Hörnigk, and Bettina Mausch (Berlin: Theater der Zeit, 2001), 7–9 (7).

[7] Theodor Lessing, "Zwei Münchener Dichterinnen: Ernst Rosmer und Helene Böhlau," in *Die Gesellschaft* 13/III (1898), 16–28 (21); Otto Heller, *Studies in Modern German Literature* (Boston: Ginn, 1905), 280.

[8] See for example Gustav Morgenstern, "Anna Croissant-Rust" in *Die Gesellschaft* 13/III (1897), 211–19 (218); Paul Bornheim, "Anna Croissant-Rust" in *Das litterarische Echo* 9 (1906–7), 924–33 (926); Otto Julius Bierbaum, "Anna Crois-

sant-Rust: 'Der standhafte Zinnsoldat.' Drama in drei Acten," in *Die Zeit. Wiener Wochenschrift* 8 (1896), 158.

[9] Judith Butler, "Performative Acts and Gender Constitution: An Essay in Phenomenology and Feminist Theory," in *Writing on the Body: Female Embodiment and Feminist Theory*, ed. by Katie Conboy, Nadia Medina, and Sarah Stanbury (New York: Columbia UP, 1997), 401–18 (402).

[10] Particularly in terms of linguistic interaction. This is of course complemented by the role of the director.

[11] Judith Butler, *Bodies That Matter* (New York: Routledge, 1993), x.

[12] Sarah Colvin, "Disturbing Bodies: Mary Stuart and Marilyn Monroe in Plays by Liz Lochhead, Marie von Ebner-Eschenbach and Gerlind Reinshagen," in *Forum for Modern Language Studies* 35 (1999), 251–60 (251).

[13] Brecht, "Das epische Theater," in *Die Stücke von Bertolt Brecht in einem Band* (Frankfurt a. M.: Suhrkamp, 1987 [1978]), 983–98 (986).

[14] Irigaray, *This Sex Which Is Not One*, transl. by Catherine Porter (Ithaca, NY: Cornell UP, 1985 [1977]), 76.

[15] In Reinshagen, *Gesammelte Stücke* (Frankfurt a. M.: Suhrkamp, 1986), 576–630.

[16] Elin Diamond, *Unmaking Mimesis: Essays on Feminism and Theatre* (London: Routledge, 1997), xvi.

[17] Jelinek, *Krankheit oder Moderne Frauen*, in *Theaterstücke*, ed. by Ute Nyssen (Reinbek bei Hamburg: Rowohlt, 1992), 236.

[18] For corroboration of this across the history of women's playwriting in German compare especially Kord, *Ein Blick hinter die Kulissen* (Stuttgart: Metzler, 1992) and *Sich einen Namen machen: Anonymität und weibliche Autorschaft, 1700–1900* (Stuttgart: Metzler, 1996); Dagmar von Hoff, *Dramen des Weiblichen: Deutsche Dramatikerinnen um 1800* (Opladen: Westdeutscher Verlag, 1989); Katrin Sieg, *Exiles, Eccentrics, Activists: Women in Contemporary German Theater* (Ann Arbor: U of Michigan P, 1994).

Works Cited

Works by Women Dramatists 1860–1945

With locations of texts cited in parentheses. For alternative locations of some texts, see Susanne Kord, *Ein Blick hinter die Kulissen: Deutschsprachige Dramatikerinnen im 18. und 19. Jahrhundert* (Stuttgart, 1992), Appendix B.

Bernstein-Porges, Elsa (alias Ernst Rosmer). *Wir Drei. Fünf Akte.* Munich: E. Albert n.d. [1893] (Berlin, Staatsbibliothek).

———. *Milost Pan.* In Ernst Rosmer, *Madonna. Novellen.* Berlin: S. Fischer, 1894 (Berlin, Staatsbibliothek).

———. *Dämmerung: Schauspiel in 5 Akten.* Berlin: S. Fischer, 1894 (Oxford, Taylor Institution Library).

———. *Königskinder: Ein deutsches Märchen in drei Akten.* Berlin: S. Fischer, 1895 (Marbach, Deutsches Literaturarchiv).

———. *Themistokles: Tragödie in fünf Akten.* Berlin: S. Fischer, 1897 (Frankfurt a. M., Staats- und Universitätsbibliothek).

———. *Johannes Herkner: Schauspiel in fünf Akten.* Berlin: S. Fischer, 1904 (Berlin, Staatsbibliothek).

———. *Maria Arndt. Schauspiel.* Berlin: S. Fischer, 1908 (Berlin, Staatsbibliothek).

———. *Achill: Tragoedie in drei Akten.* Berlin: S. Fischer, 1910 (Berlin, Staatsbibliothek).

Breden, Christiane von (alias Ada Christen). *Faustina: Drama in fünf Akten.* Vienna: Jakob Dirnboeck, 1871 (Marbach, Deutsches Literaturarchiv).

Croissant-Rust, Anna. *Der standhafte Zinnsoldat. Drama.* Berlin: Schuster & Loeffler, 1896 (Marbach, Deutsches Literaturarchiv).

———. *Der Bua: Oberbayerisches Volksdrama in 4 Akten.* Berlin: Schuster & Loeffler, 1897 (Marbach, Deutsches Literaturarchiv).

———. "Rückschau." In *Die Brücke. Monatsschrift für Zeitinterpretation* 2 (1912), 4–8 (Marbach, Deutsches Literaturarchiv).

delle Grazie, Marie Eugenie. *Saul. Tragödie in 5 Acten.* Vienna: Konegen, 1885 (Vienna University Library).

———. *Moralische Walpurgisnacht: Ein Satyrspiel.* Leipzig: Breitkopf & Härtel, 1896 (Vienna University Library).

———. *Der Schatten: Drama in 3 Akten und einem Vorspiel.* Leipzig: Breitkopf & Härtel, 1901 (Vienna University Library).

———. *Schlagende Wetter: Drama in fünf Akten* (1898). In delle Grazie, *Sämtliche Werke,* vol. 7. Leipzig: Breitkopf und Härtel, 1904 (Berlin, Staatsbibliothek).

———. *Zu spät: Vier Einakter.* In delle Grazie, *Sämtliche Werke,* vol. 7. Leipzig: Breitkopf und Härtel, 1904 (Berlin, Staatsbibliothek).

———. *Narren der Liebe: Lustspiel in vier Akten.* Leipzig: Breitkopf & Härtel, 1904 (Berlin, Staatsbibliothek).

———. *Ver sacrum. Drama in 3 Akten.* Leipzig: Breitkopf & Härtel, 1906 (Vienna University Library).

Druskowitz, Helene. *Die Emancipations-Schwärmerin: Lustspiel in fünf Aufzügen.* In Druskowitz, *Die Emancipations-Schwärmerin und dramatische Scherze,* Dresden: Rudolf Petzold, n.d. [1889], 4–80 (Zurich, Zentralbibliothek).

———. *Er dozirt!* In Druskowitz, *Die Emancipations-Schwärmerin und dramatische Scherze,* Dresden: Rudolf Petzold, n.d. [1889], 83–90 (Zurich, Zentralbibliothek).

———. *Einsamkeit — das einzige Glück.* In Druskowitz, *Die Emancipations-Schwärmerin und dramatische Scherze,* Dresden: Rudolf Petzold, n.d. [1889], 91–100 (Zurich, Zentralbibliothek).

———. *Unerwartet.* In Druskowitz, *Die Emancipations-Schwärmerin und dramatische Scherze,* Dresden: Rudolf Petzold, n.d. [1889], 101–10 (Zurich, Zentralbibliothek).

———. *International: Dramatischer Scherz in drei Akten.* Leipzig: Metzger & Wittig, 1980 (Zurich, Zentralbibliothek).

———. *Der Mann als logische und sittliche Unmöglichkeit und als Fluch der Welt,* ed. by Hinrike Gronewold and Traute Hensch. Freiburg: Kore, 1988.

Ebner-Eschenbach, Marie von. *Maria Stuart in Schottland.* Vienna: Ludwig Mayer, 1860 (Edinburgh, National Library of Scotland).

———. *Marie Roland: Trauerspiel in fünf Aufzügen.* Vienna: Wallishausser, 1867 (Marbach, Deutsches Literaturarchiv).

———. *Ohne Liebe: Lustspiel in 1 Akt.* Berlin: Eduard Bloch, 1891.

———. *Das Waldfräulein,* ed. by Karl Gladt. Vienna: Belvedere, 1969.

———. *Das Waldfräulein,* in *Aphorismen — Erzählungen — Theater,* ed. by Roman Roçek. Vienna: Böhlau, 1988.

———. *Tagebücher*, ed. by Karl Konrad Polheim. Tübingen: Niemeyer, 1989.

———. *Ein Spätgeborner*. In *Erzählungen / Neue Erzählungen* (*Sämtliche Werke*, vol. 1). Berlin: Paetel, 1920; repr. Freiburg: Freiburger Echo Verlag, 1999, 11–73.

Fleisser, Marieluise. "Fegefeuer in Ingolstadt." In *Zeit und Theater: Von der Republik zur Diktatur, 1925–33*, ed. by Günther Rühle. Berlin: Propyläen, 1972, 105–54.

———. *Pioniere in Ingolstadt*, ed. with an introduction, notes and vocabulary by David Horton. Manchester: Manchester UP, 1992.

———. *Der Tiefseefisch: Text — Fragmente — Materialien*, ed. by Wend Kässens and Michael Töteberg. Frankfurt a. M.: Suhrkamp, 1980.

———. *Gesammelte Werke*, 4 vols., ed. by Günther Rühle. Frankfurt a. M.: Suhrkamp, 1994 [1972–89].

Itzerott, Marie. *Delila: Dramatisches Gedicht in 5 Aufzügen*. Oldenburg and Leipzig: Schulzesche Hof-Buchhandlung und Hof-Buchdruckerei, 1899 (Berlin, Staatsbibliothek).

———. *Dido: Drama in vier Aufzügen mit einem Vorspiel*. Strasbourg: Heitz, 1901 (Berlin, Staatsbibliothek).

———. *Hilde Brandt: Schauspiel in 4 Aufzügen*. Strasbourg: Heitz, 1905 (Berlin, Staatsbibliothek).

Kühne, Julie (alias Thure und Dierenow). *Elfriede Laub oder Weib und Mensch. Drama in 5 Aufzügen*. Leipzig: Oswald Mutze, n.d. [1873] (Berlin, Staatsbibliothek).

———. *Die Badegesellschaft. Charakter-Lustspiel und Sittengemaelde in fünf Aufzügen*. Leipzig: Oswald Mutze, 1875 (Berlin, Staatsbibliothek).

———. (alias Friedrich Masche). *Das Rattenschloß oder Der Einzug der Franzosen in Berlin: Humoristisch-satirisches Lustspiel in vier Aufzügen*. Leipzig: Oswald Mutze, 1876 (Berlin, Staatsbibliothek).

———. *Sie will wie er, und er ihr Glück oder Hexe und Teufel: Lustspiel in fünf Aufzügen*. Leipzig: Oswald Kühne, 1882 (Berlin, Staatsbibliothek).

———. *Villa Frankreich. Geschichtliche Komödie in 4 Aufzügen*. Kassel: Friedr. Scheel, 1896 (Berlin, Staatsbibliothek).

Lask, Berta. *Senta: Eine Lebenslinie in acht Szenen*. Hannover: Paul Steegemann, 1921 (Marbach, Deutsches Literaturarchiv).

———. *Giftgasnebel über Sowjet-Rußland: Revue-Drama in 35 Scenen*. Berlin: Ernst Friedrich, 1927 (Berlin, Staatsbibliothek).

———. *Leuna 1921: Drama der Tatsachen*. Berlin: Vereinigung Internat. Verlagsanstalten, 1927 (Marbach, Deutsches Literaturarchiv).

————. *Leuna 1921: Drama in fünf Akten. Mit einem Nachwort von Johannes Schellinger.* Berlin: Dietz, 1961.

Lasker-Schüler, Else. *Mein Herz: Ein Liebesroman mit Bildern und wirklich lebenden Menschen.* Munich: Heinrich F. S. Bachmair, 1912.

————. *Arthur Aronymus: Die Geschichte meines Vaters.* Berlin: Rowohlt, 1932.

————. *Verse und Prosa aus dem Nachlaß,* ed. by Werner Kraft. Munich: Kösel, 1961.

————. *Ichundich: Eine theatralische Komödie,* ed. by Margarete Kupper. Munich: Kösel, 1980.

————. *Die Wupper und andere Dramen.* Edited with an afterword by Margarete Kupper. Munich: dtv, 1986.

————. *Die Wupper* (1909). In *Dramen,* ed. by Georg-Michael Schulz (*Werke und Briefe: Kritische Ausgabe,* ed. by Norbert Oellers, Heinz Röllecke, and Itta Shedletzky, vol. 2). Frankfurt a. M.: Jüdischer Verlag / Suhrkamp, 1997, 7–72.

————. *Arthur Aronymus und seine Väter.* In *Dramen,* ed. by Georg-Michael Schulz (*Werke und Briefe: Kritische Ausgabe,* ed. by Norbert Oellers, Heinz Röllecke, and Itta Shedletzky, vol. 2). Frankfurt a. M.: Jüdischer Verlag / Suhrkamp, 1997, 73–181.

————. *IchundIch: Ein Schauspiel.* In *Dramen,* ed. by Georg-Michael Schulz (*Werke und Briefe: Kritische Ausgabe,* ed. by Norbert Oellers, Heinz Röllecke, and Itta Shedletzky, vol. 2). Frankfurt a. M.: Jüdischer Verlag / Suhrkamp, 1997, 183–235.

Marholm, Leonard (alias for Laura Mohr-Hansson). *Johann Reinhold Patkul: Tragödie in zwei Theilen.* Riga: J. Deubner, 1878 (Berlin, Staatsbibliothek).

Marholm, Laura (alias for Laura Mohr-Hansson). *Karla Bühring: Ein Frauendrama in vier Acten.* Paris: Langen, 1895 (Oxford, Taylor Institution Library).

————. (alias for Laura Mohr-Hansson). *Das Buch der Frauen: Zeitpsychologische Portraits,* 4th ed. Paris: Langen, 1896 (1895) (Marbach, Deutsches Literaturarchiv).

————. (alias for Laura Mohr-Hansson). *Wir Frauen und unsere Dichter,* 2nd ed. Berlin: Carl Duncker, 1896 (1895) (Berlin, Staatsbibliothek).

————. *Frau Lilly als Jungfrau, Gattin und Mutter.* Berlin: Carl Duncker, 1897 (Berlin, Humboldt University Library).

————. (alias for Laura Mohr-Hansson). *Zur Psychologie der Frau,* 2 vols., 2nd ed. Berlin: Carl Duncker, 1903 (1897) (Berlin, Staatsbibliothek).

Märten, Lu. *Bergarbeiter: Schauspiel in einem Akt.* 2nd ed. Frankfurt a. M.: Taifun, 1924 (Marbach, Deutsches Literaturarchiv).

————. *Bergarbeiter: Schauspiel in einem Akt*. In: *Aus dem Schaffen früher sozialistischer Schriftstellerinnen*, ed. by Cäcilia Friedrich. Berlin: Akademie-Verlag, 1966.

Paar, Mathilde. *Helene: Schauspiel in vier Akten*. Berlin: Friedrich Luckhardt, 1882 (Berlin, Staatsbibliothek).

Prellwitz, Gertrud. *Zwischen zwei Welten: Eine Weltanschauung im dramatischen Bilde*. Freiburg i. Br.: Friedrich Ernst Fehsenfeld, 1901 (Frankfurt a. M., Staats- und Universitätsbibliothek).

————. *Michel Kohlhas: Ein Trauerspiel in 5 Akten*. Freiburg i. Br.: Friedrich Ernst Fehsenfeld, 1905 (Berlin, Humboldt University Library).

————. *Seine Welt. Ein Lustspiel in 5 Akten*. Berlin: Erkner, 1911 (Berlin, Humboldt University Library).

Viebig, Clara. *Barbara Holzer. Schauspiel in drei Akten*. Berlin: Fontane & Co., 1897 (Berlin, Staatsbibliothek).

————. *Pharisäer: Komödie in drei Akten*. Berlin: Egon Fleischel & Co., 1903 (1899) (Oxford, Taylor Institution Library).

————. *Die Bäuerin: Drama in einem Akt*. In *Bühne und Welt* 6 (1903–4), 365–75. (Marbach, Deutsches Literaturarchiv).

————. *Der Kampf um den Mann*. 5th ed. Berlin: Egon Fleischel & Co., 1905. (Frankfurt a. M., Staats- und Universitätsbibliothek).

————. *Das letzte Lied: Schauspiel in vier Akten*. Berlin: Egon Fleischel & Co., 1908 (Oxford, Taylor Institution Library).

————. *Das letzte Glück: Schauspiel in vier Akten*. Berlin: Egon Fleischel & Co,. 1909 (Oxford, Taylor Institution Library).

————. *Eine Zuflucht*. In *Einakter des Naturalismus*, ed. by Wolfgang Rothe. Stuttgart: Reclam, 1973.

Early Critical Texts Cited

Andreas-Salomé, Lou. "Ketzereien gegen die moderne Frau." In *Die Zukunft* 26 (1899), 237–40.

Bierbaum, Otto Julius. "Anna Croissant-Rust: 'Der standhafte Zinnsoldat.' Drama in drei Acten." In *Die Zeit. Wiener Wochenschrift* 8 (1896), 158.

Bornheim, Paul. "Anna Croissant-Rust." In *Das litterarische Echo* 9 (1906–7), 924–33.

Braun, Lily. *Das geistige Leben des Weibes. Sonderdruck aus "Mann und Weib."* *Herausgegeben von Professor Dr. R. Koßmann und Privatdocent Dr. Jul. Weiß.* N.p., 1908.

Bülow, Frieda Freiin von. "Männerurtheil über Frauendichtung." In *Die Zukunft* 26 (1899), 26–29.

Burckhardt, Max. "Schlagende Wetter." In Burckhardt, *Theater: Kritiken, Vorträge und Aufsätze*, 1 (1898–1901). Vienna: Manzsche 1905, 182–85.

———. "Zu spät." In Burckhardt, *Theater: Kritiken, Vorträge und Aufsätze*, vol. 2 (1902–1904). Vienna: Manzsche 1905, 148.

Cauer, Minna. *Die Frau im neunzehnten Jahrhundert*. Berlin: Cronbach, 1898.

Dittmar, Louise. *Das Wesen der Ehe. Nebst einigen Aufsätzen über die soziale Reform der Frauen* (Leipzig 1849). Reprinted in *Frauenemanzipation im deutschen Vormärz: Texte und Dokumente*, ed. by Renate Möhrmann. Stuttgart: Reclam, 1978.

Dohm, Hedwig. *Die Antifeministen: Ein Buch der Verteidigung*. Berlin: Dümmler, 1902.

Ebner, Theodor. "Literarische Amazonen." In *Die Gegenwart* 56 (1899), 8–10.

Heller, Otto. *Studies in Modern German Literature*. Boston: Ginn & Company, 1905.

Hoppe, Else. "Die Frau als Dramatikerin." In *Die Literatur* 10 (1929), 563–64.

Kerr, Alfred. "Ernst Rosmer." In *Das neue Drama*, 3rd ed. Berlin: Fischer, 1909 (1904), 215–17.

Krack, Otto. "Schreibende Frauen." In *Die Zukunft* 24 (1898), 324–30.

Lask, Berta. "Erinnerungen an Piscators Proletarisches Theater." In *Die Rote Fahne* 25 January 1925. Reprinted in *Deutsches Arbeitertheater 1918–1933*, vol. 1, ed. by Ludwig Hoffmann and Daniel Hoffmann-Ostwald. 2nd ed. Berlin: Henschel, 1972, 75–76.

Lessing, Theodor. "Zwei Münchener Dichterinnen: Ernst Rosmer und Helene Böhlau." In *Die Gesellschaft* 13/III (1898), 16–28.

Lothar, Rudolf, *Das deutsche Drama der Gegenwart*. Munich and Leipzig: Georg Müller, 1905.

Mar, Alexander. "Ein merkwürdiges Buch. 'Der Balkon.' Drei Akte von Gunnar Heiberg." In *Die Gesellschaft* 11 (1895), 1511–21.

Mensch, Ella. *Die Frau in der modernen Literatur: Ein Beitrag zur Geschichte der Gefühle*. Berlin: Carl Duncker, 1898.

———. "Der Misserfolg der Frau als Dramenschriftstellerin." In *Bühne und Welt* 13 (1910–11), 155–59.

Morgenstern, Gustav. "Anna Croissant-Rust." In *Die Gesellschaft* 13/III (1897), 211–19.

Pauli, Hans. "Frauen-Litteratur." In *Neue Deutsche Rundschau* 7 (1896), 276–81.

Scheuffler, G. *Clara Viebig: Zeit und Jahrhundert*. Erfurt: Max Beute, 1927.

Schlenther, Paul. "Frauenarbeit im Theater." In *Die Frau* 1 (1893–94), 150–55.

Spiero, H. *Geschichte der Frauendichtung seit 1800*. Leipzig: Teubner, 1913.

Wiegand, Johannes. *Die Frau in der modernen Literatur: Plaudereien*. Bremen: Carl Schünemann, 1903.

Zepler, Wally. "Die neue Frau in der neuen Frauendichtung." In *Sozialistische Monatshefte* 20 (1914), 53–65.

Secondary Literature Cited

Arnold, Heinz Ludwig. *Marieluise Fleißer* (Text und Kritik 64). Munich: Text und Kritik, 1979.

Bänsch, Dieter. *Else Lasker-Schüler: Kritik eines etablierten Bildes*. Stuttgart: Metzler, 1971.

Barreca, Regina, ed. *Last Laughs: Perspectives on Women and Comedy*. New York: Gordon & Reach, 1988.

Bauschinger, Sigrid. *Else Lasker-Schüler: Ihr Werk und ihre Zeit*. Heidelberg: Stiehm, 1980.

Bennett, Benjamin. *Theater as Problem: Modern Drama and its Place in Literature*. Ithaca and London: Cornell UP, 1990.

Boon, Richard, and Jane Plastow, eds. *Theatre Matters: Performance and Culture on the World Stage*. Cambridge: Cambridge UP, 1998.

Bovenschen, Sylvia. *Die imaginierte Weiblichkeit: Exemplarische Untersuchungen zu kulturgeschichtlichen und literarischen Präsentationsformen des Weiblichen*. Frankfurt a. M.: Suhrkamp, 1979.

Brantly, Susan Carol. "The Life and Writings of Laura Marholm." Unpublished doctoral thesis, Yale University 1987.

Brauner, Sigrid. *Fearless Wives and Frightened Shrews: The Construction of the Witch in Early Modern Germany*, edited with an introduction by Robert H. Brown. Amherst: U of Massachusetts P, 1995.

Brecht, Bertolt. "Das epische Theater." In *Die Stücke von Bertolt Brecht in einem Band*. Frankfurt a. M.: Suhrkamp, 1987 [1978], 983–98.

Brinker-Gabler, Gisela, et al. *Lexikon deutschsprachiger Schriftstellerinnen 1800–1945*. Munich: dtv, 1986.

Brinker-Gabler, Gisela, ed. *Deutsche Literatur von Frauen*. 2 vols. Munich: Beck, 1988.

Bronfen, Elisabeth. *Over Her Dead Body: Death, Femininity and the Aesthetic*. New York: Routledge 1992.

Brüns, Elke. *Außenstehend, ungelenk, kopfüber weiblich: Psychosexuelle Autorpositionen bei Marlen Haushofer, Marieluise Fleißer und Ingeborg Bachmann.* Stuttgart: Metzler, 1998.

Buck, Theo. "Dem Kleinbürger aufs Maul geschaut: Zur gestischen Sprache der Marieluise Fleißer." In *Marieluise Fleißer*, ed. Heinz Ludwig Arnold, 35–53.

Butler, Judith. *Gender Trouble: Feminism and the Subversion of Identity.* New York: Routledge, 1990.

———. *Bodies That Matter: On the Discursive Limits of "Sex."* New York: Routledge, 1993.

Cardinal, Agnès. "Shadow Playwrights of Weimar: Berta Lask, Ilse Langner, Marieluise Fleißer." In *Women in European Theatre*, ed. Elizabeth Woodrough. Oxford: Europa, 1995, 65–73.

Case, Sue-Ellen, ed. *The Divided Home/Land: Contemporary German Women's Plays.* Ann Arbor: U of Michigan P, 1992.

Clark, Stuart. "Inversion, Misrule and the Meaning of Witchcraft." In *Past and Present* 87 (1980), 98–127.

Cocalis, Susan L. "'Weib ist Weib': Mimetische Darstellung contra emanzipatorische Tendenz in den Dramen Marieluise Fleißers." In *Die Frau als Heldin und Autorin*, ed. by Wolfgang Paulsen. Bern: Francke, 1979, 201–10.

Cocalis, Susan L., and Ferrel Rose, eds. *Thalia's Daughters: German Women Dramatists from the Eighteenth Century to the Present.* Tübingen: Franke, 1996.

Colvin, Sarah. "The Power in the Text: Reading Women Writing Drama." In *Gendering German Studies*, ed. by Margaret Littler. Oxford: Blackwell, 1997, 67–81.

———. *The Rhetorical Feminine: Gender and Orient on the German Stage, 1647–1742.* Oxford: Clarendon 1999.

———. "Women and Drama at the Turn of the Century, or Thresholds of Gender and Genre." In *Schwellen: Germanistische Erkundungen einer Metapher*, ed. by Nicholas Saul, Daniel Steuer, Frank Möbus, and Birgit Illner. Würzburg: Königshausen & Neumann, 1999, 265–78.

———. "Disturbing Bodies: Mary Stuart and Marilyn Monroe in Plays by Liz Lochhead, Marie von Ebner-Eschenbach and Gerlind Reinshagen." In *Forum for Modern Language Studies* 35 (1999), 251–60.

———. "'Lachend über den Abgrund springen': Comic Complexity and a Difficult Friendship in Charlotte von Stein's *Neues Freiheitssystem oder die Verschwörung gegen die Liebe.*" In *Goethe at 250 / Goethe mit 250*, ed. by T. J. Reed, Martin Swales, and Jeremy Adler. Munich: Iudicium, 2000, 199–208.

———. "Ein Bildungsmittel ohnegleichen: Marie von Ebner-Eschenbach and the Theatre." In *Harmony in Discord: German Women Writers of the 18th and 19th Centuries*, ed. by Laura Martin. Oxford: Peter Lang, 2001, 161–82.

Dane, Gesa. "Die Dichterin als Rabbinerin: Geschichte und Erinnerung in Else Lasker-Schüler's 'IchundIch.'" In *Text und Kritik* 4 (1994), 55–64.

Dawson, Ruth P. "Frauen und Theater: Vom Stegreifspiel zum bürgerlichen Rührstück." In Brinker-Gabler, *Deutsche Literatur von Frauen*, vol. 1, 421–34.

Devrient, Eduard. *Aus seinen Tagebüchern. Karlsruhe 1852–1970*, ed. by Rolf Kabel. Weimar: Böhlau, 1964.

Diamond, Elin. *Unmaking Mimesis: Essays on Feminism and Theatre*. London: Routledge, 1997.

Döpper-Henrich, Angelika *"Entfremdung" in den dramatischen Schriften Marieluise Fleißers*. Frankfurt a. M.: Haag & Herchen, 1996.

Elam, Keir. *The Semiotics of Theatre and Drama*. London: Routledge, 1994 (1980).

Engelhardt Barbara, Therese Hörnigk, and Bettina Mausch, eds. *Theater-FrauenTheater*. Berlin: Theater der Zeit, 2001.

Feßmann, Meike. *Spielfiguren: Die Ich-Figurationen Else Lasker-Schülers als Spiel mit der Autorrolle: Ein Beitrag zur Poetologie des modernen Autors*. Stuttgart: M&P, 1992.

Finney, Gail. *Women in Modern Drama: Freud, Feminism, and European Theater at the Turn of the Century*. Ithaca: Cornell UP, 1989.

Fischer-Lichte, Erika. "Frauen erobern die Bühne: Dramatikerinnen im 20. Jahrhundert." In *Deutsche Literatur von Frauen*, ed. by Gisela Brinker-Gabler, vol. 2. Munich: Beck, 1988, 379–93.

Fleig, Anne. *Handlungs-Spiel-Räume: Dramen von Autorinnen im Theater des ausgehenden 18. Jahrhunderts*. Würzburg: Königshausen und Neumann, 1999.

Freud, Sigmund, "Femininity." (1933) In *The Essentials of Psycho-Analysis: The Definitive Collection of Sigmund Freud's Writing*, ed. by Anna Freud. London: Penguin, 1991 [1986], 412–32.

Gardiner, Judith Kegan. "On Female Identity and Writing by Women." In *Writing and Sexual Difference*, ed. by Elizabeth Abel. Brighton: Harvester, 1982, 177–92.

Giebel, Dörte. "Das Ende meiner Mädchenjahre." In *Hamburger Frauenzeitung* 56 (1999), 32–33.

Giesing, Michaela. "Theater als verweigerter Raum: Dramatikerinnen der Jahrhundertwende in deutschsprachigen Ländern." In Gnüg/Möhrmann, *Frauen Literatur Geschichte* (1985), 240–59.

———. "Verhältnisse und Verhinderungen — deutschsprachige Dramatikerinnen um die Jahrhundertwende." In Gnüg/Möhrmann, *Frauen Literatur Geschichte* (1999), 261–78.

Gilbert, Sandra M., and Susan Gubar. *The Madwoman in the Attic: The Woman Writer and the Nineteenth-Century Imagination.* New Haven: Yale UP, 1979.

Ginsberg, Ernst, ed. *Else Lasker-Schüler: Dichtungen und Dokumente.* Munich: Kösel, 1951.

Gnüg, Hiltrud, and Renate Möhrmann, eds. *Frauen Literatur Geschichte: Schreibende Frauen vom Mittelalter bis zur Gegenwart.* Stuttgart: Metzler, 1985.

———. *Frauen Literatur Geschichte: Schreibende Frauen vom Mittelalter bis zur Gegenwart,* 2nd completely revised edition. Stuttgart: Metzler, 1999.

Goodman, Kay. "Motherhood and Work: The Concept of the Misuse of Women's Energy, 1895–1905." In *German Women in the Eighteenth and Nineteenth Centuries: A Social and Literary History,* ed. by Ruth-Ellen B. Joeres and Mary Jo Maynes. Bloomington, Ind.: Indiana UP, 1986.

Göttel, Sabine. *"Natürlich sind es Bruchstücke": Zum Verhältnis von Biographie und literarische Produktion bei Marieluise Fleißer.* St. Ingbert: Röhrig, 1997.

Greenhalgh, Susanne. "Occupying the Empty Space: Feminism and Drama." In *Teaching Women: Feminism and English Studies,* ed. by Anne Thompson and Helen Wilcox. Manchester: Manchester UP, 1989, 170–79.

Gronewold, Hinrike. "Helene von Druskowitz (1856–1918): 'Die geistige Amazone.'" In *Wahnsinns Frauen,* ed. by Sybille Duda and Luise F. Pusch. Frankfurt a. M.: Suhrkamp, 1992, 96–122.

Hallersleben, Markus. *Else Lasker-Schüler: Avantgardismus und Kunstinszenierung.* Tübingen: Franke, 2000.

Hedgepeth, Sonja M. *"Überall blicke ich nach einem heimatlichen Boden aus": Exil im Werk Else Lasker-Schülers.* New York: Lang, 1994.

Hoff, Dagmar von. *Dramen des Weiblichen: Deutsche Dramatikerinnen um 1800.* Opladen: Westdeutscher Verlag, 1989.

Hoffmeister, Donna L. *The Theater of Confinement: Language and Survival in the Milieu Plays of Marieluise Fleißer and Franz Xaver Kroetz.* Columbia, SC: Camden House, 1983.

Irigaray, Luce. *This Sex Which is Not One,* transl. by Katharine Porter. Ithaca, NY: Cornell UP, 1985.

Jones, Calvin N. *The Literary Reputation of Else Lasker-Schüler: Criticism 1901–1993.* Columbia, SC: Camden House, 1994.

Kambas, Chryssoula. *Die Werkstatt als Utopie: Lu Märtens literarische Arbeit und Formästhetik seit 1900.* Tübingen: Niemeyer, 1988.

Klostermaier, Doris. *Marie von Ebner-Eschenbach: The Victory of a Tenacious Will.* Riverside, CA: Ariadne, 1997.

Klüsener, Erika. *Else Lasker-Schüler.* Reinbek bei Hamburg: Rowohlt, 1998 (1980).

Koch, Angelika. *Die Bedeutung des Spiels bei Else Lasker-Schüler im Rahmen von Expressionismus und Manierismus.* Bonn: Bouvier, 1971.

Kord, Susanne. "Fading Out: Invisible Women in Marieluise Fleißer's Early Dramas." In *Women in German Yearbook* 5 (1989), 57–72.

——. *Ein Blick hinter die Kulissen: Deutschsprachige Dramatikerinnen im 18. und 19. Jahrhundert.* Stuttgart: Metzler, 1992.

——. "Performing Genders: Three Plays on the Power of Women." In *Monatshefte* 86 (1994), 95–115.

——. *Sich einen Namen machen: Anonymität und weibliche Autorschaft, 1700–1900.* Stuttgart: Metzler, 1996.

——. "Frühe dramatische Entwürfe — Drei Dramatikerinnen im 18. Jahrhundert." In Gnüg/Möhrmann, *Frauen Literatur Geschichte* (1999), 231–47.

Korn, Benjamin. "Es geht um das Leben. Nur deshalb geht es um die Kunst: Zum 50. Todestag der Dichterin, der Dramatikerin Else Lasker-Schüler." In *Theater heute* 1 (1995), 20–23.

Kraft, Helga. *Ein Haus aus Sprache: Dramatikerinnen und das andere Theater.* Stuttgart: Metzler, 1996.

——. "Mimesis unterminiert: Drama und Theater von Frauen." In Gnüg/Möhrmann, *Frauen Literatur Geschichte* (1999), 279–98.

Krumbholz, Martin. "Hölle, Jahrmarkt, Garten Eden: Zum dramatischen Werk der Else Lasker-Schüler." In *Text und Kritik* 4 (1994), 42–53.

Kupper, Margarete. "*IchundIch*: Nachlaßschauspiel." In *Jahrbuch der deutschen Schillergesellschaft* 14 (1970), 24–99.

Laegreid, Sissel. *Nach dem Tode — oder vor dem Leben: Das poetische Projekt Else Lasker-Schülers.* Frankfurt a. M.: Lang, 1997.

Lenk, Elisabeth. "Die sich selbst verdoppelnde Frau." In Lenk, *Kritische Phantasie: Gesammelte Essays.* Munich: Matthes & Seitz, 1986, 149–60.

Lindtberg, Leopold. "So glänzte der Traum des Arthur Aronymus." In Schmid, Michael, ed., *Lasker-Schüler: Ein Buch zum 100. Geburtstag der Dichterin.* Wuppertal: Peter Hammer, 1969, 73–86.

Lorenz, Dagmar C. G. "Jewish Women Authors and the Exile Experience: Claire Goll, Veza Canetti, Else Lasker-Schüler, Nelly Sachs, Cornelia Edvardson." In *German Life and Letters* 51 (1998), 225–39.

McGowan, Moray. "Kette und Schuß: Zur Dramatik der Marieluise Fleißer." In *Marieluise Fleißer* (Text und Kritik 64), ed. by Heinz Ludwig Arnold. Munich: Text und Kritik, 1979, 11–34.

——. *Marieluise Fleißer.* Munich: Beck, 1987.

Marney, Julie. "Performing Subjectivities: Feminism, Postmodernism and the Practice of Identity." Unpublished doctoral dissertation, University of Edinburgh 2000.

Mayer-Flaschberger, Maria. *Marie Eugenie delle Grazie: Eine österreichische Dichterin der Jahrhundertwende: Studien zu ihrer mittleren Schaffensperiode.* Munich: Verlag des Süddeutschen Kulturwerks, 1984.

Mennemeier, Franz Norbert. *Modernes deutsches Drama: Kritiken und Charakteristiken.* Vol. 1, 1910–1933. 2nd ed. Munich: Fink, 1979.

Michalska, Urzula, *Clara Viebig: Versuch einer Monographie.* Poznań: Uniwersyset im. Adama Mickiewicza, 1968.

Middell, Eike. "*IchundIch* von Else Lasker-Schüler." In *Sinn und Form* 33 (1981), 637–52.

Möhrmann, Renate. *Die Schauspielerin: Zur Kulturgeschichte der weiblichen Bühnenkunst.* Frankfurt a. M.: Insel, 1989.

Müller, Ulrike. *Auch wider dem Verbote: Else Lasker-Schüler und ihr eigensinniger Umgang mit Weiblichkeit, Judentum und Mystik.* Frankfurt a. M.: Lang, 1997.

Neubaur, Petra. "Vogue la galère: Die 'Frauenfrage' als Modeströmung: Skepsis und Ambivalenz in Helene Druskowitz' 'Die Emanzipations-Schwärmerin' (1890 [sic])." In *Frau — Literatur — Wissenschaft im alpen-adriatischen Raum,* 11: *Zuschnitte/Moden* (May 1997), ed. by Bettina Wellacher, Jolanda Woschitz, Ulrike Oberheber, and Elisabeth Frei. Klagenfurt: University of Klagenfurt, 1997.

O'Brien, Mary. "'Ich war verkleidet als Poet . . . ich bin Poetin!!': The Masquerade of Gender in Else Lasker-Schüler's Work." In *The German Quarterly* 65.1 (1992), 1–17.

Parr, Andrea. *Drama als "Schreitende Lyrik": Die Dramatikerin Else Lasker-Schüler.* Frankfurt a. M.: Lang, 1988.

Pfister, Eva. "'Unter dem fremden Gesetz': Zu Produktionsbedingungen, Werk und Rezeption der Dramatikerin Marieluise Fleißer." Doctoral thesis, University of Vienna 1981.

Plumpe, Gerhard. "Kunstform und Produktionspraxis im Blick auf Lu Märten." In *Arbeitsfeld: Materialistische Literaturtheorie: Beiträge zu ihrer Gegenstandsbestimmung,* ed. by Klaus-Michael Bogdal, Burkhardt Lindner, and Gerhard Plumpe. Wiesbaden: Athenaion, 1975, 193–228.

Purdie, Susan. *Comedy: The Mastery of Discourse.* New York: Harvester Wheatsheaf, 1993.

Pusch, Luise. *Das Deutsche als Männersprache.* Frankfurt: Suhrkamp, 1984.

Reichard, Georg. "Die Dramen Marie von Ebner-Eschenbachs auf den Bühnen des Wiener Burg- und Stadttheaters." In *Marie von Ebner-Eschenbach: Ein Bonner Symposion zu ihrem 75. Todesjahr,* ed. by Karl Konrad Polheim. Berne: Peter Lang, 1994, 97–122.

Reiss-Suckow, Christine. *"Wer wird mir Schöpfer sein!!" Die Entwicklung Else Lasker-Schülers als Künstlerin.* Konstanz: Hartung-Gorre, 1997.

Robertson, Ritchie. "Historicizing Weininger: The Nineteenth-Century German Image of the Feminized Jew." In *Modernity, Culture and "the Jew,"* ed. by Bryan Chevette and Laura Marcus. Oxford: Polity, 1998, 23–39.

Rose, Ferrel. *The Guises of Modesty: Marie von Ebner-Eschenbach's Female Artists.* Columbia, SC: Camden House, 1994.

———. "The Disenchantment of Power: Marie von Ebner-Eschenbach's Maria Stuart in Schottland." In Cocalis/Rose, eds. *Thalia's Daughters,* 147–46.

Rossbacher, Karlheinz. *Literatur und Liberalismus: Zur Kultur der Ringstrassenzeit in Wien.* Vienna: J&V, 1992.

Rühle, Günther, ed. *Materialien zum Leben und Schreiben der Marieluise Fleißer.* Frankfurt a. M.: Suhrkamp, 1973.

Russ, Joanna. *How to Suppress Women's Writing.* London: The Women's Press, 1994 (1983).

Russo, Mary. "Female Grotesques: Carnival and Theory." In *Writing on the Body: Female embodiment and feminist theory,* ed. by Katie Conboy, Nadia Medina, and Sarah Stanbury. New York: Columbia UP, 1997, 318–36.

Sabelus, Annette. "'Mir persönlich brachten sie allerhand Verdruß': Zu den Bearbeitungen von Marieluise Fleißers *Pioniere in Ingolstadt* durch Rainer Werner Fassbinder." In *Reflexive Naivität: Zum Werk Marieluise Fleißers,* ed. by Maria E. Müller and Ulrike Vedder. Berlin: Erich Schmidt, 2000, 254–71.

Sauer, Jutta. *"Etwas zwischen Männern und Frauen": Die Sehnsucht der Marieluise Fleißer.* Cologne: PapyRossa, 1991.

Schmid, Heike. *Gefallene Engel: Deutschsprachige Dramatikerinnen im ausgehenden 19. Jahrhundert.* St. Ingbert: Röhrig, 2000.

Scott-Jones, Marilyn. "Laura Marholm and the Question of Female 'Nature.'" In *Beyond the Eternal Feminine: Critical Essays on Women and German Literature,* ed. by Susan L. Cocalis and Kay Goodman. Stuttgart: Hans-Dieter Heinz, 1982, 203–23.

Searle, John R. *Speech Acts: An Essay in the Philosophy of Language.* Cambridge: Cambridge UP, 1969.

Sheppard, Richard. "Straightening Long-Playing Records: The Early Politics of Berta Lask and Friedrich Wolf." In *German Life and Letters* 45 (1992), 279–87.

Sieg, Katrin. *Exiles, Eccentrics, Activists: Women in Contemporary German Theater.* Ann Arbor: U of Michigan P, 1994.

Skrine, Peter. "Elsa Bernstein and Königskinder." In *Königskinder or The Prince and the Goosegirl.* English National Opera program notes 1992.

———. "Elsa Bernstein: Germany's Major Woman Dramatist?" In *German Women Writers 1900–1933: Twelve Essays,* ed. by Brian Keith-Smith. Lampeter: Edwin Mellen, 1993, 43–63.

Spender, Dale. *Man Made Language,* 2nd ed. London: Pandora, 1985.

———. *The Writing or the Sex? Or Why You Don't Have to Read Women's Writing to Know It's No Good.* New York: Pergamon, 1989.

Streller, Karl-Heinz, and Erika Massalsky. *Geschichte des VEB Leuna-Werke "Walter Ulbricht" 1916–1945.* Leipzig: VEB deutscher Verlag für Grundstoffindustrie, 1989.

Stürzer, Anne. *Dramatikerinnen und Zeitstücke: Ein vergessenes Kapitel der Theatergeschichte von der Weimarer Republik bis zur Nachkriegszeit.* Stuttgart: Metzler, 1993.

Tanzer, Ulrike. *Frauenbilder im Werk Marie von Ebner-Eschenbachs.* Stuttgart: Hans-Dieter Heinz, 1997.

Thiel, Heinz. "'Ich und Ich' — ein versperrtes Werk?." In *Lasker-Schüler: Ein Buch zum 100. Geburtstag der Dichterin,* ed. by Michael Schmid. Wuppertal: Peter Hammer, 1969, 123–55.

Toegel, Edith. "The 'Leidensjahre' of Marie von Ebner-Eschenbach: Her Dramatic Works." In *German Life and Letters* 46 (1993), 107–19.

Tylee, Claire M., Elaine Turner, and Agnès Cardinal, eds. *War Plays by Women: An International Anthology.* London: Routledge, 1999.

Tyson, Peter K. "Else Lasker-Schüler's *Die Wupper*: Between Naturalism and Expressionism." In *AUMLA: Journal of the Australasian Universities Modern Language & Literature Association* 64 (1985), 144–53.

Von Hoff, Dagmar. *Dramen des Weiblichen: Deutsche Dramatikerinnen um 1800.* Opladen: Westdeutscher Verlag, 1989.

Waugh, Patricia. *Practising Postmodernism, Reading Modernism.* London: Edward Arnold, 1992.

Weigel, Sigrid. "Der schielende Blick: Thesen zur Geschichte weiblicher Schreibpraxis." In *Die verborgene Frau: Sechs Beiträge zu einer feministischen Literaturwissenschaft,* ed. Inge Stefan and Sigrid Weigel. Berlin: Argument, 1988.

Wilshire, Bruce. *Role-Playing and Identity: The Limits of Theater as Metaphor.* Bloomington, IN: Indiana UP, 1991 (1982).

Woolf, Virginia. "Professions for Women." In Virginia Woolf, *Collected Essays.* London: Chatto & Windus, 1966, vol. 2, 284–89.

Wurst, Karin. *Frauen und Drama im 18. Jahrhundert, 1770–1800.* Cologne: Böhlau, 1991.

Zetkin, Klara. "Ein Arbeiterdrama: 'Bergarbeiter,' Schauspiel in einem Akt von Lu Märten." In *Aus dem Schaffen früher sozialistischer Schriftstellerinnen,* ed. by Cäcilia Friedrich. Berlin: Akademie, 1966, 160–64.

Zophoniasson-Baierl, Ulrike. *Elsa Bernstein alias Ernst Rosmer: Eine deutsche Dramatikerin im Spannungsfeld der literarischen Strömungen des Wilhelminischen Zeitalters.* Berne: Peter Lang, 1985.

Index